LAND IN CALIFORNIA

LAND IN CALIFORNIA

THE STORY OF MISSION LANDS
RANCHOS, SQUATTERS, MINING CLAIMS, RAILROAD GRANTS
LAND SCRIP, HOMESTEADS

By W. W. ROBINSON

UNIVERSITY OF CALIFORNIA PRESS
Berkeley   Los Angeles   London

University of California Press
Berkeley and Los Angeles, California

University of California Press, Ltd.
London, England

❖

This book was originally published in the series
The Chronicles of California

First Paperback Printing 1979
ISBN: 0-520-03875-4

Printed in the United States of America

1 2 3 4 5 6 7 8 9

Preface

IN THE *collection and choice of material for* Land in California, *and in its writing, I am indebted to many persons, some of whom gave good advice upon the preparation of the manuscript as a whole, others of whom lent a hand upon particular parts.*

John Walton Caughey suggested the project and was most helpful in keeping me in the straight and narrow path during the course of my effort. Herbert Eugene Bolton, with encouragement and counsel, and Robert Glass Cleland, with friendly and interested assistance, played important parts in enabling me to carry through this study. Frederick Webb Hodge was generous with help on the Indian phase, J. N. Bowman gave excellent pointers and helped me avoid some pitfalls on rancho and Land Commission subjects.

Leslie E. Bliss, Robert O. Schad, and Carey S. Bliss, of the Huntington Library; George P. Hammond and Eleanor Bancroft, of the Bancroft Library; Mabel R. Gillis, of the California State Library; Lawrence Clark Powell, of the University of California Library, Los Angeles; Laura C. Cooley, of the Los Angeles Public Library; Anna Begue Packman, Secretary of the Historical Society of Southern California; Helen S. Giffen, of the Society of California Pioneers; and Ella L. Robinson, of the Southwest Museum Library, were all good enough to place interesting and important library resources at my disposal.

C. W. Calbreath, of the United States District Court, San Francisco; P. M. Hamer and W. L. G. Joerg, of the National Archives, Washington, D.C.; Joel David Wolfsohn, of the Bureau of Land Management, Washington,

Preface

D.C.; and D. M. B. Peatross, of the Public Survey Office, Glendale, extended their help. Charles K. Adams and W. W. Reyburn threw light on railroad titles. Robert J. Woods allowed me to browse contentedly in his lush Californiana. William W. Clary was generous with his material on tidelands.

A number of men in the title insurance business in various California cities gave special help, among them: Benj. J. Henley and the late Donzel Stoney, of San Francisco; Jas. D. Forward and George Heyneman, of San Diego; W. W. McEuen, of El Centro; Allen S. Mobley, of San Luis Obispo; L. R. Pettijohn, of Hanford; C. J. Hironymous, of Stockton; Stuart O'Melveny, W. Herbert Allen, Walter Clark, Lawrence Otis, and Ben Utter, of Los Angeles; George P. Anderson, of Ukiah; Geo. A. Parker, of Santa Ana; and Floyd Cerini, Executive Secretary of the California Land Title Association.

In the reprinting of part of "The Strange Case of Thomas Valentine" permission was obtained from the Automobile Club of Southern California, through Phil Townsend Hanna, editor and general manager of Westways, in which the article originally appeared.

Through the courtesy of Edward Weston, three of his photographs are used. The drawings for the chapter vignettes are the work of Irene Robinson.

Title Insurance and Trust Company, Los Angeles, also permitted reproduction of a number of pictures from its Historical Collection.

Constance Riebe gave secretarial assistance. Lucie E. N. Dobbie, University of California Press, gave editorial help.

W. W. ROBINSON

Los Angeles, 1948

Contents

Illustrations

CHAPTER I

Whose California?

THE STORY OF California can be told in terms of its land. Better still, it can be told in terms of men and women claiming the land. These men and women form a procession that begins in prehistory and comes down to the present moment.

Heading the procession are Indians, stemming out of a mysterious past, speaking a babel of tongues, and laying claims to certain hunting, fishing, and acorn-gathering areas—possessory claims doomed to fade quickly before conquering white races.

Following the brown-skinned Indians are Spanish-speaking soldiers, settlers, and missionaries who, in 1769, began coming up through Lower California and taking over the fertile coast valleys and the harbors of California. Their laws were the Laws of the Indies controlling Spanish colonization and governing ownership of land. Missions, presidios, pueblos, and ranchos were born in the period of these people.

A few Russians are in the procession because of their temporary establishment—without consent of Spain—of Fort Ross, north of San Francisco Bay. These men, hunters of seals and otters, came down the coast in 1812 and left in 1841, after selling their equipment to Swiss-adventurer John A. Sutter.

Citizens of Mexico are in line, too, for in 1822 the flag of Spain yielded to that of Mexico at California's capital city of Monterey. They carried on the Spanish tradition in landownership, with embellishments of their own. Ranchos had their flowering during California's Mexican regime.

Americans follow, some before, but most of them after, the Mexican War. As a result of the war California became a part of the Union and a board of commissioners was set up to help segregate private land claims (of Spanish and Mexican origin) from public lands of the United States. Of these Americans there was and is no end—nor of the law books that hold their beliefs about landownership.

Today, all publicly and privately owned land in California may be grouped according to origin of title.

First of all there are the lands—mostly rancho and pueblo—the titles to which were granted by, or derived from, Spanish or Mexican authority before the American period in California's history, and which later received United States confirmation. Rancho land took in some of the best pasture and agricultural areas of the state.

Then there are the "public lands"—so called—of the United States. These lands were unconveyed under Spanish or Mexican authority and are outside rancho and original pueblo areas, though once a part of the land vested in the King of Spain and later the Mexican nation.

They passed directly to the United States with the cession of California by Mexico under the Treaty of Guadalupe Hidalgo in 1848. Most of the public domain in California has been conveyed by the United States directly to individuals or to corporate or governing bodies or has been reserved. Public lands include those conveyed under American laws governing preëmption, homestead, desert, timber culture, and timber and stone entries, military bounty warrants and scrip, mining claims, federal townsites, railroad titles, and Indian reservations. Some of the public lands are now within national forests or national parks set apart for the all-time benefit of the people.

In addition, there are what are called "state lands." These include those which Congress, early in California's American period, granted to the State of California out of the public domain to supply it with the means to raise funds for education and reclamation. These lands also include those in which the state has, or had, at least a qualified ownership, such as lands under inland navigable waters, rivers, harbors, even tidelands down to the low-water mark.

Within the boundaries of California, as defined in its constitution, is the three-mile wide coastal strip of submerged land extending oceanward from the line of low-water mark. Until June 23, 1947, this strip was thought to be owned by the State of California as a sovereign power. On that date the United States Supreme Court denied this ownership and asserted paramount rights of the federal government. This decision is subject, of course, to possible later Congressional action.

How and why the rich land of California came into the hands of its present owners is the story to be told here—with comment along the way about Indians, missions, presidios, pueblos, ranchos, squatters, miners, railroad companies, settlers, subdividers, real estate brokers, recording systems, title companies, and bulging cities.

CHAPTER II

First Owners

BEFORE THERE were white men in California, that is, before the year 1769, there were Indians, at least 150,000 of them. Some authorities have estimated their number then as high as 250,000.

What we know about the cultures of these California Indians and their relation to other Indian cultures we owe to the anthropologist.

The Mohaves, living in the southeastern part of the state, were an organized tribe, it seems, but in most parts of California the tribal system was probably only in its beginnings or did not exist at all. For example, the Yurok and Karok people of northern California did not recognize any organization higher than that of individuals or of kindred. Even the village was not a unit. Prewhite California was a babel of tongues, with a new language every few miles. In fact there were a greater number of unrelated languages in California than in any equal area in the world.

Through occupancy and use, the California tribes, groups, villages, even individuals, had gradually established claims to, or the rights to possess, certain acorn-gathering lands, certain hunting grounds where deer abounded, certain fishing streams, certain fields, forests, and chaparral-clad hills that could give men and women the wherewithal to feed and clothe themselves as well as to furnish them medicines and materials for their arts.

The Indian conception of the earth as the mother who provides food for her children is presented by the late Alice C. Fletcher in a general discussion of land tenure among American Indians in the all-encompassing *Handbook of American Indians North of Mexico* edited by Frederick Webb Hodge. "In this primitive and religious sense," explains this authority, "land was not regarded as property, it was like the air, it was something necessary to the life of the race, and therefore not to be appropriated by any individual or group of individuals to the permanent exclusion of all others." Occupancy, therefore, was the only land tenure recognized by Indians. Generally speaking, so long as they lived on certain village sites or so long as they went regularly to certain hunting grounds, the members of a tribe could claim them against intruders. Actually, the struggle over rights to hunting grounds was the cause of most Indian wars in America.

Bearing these fundamental generalizations about land tenure in mind, it will be worth while to consider the viewpoints of different California groups regarding property, especially real property. We must look primarily to A. L. Kroeber, whose studies of these groups—from those at the northerly boundary of the state to those at the Mexican border—are to be found in his monumental *Handbook of the Indians of California.*

Among the individualistic Yuroks, who lived in houses of split redwood planks along the Klamath River and on the shore of the Pacific Ocean in the extreme northern part of California, much thought was given to the acquisition and use of all kinds of property, both personal and real. River land of any value for hunting deer and elk was privately claimed. A mile or more back from the river, lands were unclaimed. Rich men might hold three or four inherited tracts; poor people, a single tract or no tract at all. Good fishing places might be held jointly, each owner using them in turn for a day. No new fishing places could be established, and fishing that interfered with established rights was forbidden. Certain areas esteemed for seed gathering were bought and sold, reports Kroeber. It is related that one villager, having killed a man, fled to the coast, bought himself a stream, and made his home there.

The money used by the Yuroks in buying and selling was dentalium shells. A fishing place, for example, was worth one to three strings of such shells—a twelve-dentalium string in the American period equaling ten American dollars. A house had a three-string value, though a well-conditioned one of redwood planks might have a valuation of five strings. A tract bearing acorns was said to be worth one to five strings.

Among the Yuroks most of the estate of a man who died went to his sons. The daughters, however, received a share and something was given to the nearer relatives, at least male relatives. The house itself, real property, was inherited by the son, says Kroeber. Only if there were no adult sons or daughters was the brother of the dead man the inheritor.

Among the Indians of Hoopa (or Hupa) Valley on the Trinity River, the power of each headman depended on the amount of property he owned. He had special hunting and fishing rights and certain lands where his women might gather acorns and seeds. Varying lengths of river shore were held as private fishing rights by heads of families, and these passed from father to son.

The Pomo Indians, living in redwood-bark houses along the Russian River, owned a famous and prized salt deposit. Its salt was free to their particular friends; all others paid for the salt they took.

Among the Shastas, several fish dams were built in the upper Klamath River. Each dam was the property of one family. All salmon caught in the willow traps belonged to the head of the family, but he was expected to give fish to everyone asking. The Atsugewi Shastas, living along streams that drained into the Pit River, had no private or family ownership in land, but they recognized claims to certain places where edible roots and seeds were to be found and to certain eagles' nests, the right to take from which passed from father to son. This claim is reminiscent of property rights among the Pueblo Indians who considered the nests of eagles to be the property of the clan within whose domain they were found, and the birds themselves to belong to the clan.

Land was free, and common to all members of the community, among the Maidu Indians whose lean-to shelters of bark and brush were found in the territory between the Sacramento River and the crest of the Sierra Nevada. Fish holes, however, sometimes were claimed individually, and certain families had the right to build fences for deer drives. Individual hunters were not restricted.

The warlike Mohaves planted corn, beans, pumpkins, and watermelons along the Colorado River. This farm land was claimed individually and was bought and sold for beads or for captives and spoils brought back from war. Mohave farmers had boundary disputes—like present-day Imperial Valley farmers—an aftermath of river floods that washed away landmarks or changed the shape of the land. These disputes were settled by dragging or shoving the claimant across the disputed territory, each farmer being helped by his friends. The stake might be the entire arable holdings of both contestants. Losers, if they wished, might then fight the victors, each side armed with thick willow poles and short sticks. Title to the disputed tract was finally established by driving an opponent back across it. The dispossessed went to his friends who might permit him to share their fields.

Property transfers among California Indians, whether involving personal possessions or claims to land, took place when the property owner died. They also took place when the proper consideration—dentalium shells, clamshell disc beads, slaves, captives, spoils of war or other property—passed between buyer and seller. Furthermore, a man became richer or poorer in property as a result of wagering on a game. California Indians, northern, central and southern, like all American Indians, were inveterate players of games—and the stakes were anything from a white deerskin to a wife. Although the games were both those of dexterity, like the hoop-and-pole game, and of chance (dice or guessing), the guessing games were universal favorites. Reckless betting upon which hand held which stick—perhaps one with a painted center among two shuffled and divided handfuls of sticks—could strip a man ultimately of all his personal property and all his claims to fishing holes and acorn-gathering lands.

The Indians of California, like those of the rest of

America, had fully developed ideas of personal property ownership, yet they also had, it has been pointed out, a definite sense of ownership in lands that were directly used by a tribe, a group, a village, or even an individual. These ideas were not peculiar to California Indians. In fact, the cultures of California—including real property beliefs—were related to more widely spread cultures outside the state. The Yurok and northwestern culture, for example, was part of the north Pacific Coast civilization centering in British Columbia and was influenced by habits and strong property beliefs of that area. Northwestern California culture predominated over that of southwestern Oregon, however, probably because the Klamath River was the largest stream entering the Pacific south of the Columbia and north of the Sacramento rivers. The Klamath valley region supported a larger population with a more active social life than the area that adjoined on the north. Yurok culture and that of their neighbors, the Hoopa and Karok, formed the southern tip of the culture common to the Pacific Coast from Oregon to Alaska. The central California Indian culture, less vigorous than the British Columbian, was more isolated because of the physical boundaries of central California. This area, however, and that of the Shoshoneans of the Great Basin adjoining on the east, had cultural kinship. The cultures of the southern Californian and lower Colorado River Indians had ties with those of the southwest, though the southwestern basis was ultimately Mexican in character.

The first white men to look upon California and California Indians were sixteenth-century Spanish explorers, but actual occupancy by Spaniards did not begin until 1769.

In that year a land expedition coming up through Lower California, under Captain Gaspar de Portolá, reached the port of San Diego. Spanish-speaking soldiers, missionaries, and settlers, under an active expansionist program, gradually occupied the fertile coast valleys and established outposts on the good harbors of California between the San Diego and San Francisco areas. Presidios and pueblos were established, and twenty-one Franciscan missions into which near-by Indians were shepherded.

The Spanish newcomers gave, in practice, as little heed to the Indians' tribal, communal, or individualistic claims to the land as the Indians themselves had given to the occupation by animals of the fields, forests, caves, burrows, or nests that interfered with the wishes or needs of brown-skinned men. They brought with them to California the Laws of the Indies, controlling Spanish colonization and governing colonial ownership and use of land. These laws were full of pious recognition of the rights of Indians to their possessions, the right to as much land as they needed for their habitations, for tillage, and for the pasturage of their flocks. So far as the California Indians were concerned, this meant, practically, that when they were "reduced," that is, converted to Christianity and established within or around a mission area, they would have these theoretical property rights. There was, of course, no recognition of Indian rights to land not actually occupied or necessary for their use, nor was there any policy of purchasing Indian titles. Obviously only Christianized California Indians could share in any of the provisions of Spanish law.

The brief span of years between 1769 and 1822 saw established in California the chain of missions, inaugurated and planned by Fray Junípero Serra, along with

four presidios and three pueblos. These years saw the
Indian villages of the mission-controlled area—about one
sixth of California—abandoned for the Indian quarters
of the missions. At each mission there were from a few
hundred to two or three thousand Indians. Here, without individual property rights, they worked at the tasks
assigned them in the fields or shops and were given food
and clothing. The lands, theoretically, were held by the
missions in trust for the Indians, a temporary arrange-
ment that envisioned the natives becoming self-sustaining
units. Distant or reluctant natives—the great majority—
kept to aboriginal living and had no property rights that
were recognized by Spanish authorities.

Those tribes that became completely devoted to mission life are today gone. Disease and disruption of native
ways of living swept them away. Kroeber says: "The brute
upshot of missionization, in spite of its kindly flavor and
humanitarian roots, was only one thing: death." Another
authority, S. F. Cook, in his exhaustive *The Conflict Between The California Indian And White Civilization*,
states that from 1779 to 1833 there were 29,100 births at
the missions, and 62,600 deaths.

Since eighteenth- and nineteenth-century missionization of Indians destroyed native cultures, there is little
information about real property ideas among the groups
that gave up their villages for the mission compound. The
Gabrielinos, for example, the most advanced of the Sho-
shonean peoples in southern California, held the most
fertile land there, a stretch of pleasant coast, and Santa
Catalina, the best of the Santa Barbara Channel islands.
Yet only the scantiest source material is available about
their holding of real property before they substituted
the mission for the ranchería.

In California Spanish rule yielded to Mexican in 1822. Henceforth, until the American conquest, California was a Mexican province, the first few months being under an imperial regime. The laws of Spain carried over into those of Mexico, with California landowners and land users—white or Indian—governed by the rulings of Mexico City.

On the secularization of the missions by the Mexican government, during the years 1834–1836, some of the mission holdings were distributed among Indian heads of families and those more than twenty-one years of age. Several Indian pueblos were then established. These proved temporary, for the Indians were largely incapable of assuming responsibility. There were exceptions, however, for a number of Christianized Indians received Mexican grants of ranchos.

With the close of the Mexican War and the signing of the Treaty of Guadalupe Hidalgo in 1848, California became a part of the United States, the California Indians becoming subject to its jurisdiction. They numbered then perhaps 110,000.

The Indians' right to occupy their lands until voluntary relinquishment—traditionally recognized by the federal government since the early days of the republic—did not prevent their being quickly dispossessed. The United States from the beginning admitted the Indians' right to occupy lands possessed by them, but it held—and the courts held—that the absolute title to the soil was vested in the government. Since the Indians could occupy land until voluntary relinquishment or until their rights were extinguished by "justifiable conquest," the young republic had early to adopt a policy that would enable it to wipe out Indian claims to territory not in actual use. The policy adopted—and followed until March 3, 1871—was to recognize the tribes as nations and to enter into treaties with them as such. By these treaties specified lands were agreed upon as tribal, with a cession to the United States, for proper compensation, of outside areas.

Accordingly, when California became a part of the Union, three commissioners were appointed under the provisions of the Act of September 30, 1850, to effect a just settlement with the California Indians. Redick McKee, G. W. Barbour, and O. M. Wozencraft, representing the United States, proceeded to negotiate with the headmen of California tribes. Between March 19, 1851, and January 7, 1852, they met 402 tribal heads at various central meeting places, and entered into eighteen treaties. It has been estimated that one half to one third of the Indians of California were involved in these treaties. Under the treaties the Indians relinquished their claims to lands in the United States, but they were to have the right to use and occupy certain areas specifically described, and were promised supplies, tools, livestock, clothing, the services of agents, teachers, and carpenters, together with necessary buildings. By these treaties a large part of the acreage of California was surrendered in return for promises—promises that were not kept. The Indians and the treaty negotiators acted apparently in good faith but the United States Senate refused to ratify a single treaty.

The mighty Gold Rush was on, with newcomers swarming over part of the areas proposed to be set apart as Indian reservations and with old-timers angry at the idea of good lands being awarded to "degraded" Indians. Most Californians had no use for the government's treaty making with the Indians. The editor of the Los Angeles *Star* represented this viewpoint when on March 13, 1852, he wrote:

We believe the action of the commissioners to be pregnant with the most disastrous consequences, and we can see no solution of the difficulties that will grow up around us, if the General Government ratify these treaties, except a general and exterminating war ... To place upon our most fertile soil the most degraded race of aborigines upon the North American Continent, to invest them with the rights of sovereignty, and to teach them that they are to be treated as powerful and independent nations, is planting the seeds of future disaster and ruin ... We hope that the general government will let us alone—that it will neither undertake to feed, settle or remove the Indians amongst whom we in the South reside, and that they will leave everything just as it now exists, except affording us the protection which two or three cavalry companies would give.

A special committee appointed by the California legislature reported against the policy followed by the commissioners, and the legislature, by an overwhelming vote, recommended that Congress be prevented from confirming the Indian reservations. The resolutions from California did their work and on July 8, 1852, the Senate of the United States rejected each of the eighteen treaties.

Meanwhile the Indians who had been induced to remove to specified reservations met the opposition of any white pioneers claiming or in possession of such areas. Lands ceded by the Indians, if not within privately granted ranchos, remained a part of the public domain. Lands promised for Indian use and occupancy—but not given—were also largely "public lands" and remained such. On top of all this the courts held that the failure of the California Indians—an almost wholly illiterate people—to present their claims before the Board of Land

Commissioners, whose hearings took place in the 1850's, debarred them from later establishing any interest in California lands, even the right of occupancy.

The Indians of California, accordingly, who once occupied, after a fashion, three-quarters of the state's more than 100,000,000 acres of land—along the seashore, in the mountains and the deserts, and along the Sacramento, San Joaquin, Russian, Pit, Klamath, Trinity, and other rivers—were exposed to eviction, persecution, exploitation, enslavement, and massacre. Many became homeless wanderers. By 1910 California Indians numbered 16,350.[1]

When the United States did get around to setting aside, as Indian reservations, certain lands out of the public domain or out of privately owned land bought for that purpose, too often miners and settlers had already taken the best. What was left was sometimes, as in southern California especially, waste land, desert, mountain, grazing, isolated, or waterless areas.

The year-by-year story of what lands the Indians of California relinquished to the United States, of what lands were set aside out of the public domain or elsewhere for their use as "reservations"—between the years 1851 and 1894—and of the transfer of tribes from one reservation to another is told in Charles C. Royce's exhaustive *Indian Land Cessions in the United States.* Descriptions and maps of the tracts involved accompany the schedule of cessions. This study includes the first "treaty" reservation, a tract between the Merced and Tuolumne rivers, established March 19, 1851. It tells of Superintendent E. F. Beale's establishment of a "reserve," the first of its

---

[1] The population had apparently increased to 23,281 by 1940, according to the report of the Commissioner of Indian Affairs made on June 30, 1940. This figure possibly does not represent an actual increase, but, instead, the inclusion of many Indians who had not been enrolled before.

kind, at Tejon Pass. A listing of important cessions or dispositions of Indian lands after the year 1894 is presented in Daniel M. Greene's *Public Land Statutes of the United States,* a compilation for the United States Department of the Interior.

The map of California today shows several hundred thousand acres of land in Indian reservations. The largest is the Hoopa (Hupa) Valley reservation in Humboldt County. Other reservations are the Round Valley, in Mendocino County, the Tule River in Tulare County, the Yuma in the southeast corner of Imperial County, and the large group of "mission" Indian reservations in Riverside and San Diego counties. The last group numbers less than thirty and includes, among others, the Morongo, Soboba, Agua Caliente (Palm Springs), Santa Ysabel, and Pala reservations. Each reservation was established after a long struggle by or on behalf of the Indians. Lands within these reservations could be disposed of only under the provisions of special acts of Congress.[2]

Although there was Congressional legislation in 1875 and in 1884 to enable certain Indians to secure homesteads on the public domain, the restrictions in the acts defeated their purposes. Probably, too, no California Indian was ever informed of his rights.

Allotments of lands to Indians were provided for by Congress in 1887. These allotments could be within established reservations or outside on the public domain. Their size ranged from 40 to 160 acres, depending upon whether the land was "irrigable," "non-irrigable agricultural," or "grazing." A large number of allotments ultimately were made in California, mostly in the

---

[2] The Office of Indian Affairs had under its jurisdiction on January 1, 1940, 666,817 acres of California land: 198,368 "trust allotted"; 458,934 "tribal"; and 9,515 "government owned."

northeastern counties, by special agents sent out from Washington.[3] The act provided for the issuance of patents in the names of the allottees, but the United States was to hold the land allotted in trust for twenty-five years. In some cases the allotments were of great value, but many were absolute desert, and to most of California's Indians the allotment laws brought little relief.

As land in California became more sought after by white settlers, life became harder for the Indian population. When ejected from one tract which had been filed on by some white man, the Indian families affected had to find a landowner who would tolerate their "squatting" on his lands. The wanderers thus tended to crowd into certain rancherías or settlements where living conditions were deplorable. In the 'eighties Helen Hunt Jackson had called the attention of the nation to the sad state of the California Indians by the publication of her *A Century of Dishonor* and *Ramona*. Congress took faltering steps in 1890 to give relief, and the Smiley Commission increased and enlarged the southern California reservations. A branch of the National Indian Association was established in northern California and schools for Indians were organized. The California Indian Association began an educational campaign in 1904 to secure land from Congress. Other groups joined. The most active in southern California was the Sequoya League, organized by Charles F. Lummis, David Starr Jordan, Frederick Webb Hodge, Phoebe A. Hearst, and others. Congressional appropriations for relief followed. C. E. Kelsey, General Secretary of the Northern California Indian As-

---

[3] C. E. Kelsey, special agent, reported in 1906 that 2,058 allotments had been made in California with 261 canceled, leaving 1,797 outstanding, these being in Modoc, Lassen, Plumas, Shasta, and Siskiyou counties. Kelsey also found a few Indian communities owning land in common in Humboldt, Lake, and Mendocino counties.

sociation, in charge of purchasing and allotting required lands, served until the appropriations were exhausted.

The eighteen treaties of 1851 and 1852 lay in the archives of the United States Senate until 1905. With the discovery in that year of these skeletons in the closet, various groups, such as San Francisco's Commonwealth Club of California, took steps to publicize the unfortunate situation of the remaining California Indians and to work for their relief. In 1927 the California legislature finally passed an act authorizing the attorney general, provided Congressional authority was given, to bring suit in behalf of the Indians against the United States in the Court of Claims. Congress reciprocated and passed the California Indians' Jurisdictional Act of 1928, affording a limited means of relief. Under its provisions a petition was filed in the Court of Claims—the case being entitled "The Indians of California, Claimants, by U. S. Webb, Attorney General of the State of California v. The United States, No. K-344." Following the court's decision, on October 5, 1942, that the plaintiffs were entitled to recover, subject to allowable offsets, they were awarded the sum of $5,024,842.34 on December 4, 1944. This amount was appropriated by Congress and paid into the United States Treasury to draw interest at 4 per cent per annum. It remains in the Treasury—less $27,842.50 allowed the state for expenses incurred in conducting the litigation. It is subject to reappropriation by Congress "for educational, health, industrial and other purposes for the benefit of said Indians, including the purchase of lands and building of homes," but not for per capita payments to Indians.[4] In August, 1946, Congress passed an act pro-

---

[4] From the Jurisdictional Act of 1928, 45 *Stat.* 602, 46 *Stat.* 259, and as contained in Opinion No. 47/205 issued August 29, 1947 by Fred N. Howser, Attorney General, by Hartwell H. Linney, Chief Assistant.

viding for an Indian Claims Commission of three members to be appointed by the President to hear the claims of Indians residing in the United States or Alaska against the United States.

Such is the fund and the machinery finally set up to compensate the Indians of California for the injustice practiced upon them by the rejection of the treaties negotiated in 1851–1852. Representation of Indian claims by the state attorney general and the use of sums authorized for that purpose by the state in 1947 is at present contingent upon the Indians of California uniting in one group.

If, in 1852, the Senate had approved the eighteen treaties, could we assume that all would have been well? No. If the hunting, fishing, and acorn-gathering tribes had been given some of the best lands in the state in 1852 serious trouble would have resulted for the Indians. It is certain they could not have maintained their lands against the influx of aggressive, impatient white settlers, men who saw gold in the hills and visioned farms and towns in the valleys. Conflict between civilization and primitive living was inevitable. An early awareness by the government, however, of its moral obligations as guardian of a helpless people, together with definite provision in the Act of 1851 for possessory rights of Indians, would have saved California's Indians from much of the misery that overwhelmed them.

Worthy of a place among famous Indian orations is the speech of Cecilio Blacktooth, captain of Agua Caliente, principal Indian village on Warner's Ranch in San Diego County, made by him there on March 17, 1902, a year before his tribe's forced removal to Pala Valley. On the next page is Captain Blacktooth's speech at a meeting held with Charles F. Lummis.

We thank you for coming here to talk to us in a way we can understand. It is the first time anyone has done so. You ask us to think what place we like next best to this place where we always live. You see that graveyard over there? There are our fathers and our grandfathers. You see that Eagle-Nest mountain and that Rabbit-Hole mountain? When God made them He gave us this place. We have always been here. We do not care for any other place. It may be good but it is not ours. We have always lived here. We would rather die here. Our fathers did. We cannot leave them. Our children born here—how can we go away? If you give us the best place in the world, it is not so good for us as this. My people cannot go anywhere else; they cannot live anywhere else. Here they always live; their people always live here. There is no other place. This is our home. We ask you to get it for us. If Harvey Downey say he own this place, that is wrong. The Indians always here. We do not go on his land. We stay here on ours. Everybody knows this Indian land. These Hot Springs always Indian. We cannot live anywhere else. We were born here, and our fathers are buried here. We do not think of any place after this. We want this place and not any other place. There is no other place for us. We do not want you to buy any other place for us. If you will not buy this place we will go into the mountains like quail and die there, the old people and the women and the children. Let the Government be glad and proud. It can kill us. We do not fight. We do what it says. If we cannot live here, we want to go into those mountains and die. We do not want any other home.

Blacktooth's speech appears in the *Warner's Ranch Report* made by the Congressionally approved commission of five southern Californians—Russell C. Allen, Clarence L. Partridge, Charles F. Lummis, William Collier, and R. Egan—appointed to serve without compensation and to select a new site for the Indians who were about to be evicted from their ancestral home on Rancho San José del Valle or Warner's Ranch. This rancho was a Mexican grant; the title of its owners had been upheld by the

United States Land Commission and the courts; the belated claims of the Indians had been rejected by the United States Supreme Court in 1901. The case had attracted national attention. The commission, with Lummis as chairman, chose 3,438 acres in Pala Valley, the best available place and actually a better location than Warner's Ranch.

It was inevitable that Indian claims to land in California, whether of individuals or of groups, should fade before the white invasion. What remains to them are the allotments granted and the areas substituted and set aside by the United States as reservations out of the public domain or bought by it from private owners. These reservations, too, probably will pass, with California Indians taking their place as individual landowners like California citizens of white or other races.

CHAPTER III

Missionary Empire

TODAY a Californian on vacation tour of his own state, having been escorted through one of the restored Franciscan missions, makes a contribution to the guide, and steps out into the bright sun of the road where his car is parked. He is in a mood of happy benevolence, satisfied with his excursion into the past and content with a good world.

This Californian is visiting every one of the twenty-one missions or mission sites. He began with the first of the missions, San Diego de Alcalá, founded in 1769, in the warm and fertile valley of the San Diego River, and he ends with San Francisco Solano in the sunny Sonoma Valley, the last of the missions, established in 1823. In most of the restored or partly restored mission establishments there is a priest to escort the visitor through a charming garden, gay with hollyhocks or roses, down through arched corridors, through thick-walled, cool adobe rooms—heavy with the presence of the past—the former dormitories, workshops, and storerooms of gray-robed Franciscans and brown-skinned natives, a crude but impressive church, and an old cemetery where several thousand Indians are buried five deep. The priest shows the treasured paintings, the embroidered robes, the illuminated music books bound in rawhide, the Indian-made tables and benches, the tools and relics of early days, and perhaps points to the remains of an effective irrigation system. He tells the story of the founding, the first baptism of Indians, the rise to prosperity, the vast herds of cattle, the wine making, the work and the play, and the occasional disciplining of the neophytes, the epidemics of smallpox, the sacrilege of secularization, the years of dishonor and disintegration, the final rescue by the United States of a small part of the land holdings, the partial restoration, and the hopes for the further restoration of the original buildings. Some of the missions, the visitor finds, are today parish churches, taking an active part in community work. Others are training schools for young priests.

Spain began actual colonization of this fabled and far away country in 1769. With colonization through a co-ordinated, threefold plan that called for missions, presidios, and pueblos, Spain established its claims to ownership of California.

The building of a chain of missions was begun under capable, zealous Fray Junípero Serra. Strategic spots throughout the state were chosen, the locations usually being those the Indians themselves had found best for their own needs. But this activity was not accompanied by any conveyance to missions or priests of California land. Under the Spanish theory of colonization the missionary establishments were not intended to be permanent. When the Indians were Christianized and civilized, the mission settlements were to become pueblos. They were always subject, therefore, to secularization, that is, subject to being turned over to lay administration and to having the lands disposed of as a part of the public domain. The missions were permitted, under the Spanish and Mexican governments, to occupy and use certain lands *for the benefit of the Indians,* but not to own them. They were, in effect, trustees only.

Nevertheless, long before the chain had been completed—with El Camino Real (the Royal Highway) connecting the establishments—the missionaries had so thoroughly "taken over" and had so extended their possession of the land that the "limits" of one mission tended to form those of another. This extension took place despite the fact that only a part of these lands was actually used for grazing and agriculture. The mission system grew naturally to huge proportions, though the whole of the mission-controlled area was only about one-sixth of California. The success of the system depended on the Indians leaving their villages or rancherías and living in the shadow of the church. Most of the near-by Indians did leave their rancherías, either voluntarily or through compulsion, giving up freedom for security. During the first twenty years the method of kindliness and persuasion was used to bring in the heathen. The missionaries held out the inducements of clothing, shelter, and food, along with emphasis on religious ceremony, music, and processions. After the adjacent natives had been assimilated, the fathers broadened the field of conversion and used more forcible methods, even military, to bring in recalcitrant Indians. Each mission center was an almost self-sufficing unit, extending its feudal activities over a vast surrounding area. At each mission lived a few hundred to two or three thousand dependent neophytes who worked for food, clothing, and shelter at the tasks assigned them. The Indians themselves had no individual property rights. The missions soon became wealthy in material possessions and dominated the state. With guest rooms available, they even offered the traveler the only possible hotel service.

Inevitably the missionaries resisted the giving of land concessions by the governor to individual Californians. They rightly regarded the rancho movement, which began in 1784, as a threat to the success of their effort. Rancheros, they felt, with their free and easy life, set a bad example to Indians and used land they and their neophytes needed. This attitude was expressed in a gently phrased report dated September 3, 1795, to Father Lasuén, president of the missions, from Father Santa María, who was on a site-hunting expedition that resulted in the establishment of San Fernando Mission.

What I have to say to Your Reverence is that on this expedition I observed that the whole pagandom, between this mission (San Buenaventura) and that of San Gabriel, along the beach, along the camino real, and along the border of the north, is fond of the Pueblo of Los Angeles, of the rancho of Mariano Verdugo, of the rancho of Reyes, and of the Zanja. Here we see nothing but pagans passing, clad in shoes, with sombreros and blankets, and serving as muleteers to the settlers and rancheros, so that if it were not for the gentiles there would be neither pueblo nor rancho; and if this be not accepted as true let them bring proof. Finally these pagan Indians care neither for the mission nor for the missionaries.[1]

To avoid conflict early-day rancheros sought land as far as possible from mission centers. Observe, for example, the coastal ranchos of Los Angeles County: San Pedro

---

[1] Charles Anthony (Zephyrin) Engelhardt, *San Fernando Rey* (Chicago, 1922).

and Topanga Malibu Sequit. Old records abound in disputes between priests and the holders of rancho concessions sometimes over boundaries, sometimes upon the right of individuals to take land over which missions claimed supervision for the Indians.

Mission San Gabriel objected strenuously to the presence of ranchero Manuel Nieto at Los Coyotes, where he had permission to place stock. In 1796 Nieto wrote to the governor for relief, saying: "I find myself harassed in such a way on the part of the mission that being no longer able to endure it, I appeal to your Worship's powerful protection . . . that the Reverend Father Missionaries of said mission . . . are continually warning me to abandon the place because it belongs to the Indians, and that they do not want me to stay under any title." A few years later missionaries at Carmel were calling for the expulsion of settlers from the rancho of Buena Vista. The padres of San Juan Bautista were successful in forcing Mariano Castro to abandon a settlement project at near-by La Brea, though he had a viceregal license, and to establish himself elsewhere. Boundary disputes between José María Verdugo, grantee of Rancho San Rafael (later site of Glendale and part of Burbank), and the priests of the adjoining missions of San Gabriel and San Fernando, in the years 1814 to 1817, were settled by government action and the establishment of definite ownership lines. We hear of the Church in 1819 protesting, but without avail, a cattle-grazing permit given to members of the Machado and Talamantes families for land (Los Quintos, presumably what was later called La Ballona) in the Culver City area. Consider the several years' dispute between Mission Dolores and ranchero Luís María Peralta over a section of Rancho San Antonio, on which rancho now stand part

of San Leandro, Alameda, Oakland, Piedmont, Emery-
ville, Berkeley, and Albany. The missionaries had used
this east shore property as a sheep ranch before it was
ceded to Peralta by Governor Solá in 1820.

As California's population grew and as the demand
for ranch land increased, the position of the land-monop-
olizing missions became increasingly anachronistic. The
attempts of the missions to stem the tide of private acquisition of property were doomed to the same failure that
met King Canute's fabled trials at stopping the rising
tides of the sea.

William Carey Jones in his pioneering report made
for Congress in 1850 clearly explained the temporary nature of mission titles. Later, for the benefit of the Board
of Land Commissioners hearing mission claims, Judge
Felch made a simple and concise statement of the whole
Spanish theory of missionary colonization:

The Missions were intended, from the beginning, to be temporary in their character. It *was contemplated that in ten
years from their first foundation they should cease.* It was
supposed that within that period of time the Indians would
be sufficiently instructed in Christianity and the arts of civilized life, to assume the position and character of *citizens;* that
these Mission settlements would then become PUEBLOS, and
that the Mission churches would become parish churches,
organized like the other establishments of an ecclesiastical
character, in other portions of the nation where no Missions
had ever existed. The whole Missionary establishment was
widely different from the ordinary ecclesiastical organization
of the nation. In it the superintendence and charge was com-
mitted to priests who were devoted to the special work of
Missions, and not to the ordinary clergy. The monks of the
College of San Fernando and Zacatecas, in whose charge they
were, were to be succeeded by the secular clergy of the National Church, the Missionary field was to become a DIOCESE,

the President of the Missions to give place to a BISHOP, the Mission churches to become CURACIES, and the faithful in the vicinity of each parish to become the parish worshippers.

Although actual secularization of the California missions did not begin until 1834, the demand for it had long been growing. As early as 1813 the cortes or legislature of Spain had shown impatience at the long-drawn-out existence of the missions in America and had passed a decree providing for at least partial secularization for those missions that had been established for ten years. This decree was not enforced in California. The agitation for independence from Spain stimulated the move to take over the enormously wealthy mission holdings, turn missions into parishes, and substitute secular clergy for missionary priests. Commentator Don José Martín, early-day "booster" for California, in the year 1822 was attacking the priests for enslaving Indians and for opposing establishment of haciendas by settlers. Steps toward secularization in California were taken by Governor Echeandía in 1826 and 1831 by decrees which weakened Indian dependence on the missions. Obviously California Indians were not ready for secularization and the management of their own affairs. The increasing white population, however, hungry for land and jealous of the organization that held the most and the best land, made secularization a hot and inevitable issue. Tremendous pressure was brought on the government. An ambitious Mexican attempt to colonize Alta California—long in the making—led by José María Híjar and José María Padrés and aided by Juan Bandini, California representative, spurred the Mexican congress to take decisive action.

On August 17, 1833, during Governor José Figueroa's regime, secularization, abrupt, all-inclusive and harsh, became the law in California. The following year the first regulations were issued for putting it into effect. The management of temporal affairs of the missions was to be turned over to civil administrators. Padres were to keep to their spiritual labors. Lands, other than those to be distributed to heads of Indian families and adults, were to remain at the disposal of the government. Secularization, beginning in 1834, with ten missions secularized, was completed by 1836. At many mission centers demoralization quickly set in, with the Indians—unprepared to take care of themselves—scurrying away to the towns or to the ranchos, perhaps helping themselves first to horses and other personal property, and with mission land holdings being rented, sold, or neglected by the government.

Without avail was the attempt made in 1843 by Governor Micheltorena to restore twelve of the missions, to reanimate "the skeleton of a giant," as he phrased the system. In 1845 Governor Pío Pico signed at Los Angeles detailed regulations for the sale of specific missions and the renting of certain others.[2] Thus, with secularization accomplished, with the missions destroyed, with the neophytes dispersed, one of the most idealistic adventures in colonization ever attempted came to an end.

Secularization in 1834 was the signal for a land rush in California and a shifting of population. Settlers who had been doubling up with relatives or living in presidios and pueblos flooded the governor's office with their petitions for this valley and that valley. Ricardo Vejar, for example, who had been living on Rancho Rodeo de las Aguas (now Beverly Hills) on sufferance of the owner, joined with Ygnacio Palomares and received permission to settle on and take title to Rancho San José (Pomona Valley). In-

[2] For further information on this step, see below, chap. vi.

fluential citizens were given preference, of course, for land was the gift of government. All the pueblos declined in population. It was in this same year of 1834 that 200 colonists, members of the Híjar and Padrés group, came to California to add to the land demand, some of them becoming prominent as citizens—for example, Ignacio Coronel and family, Agustín Olvera, Victor Prudon, and José María Covarrubias. Between 1834 and 1842 more than 300 ranchos were granted to Mexican citizens, and largely carved out of mission-held land.

The claims of the Catholic Church to acreage at each of the twenty-one missions were presented in 1853 by Archbishop Joseph Sodoc Alemany to the Board of United States Land Commissioners. This Board was created under the Act of 1851 to segregate privately owned land from that which was public domain. Confirmation was limited practically to the exact area of land covered by the church buildings, cemeteries, and gardens, ranging from 6.48 acres allowed Mission San Rafael in Marin County to 283.13 acres allowed Mission Santa Barbara in Santa Barbara County. Patents from the United States followed official survey of these small allotments—all that was salvaged from the pastoral-age land empire that had been founded by tireless and heroic Fray Junípero Serra.[3]

---

[3] The following list of California missions, in the order of founding, gives the quantity of land the title to which was confirmed by the United States, the acreage being that shown in the *Corrected Report of Spanish and Mexican Grants in California Complete to February 25, 1886*, prepared by the State Surveyor General and published in Sacramento in 1886 as a supplement to the Official Report of 1883–84:

San Diego de Alcalá, 1769, 22.21 acres
San Carlos Borroméo, or Carmelo, 1770, 9 acres
San Antonio de Padua, 1771, 33.19 acres
San Gabriel Arcángel, 1771, 190.69 acres
San Luís Obispo, 1772, 52.72 acres
San Francisco de Asís, or Dolores, 1776, 8.54 acres
San Juan Capistrano, 1776, 44.40 acres

The California visitor today, who has completed his pleasant tour of the twenty-one missions or mission sites, will probably not go deeply into their history. Nor will he concern himself with missionary theories of land-ownership or of trusteeship for Indians. He will be interested, probably and properly, in their preservation and further restoration—symbols of an idealistic adventure. He will feel sure, too, that more of them will become parish churches and training schools, performing useful functions year by year as well as preserving indefinitely the story of one phase of the Spanish colonization of California.

Santa Clara de Asís, 1777, 19.95 acres
San Buenaventura, 1782, 36.27 acres
Santa Barbara, 1786, 283.13 acres
La Purísima Concepción, 1787, 14.04 acres
Santa Cruz, 1791, 16.94 acres
La Soledad, 1791, 34.47 acres
San José, 1797, 28.33 acres
San Juan Bautista, 1797, 55.23 acres
San Miguel Arcángel, 1797, 33.97 acres
San Fernando Rey, 1797, 76.94 acres
San Luís Rey, 1798, 53.39 acres
Santa Inés, 1804, 17.35 acres
San Rafael Arcángel, 1817, 6.48 acres
San Francisco Solano, 1823, 14.20 acres

Archbishop Alemany filed the claim of the Church with the Land Commission on February 19, 1853 (Case No. 609). Confirmation by the Commission took place December 18, 1855. The appeal to the District Court was dismissed March 16, 1857, Northern District, and March 15, 1858, Southern District (Case Nos. 425, N.D. and 388, S.D.). Patents for each mission area were issued to Archbishop J. S. Alemany. Also confirmed to the Church were Cañada de los Pinos or College Rancho in Santa Barbara County, comprising 35,499.37 acres, and La Laguna in San Luis Obispo County, comprising 4,157.02 acres. Patents for these areas were also issued to Archbishop J. S. Alemany.

CHAPTER IV

Four Square Leagues

PROBABLY NO ONE, unless he were a missionary priest, wanted to go to California in the year 1769, when Spain was beginning its occupation of that far-flung, far-distant land.

But Spain's plans for colonization of Alta California were part of the expansionist program of José de Gálvez, adviser to King Charles III, working through the obliging viceroy of New Spain. That program called not only for missionaries to establish missions and civilize the Indians, but also for soldiers to found frontier outposts and settlers to start farming communities. Soldiers led the way and, carrying out royal orders, built and maintained along the coast the presidios of San Diego, Monterey, San Francisco, and Santa Barbara that permitted the building and insured the protection of missions and pueblos in the interior.

The story of the presidios and the story of the pueblos, however, is really one—so far as the account of men owning land is concerned—for presidios become pueblos. Within and around the presidios grew small settlements which came to be called presidial pueblos. These, like the deliberately planned pueblos of San José and Los Angeles, were recognized by Spain and the United States as pueblos and, as such, also entitled to four square leagues of land.[1] This area was to be measured "in a square or prolonged form according to the character of the land." The leagues were, of course, Spanish leagues. A Spanish league was about two and three-fifths miles.

The sites selected for California's four presidios commanded the sea or the bay. Visitors today to Presidio Hill Park overlooking "Old Town" and the bay of San Diego are shown a few mounds and bits of adobe wall marking the ground plan of California's first presidio, founded in 1769, under conditions of difficulty, illness, and privation, and used for garrison purposes until 1835. The building of the presidio of Monterey, situated "a gunshot from the beach," was begun in the following year—at first with only a few huts surrounded by a palisade. San Francisco, most northerly of the presidios, was established in 1776 near a high and perpendicular cliff, on a site chosen by Juan Bautista de Anza. Diarist Father Font described it not only as a place from which one could watch the spouting of whales and the play of dolphins, sea otters, and sea lions but from which one could spit into the sea. Fourth and last of the presidios to be founded was that

---

[1] The Spanish law which assigned four square leagues of land to each organized pueblo is found in Book 4 of the Laws of the Indies (*Recopilacion de Leyes de los Reynos de las Indias*), Title 5, Laws 6 and 10. Official construction of the law is found in an opinion given on October 27, 1785, by Galindo Navarro, attorney of the Commandancy, and transmitted to California's governor, Don Pedro Fages. Translations are available in John W. Dwinelle's *The Colonial History of San Francisco* (San Francisco, 1863), see his Addenda, Nos. I, II, VI. Also see Hart *v.* Burnett, 15 Cal. 530.

of Santa Barbara, in 1782, near the shore of a bay and close by springs of good water and a large native village.

Soldiers, sailors, priests, and settlers participated in the ceremonies that attended the beginnings of the presidios that were to become pueblos. The actual construction of presidios followed an established pattern. The features of a presidio, as described by the French visitor Duflot de Mofras, were an outer, surrounding ditch, the enclosure forming a quadrilateral; a rampart twelve to fifteen feet high and three feet thick; small bastions; an armament of bronze cannon, eight-, twelve-, and sixteeen-pounders; within the enclosure a church, barracks, houses for colonists, storehouses, workshops, stables, wells, and cisterns; outside were some houses and, at greater distance, the "King's Farm" (*el rancho del rey*) which furnished pasturage to horses and cattle.

The account of the beginning of the presidio of San Francisco is well detailed. Soldiers, colonists, and cattle went by land from Monterey, and equipment was shipped from the same port on the *San Carlos*. A temporary chapel and tule huts were put up, then a square measuring 92 varas each way was marked out for the presidio, which was to include divisions for church, royal offices, warehouses, guardhouse, and houses for soldier settlers. Sailors and carpenters built a warehouse for supplies, a house for the commanding officer, and a chapel. The soldiers were free to erect their own dwellings. By September, 1776, the presidio had become a little village of flat-roofed log houses and buildings—perhaps resembling, we are reminded by historian Herbert E. Bolton, some of its contemporaries in the Ohio Valley.

California's presidios were first of all military outposts. But they were also recognized as pueblos, the captains of the presidios being authorized to grant and distribute to soldiers and citizens house lots and lands within the four-square-league area measured from the center of the presidio square.

The presidio of San Francisco, for example, was founded by considerably more married men than that required for the founding of a pueblo. By 1825 it had 120 houses and perhaps 500 people, according to visiting Captain Benjamin Morrell. By 1834 an *ayuntamiento* or common council was functioning and the presidio had been officially recognized as a pueblo. By 1835 the population was shifting from the table land above the sea to the sheltered cove adjacent to Telegraph Hill where the village of Yerba Buena was being born. This village was within the four square leagues of land measured from the center of the plaza at the presidio. Until 1846 alcaldes and justices of the peace in Yerba Buena granted town lots to its inhabitants, the first conveyance being to William A. Richardson on June 2, 1836, of a 100-vara lot in the vicinity of the northwest corner of Grant Avenue and Washington Street. Early in 1847 Yerba Buena—"the good herb"—changed its name to San Francisco, the original designation given the presidio, the pueblo, and the bay. When California became a part of the United States, the new government recognized San Francisco as a pueblo—as did the legislature of California which raised its rank to that of a city. The United States Circuit Court in 1865 confirmed San Francisco's pueblo title to four square leagues of land—following the city's appeal from an earlier partial rejection by the Board of Land Commissioners—and in the following year Congress relinquished to the city the land confirmed.

But to go back to Spain's eighteenth-century plans for

the colonization of California. It was not enough to establish presidios at strategic points along the coast and to foster a string of missions in the interior. Farming communities—outright pueblos—fitted into the plan also and, under royal approval, were to be established in fertile valleys so that soldier garrisons need not be dependent on shipborne importations of grain from San Blas, Mexico.

Following an exchange of ideas in 1776 between Governor Neve, whose headquarters were then in Loreto, Lower California, and Viceroy Bucareli, Neve started north to establish his seat at Monterey. On the way to Monterey he looked for areas in Upper California which had good soil and abundant water for irrigation and chose a pueblo site along the Porciuncula River in the south and another along the Guadalupe in the north.

One November day Lieutenant Don José Moraga, commander of the presidio of San Francisco, started south from San Francisco under orders from the governor with sixty-six men, women, and children—soldiers and settlers with their families. The party made their last camp in a valley watered by the Guadalupe. Here they built huts of plastered palisades, earth-roofed, constructed a dam and a water ditch, prepared the fields for sowing, and so became the founders of California's first pueblo of San José, founded November 29, 1777.

It probably had not been hard to enlist these settlers, who already knew something of farming, for the site along the Guadalupe was a comparatively short distance from San Francisco and only three quarters of a league from Mission Santa Clara. Here was a pleasant valley of which the San Franciscans had some knowledge, and they came under a colonization plan (presently to be announced) that was most attractive.

To draw settlers to the Los Angeles area, however, called for extended effort and experience in the arts of persuasion on the part of the governing officials, for the recruiting grounds were a thousand miles away. Men had to be induced to leave the settled areas of Sonora and Sinaloa in Mexico and travel northward through unknown country to an unknown destination. The job of recruiting was entrusted to experienced Captain Don Fernando Javier Rivera y Moncada.

Twenty-four settlers and fifty-nine soldiers were needed. Captain Rivera was ordered to canvass a large area, to advertise the advantages of "joining up" but not to overadvertise. Do not deceive "with offers of more than can be fulfilled," he was told by his superior. He could offer settlers ten pesos a month and daily rations for three years from enlistment. He could promise to each settler "two cows, two oxen, two mares, two horses, one mule, two ewes, two goats, and the tools and utensils necessary for the labors of the field." It was give and take, however, for the government expected ultimately to be reimbursed out of crops and herds for the stock and other supplies. Soldier recruits would receive pay that would more than cover their expenses. Captain Rivera was asked to dispel some of the false interpretations already being placed by people on the regulations issued by Governor Neve for the colonization of the province of California. There were rumors, it seems, about discounts and surcharges to come out of pay, and many people were failing to take advantage of the opportunity of "gaining an honorable and happy berth and of performing a loyal service to the King."

The zeal of the government in winning men's minds is best exhibited in the governor's regulations—the *Regla-*

mento—issued in 1779 and receiving royal approval in 1781. Detailed instructions for setting up and maintaining the pueblo of Los Angeles were given, apparently applicable also to the established pueblo of San José and to pueblos not yet planned for. These instructions covered generous pay and rations to settlers, free distribution of house lots and farming land, allotment of farm animals and tools, rules for the disposal of property, and the common privileges of water, pasturage, firewood, and timber. Settlers were to be tax free for five years but they had to build houses, plant fruit trees, and in other ways improve their land and opportunities. They could not mortgage their property. They were to be armed and to maintain the defense of their district.

In the face of difficulties Rivera did a good recruiting job. The first Los Angeles man was signed up at La Villa de Sinaloa. He was Felix Villavicencio, a native of Chihuahua and he was outfitted—as were those who followed him—with everything from shoes to hair ribbons. The merchants of Los Alamos and Rosario were asked to cooperate and to keep their shelves well stocked.

Soldiers and settlers, a hardy lot, made the difficult journey through wild country, and the tule hut pueblo of Los Angeles was founded, September 4, 1781, the second pueblo in California. It was destined in ten years to be a successful farming community of 139 persons, with 29 dwellings of adobe, as well as public town hall, barracks, guardhouse, and granaries—all enclosed by an adobe wall. This community was then producing more grain than any of the missions in California, except neighboring San Gabriel.

The third pueblo, Branciforte at Santa Cruz, across the river from the mission, was established in 1797 by a party of destitute colonists from Guadalajara who had arrived by ship at Monterey in May of that year. Though ambitiously planned, the pueblo or villa, as it was sometimes called, was not long lived. Even the name itself, which honored the viceroy, was swallowed up in that of the near-by mission.

Each fully organized pueblo was entitled—without special grant—to four square leagues of land, the law providing that this area was to be measured, as already stated, in a square or prolonged form according to the character of the land. These four leagues could be divided into house lots (*solares*), farm lots (*suertes*), lands to be rented for municipal revenue (*propios*), vacant suburbs or commons (*ejidos*), and big cattle pastures (*dehesas*). The government of a pueblo, as soon as it met population requirements, was by a common council called the *ayuntamiento*. The mayor was the *alcalde*.

When the pueblos of San José and Los Angeles were five years old their people were put formally in possession of their individual house and farm lots. Late in 1782 Governor Fages appointed Lieutenant Moraga of the presidio of San Francisco as commissioner to go to San José for this official purpose. In the name of the king and in the presence of two assisting witnesses he was to give possession and good title to the nine founders of the pueblo, together with iron brands to mark their cattle. Lieutenant Moraga gave formal possession the following May, the first grant going to Ygnacio Archuleta for a house lot adjoining that on which stood the council's house and for four farm lots which were duly measured off. So, too, at the pueblo of Los Angeles, where on September 4, 1786—exactly five years after the founding—formal possession was given to the colonists by Don José Argüello of Santa Barbara, appointed commissioner for that purpose by Fages. Felix Villavicencio, who had been the first to enlist with Rivera, was the first Los Angeles settler to receive possession, his land being a house lot 20 varas wide and 40 varas long together with four farm lots each 200 varas square.

Pueblo claims to landownership were given full consideration in the act passed in 1851 by the Congress of the United States for the settlement of private land claims in California. The corporate authorities—instead of individual lot owners—were authorized to place their claims to lands granted for the establishment of a town by the Spanish or Mexican government or existing on July 7, 1846. Proof of the existence of a town on July 7, 1846, was to be prima facie evidence of a grant. For any town existing *at the time of the passing of the act,* the corporate authority was authorized to make the claim for "the land embraced within the limits of the same." There was no specific limitation to four square leagues. Accordingly, San José and Los Angeles, together with the four presidio towns and also Sonoma—a pueblo recognized as such by Mexico and formed under Mexican laws—were claimants before the Commission. Each finally received confirmation of title and a United States patent, though the land was not always in the amount asked for nor was the confirmation always without extended litigation. Los Angeles which asked for sixteen square leagues was reduced to four. San Francisco's long battle in the courts engaged the attention of the ablest attorneys and brought to light a vast quantity of historical data about the whole landholding system during the Spanish and Mexican periods.

Our courts ruled that pueblos held title in trust for the inhabitants and that the State of California succeeded to the powers Mexico formerly held to regulate the disposition of pueblo lands. Accordingly, it was necessary for the legislature of California, either through general laws or through approval of municipal charters, to determine the manner in which a former pueblo could grant its lands into private ownership. Most people who today hold title to lots within a pueblo's four-square-league (or confirmed) area can base their claims on deeds directly from the municipality itself.

A few Indian pueblos—San Juan Capistrano, San Dieguito, and Las Flores—had a feeble flowering after the secularization of the missions in 1833, under the rules issued by Governor Figueroa providing for partial conversion of missions to pueblos. The ruins of the quadrangle of adobe buildings of the Pueblita de las Flores can still be seen in a plowed field on the north side of Las Flores Creek near the coast highway in San Diego County. The story of Las Flores is told by Terry E. Stephenson from Land Commission proceedings involving Rancho Santa Margarita y Las Flores. Originating in an *estación* established by Mission San Luis Rey on El Camino Real, it was converted into an Indian pueblo by Don Santiago Argüello, civil administrator of the secularized mission, who described its boundaries as: "On the north, the gully called Temescal; south, the canyon called Sycamore; east, the Canyon Las Flores up to the fence of the garden that the padres had near a spring; west, the sea. It measured a league and a half on each side." Year by year the pueblo disintegrated, and in 1843 the Indians consented to the transfer of Las Flores' 20 square miles to Pío Pico and Andrés Pico, owners of the adjoining Rancho Santa Margarita. The pueblo was then occupied by thirty-two families of Indians who owned 54 sheep, 69 beasts of burden, 3½ yoke of oxen, 4 milk cows, a small cultivated area, and corn fields. As late as 1873 a few Indians still remained at Las Flores. It had long since been a part of Rancho Santa Margarita y Las Flores, and at that time was merely a place where passengers on the San Diego–Los Angeles stagecoach got out and stretched their legs.

Most California cities had their beginnings neither as presidio nor as pueblo. They arose in the American period and their story is that of men buying and subdividing land, whether of rancho or nonrancho origin, and of settlers on "public lands" obtaining federal grants of townsites.

CHAPTER V

First Rancheros

"LANDS FOR VETERANS," that familiar cry, was heard even in early-day Spanish California. As a result veterans of the Spanish army of occupation were the first individuals to own land in the state—if we may except the king himself. And through veterans the whole rancho movement got under way. Great ranchos, thousands of acres in extent, used by their soldier owners for the grazing of longhorned cattle, provided the pattern of the pastoral age in California and determined the character of its civilization.

Although concessions for ranchos were not given until 1784, the leaders of New Spain had given serious thought to the private distribution of lands at established presidios as early as 1773. On August 17 of that year Viceroy Bucareli authorized the military commanders of San Diego and Monterey, the two existing presidios, to assign lands to Indians and colonists, at the same time cautioning

[45]

such recipients of land not to move away from the town or mission where they were established.[1]

Under this authority, Manuel Butron, a soldier of the Monterey company, married to an Indian girl, Margarita, a Carmel Mission neophyte, was the first man in Spanish-ruled Upper California to get a plot of land he could call his own. That happened in 1775, the very year in which American colonists on the Atlantic seaboard were launching the Revolutionary War against England. Butron asked Commander Rivera for a particular 140-vara parcel near the mission in Carmel Valley. Father Serra approved, and on November 27 Butron was given possession.[2] This pioneer landowner seems soon to have abandoned his plot, however, for in 1786 he was listed as a settler in the pueblo of San José.

The rancho movement in California, that is, the settlement by individuals of tracts of land outside presidio and pueblo boundaries, began in 1784 and in what is now Los Angeles County. In that year several retirement-minded, land-hungry veterans got permission from Governor Fages, their own commander, to put their cattle on lands of their own choosing.

Among the veterans was sixty-five-year-old Juan José Domínguez, bachelor, veteran of the Portolá expedition, a man who knew what Indian fighting, hard work, poor food, and scurvy were like. It was probably in the fall of 1784 that he drove his herd of horses and 200 head of cattle from San Diego to a site near the mouth of the Los Angeles River. On the slope of a hill he built several huts

---

[1] H. W. Halleck's Report of March 1, 1849, House Ex. Doc. No. 17, App. 1; also Dwinelle, *The Colonial History of San Francisco*, Addenda III.

[2] A copy of the *expediente* of this first private land concession is in the addenda of the third edition (1866) of Dwinelle's *The Colonial History of San Francisco*.

and corrals and established what came to be known as
Rancho San Pedro. As finally surveyed there were more
than 43,000 acres in this rancho, though originally it had
included also the 31,000-acre Rancho Los Palos Verdes.

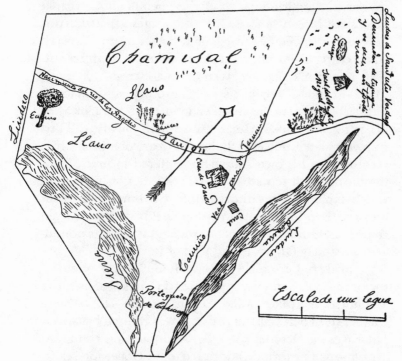

Figure 1. Diseño (typical of maps made after 1828), showing Cahuenga
Pass and part of the San Fernando Valley, Los Angeles County.

Domínguez' example was followed by Corporal José
María Verdugo, who at this time was on "detached service" at San Gabriel Mission. Verdugo looked longingly
on a tract of land, a league and a half from the mission,
the broad, grass-covered acres of which rolled back to the
wooded hills on the north. It was triangular in shape, the

southern tip being the meeting place of the Arroyo Seco and the Los Angeles River and pointing to the three-year-old pueblo of Los Angeles. In imagination Corporal Verdugo saw his own cattle pastured there, a water dam similar to the *saca de agua* of the pueblo, and irrigated fields. He placed before Governor Fages a petition for permission to keep his cattle and horses on this favored tract, citing the Domínguez concession as a precedent. The governor's answer, given on October 20, 1784, was "Yes." Corporal Verdugo sent his brother in his place to build a house, plant a garden and vineyard, and look after his cattle and horses. He remained with the army. Thirteen years later, however, he was so weary of military life, according to his own statement, suffered so much from the dropsy, and felt so keenly the burden of his family, which included six children, that Governor Borica let him retire to his rancho. Verdugo's Rancho San Rafael comprised more than 36,000 acres, and within its boundaries are today Glendale and part of Burbank.

A third soldier-ranchero was Manuel Pérez Nieto of the presidio of San Diego. His petition to keep his cattle and horses at a place called La Sanja (or La Zanja), three leagues from San Gabriel Mission, was granted by Governor Fages on October 21, 1784. Both petition and grant are typical. The former, addressed to the Governor, reads:
Sir:

Manuel Perez Nieto, soldier of the Royal Presidio of San Diego, before Your Worship with the greatest and due honour, appear and say: That in attention to the fact that I have my herd of horses, as well as of bovine stock at the Royal Presidio of San Diego, and because they are increasing and because I have no place to graze them, and likewise because I have no designated place, I request Your Worship's charity that you be pleased to assign me a place situated at three leagues distance from the Mission of San Gabriel along the road to the Royal Presidio of San Carlos de Monterey named La Sanja, contemplating Sir, not to harm neither a living soul, principally the Mission of San Gabriel, nor even less the Pueblo of the Queen of the Angels. I humbly request of Your Worship's superior government that it see fit to decide as I have requested, for if it is so, I shall receive a gift, and shall consider myself most favored; and therefore:

To Your Worship I humbly beg and request that you be pleased to decide along the tenor of my petition or as it may be to your superior pleasure, and I swear to all the necessary and that this my petition is not done in malice, nor least of all to injure any one, and not knowing how to sign I made the sign of the Cross. +

Here is the Nieto grant, attached as a marginal note to the petition:

San Gabriel, October 21, 1784

I grant the petitioner the permission of having the bovine stock and horses at the place of La Sanja, or its environs; provided no harm is done to the Mission San Gabriel nor to the Pagan Indians of its environs in any manner whatsoever; and that he must have some one to watch it, and to go and sleep at the aforementioned Pueblo.

Pedro Fages[3]

When Manuel Nieto retired from the service to his rancho he was described as "an old man," but he was not too old to raise cattle and horses successfully, nor too old to plant wheat and corn, nor too old to avoid having title disputes with the priests of San Gabriel. His adobe hut was built southwest of the present city of Whittier and within what later became Rancho Santa Gertrudes. By 1800 it was the center of a colony of white settlers. Nieto

---

[3] Petition and grant are in the National Archives, Washington, D.C., Expediente No. 103, Santa Gertrudes. The translation is by George Tays, a copy of which is in the Bancroft Library, University of California, Berkeley.

died in 1804, his vast land holdings—Los Nietos—later forming five ranchos regranted during the Mexican period to his heirs and members of his family. These five ranchos were Santa Gertrudes, Los Coyotes, Los Cerritos, Los Alamitos, and Las Bolsas. A number of cities were to arise within their boundaries, the largest of which is today Long Beach.

There may have been a fourth concession of land in this same year, 1784, the favored one being soldier Mariano de la Luz Verdugo, brother of Corporal José María Verdugo, and one of the "leather jackets" who marched north from Loreto in 1769 with the first land expedition. This concession is indicated in the letter from Governor Fages to Commandante General Ugarte, written November 20, 1784, listing individuals to whom, owing to the increase in cattle, he had given provisional grants of land. He names (1) Domínguez; (2) Nieto; (3) the *sons* of the widow Ygnacia Carillo (de Verdugo). Mariano de la Luz Verdugo's rancho—later referred to as the Portezuelo (site of part of modern Burbank), adjoining his brother's on the west—was second on the list in the 1795 report of ranchos made to Governor Borica by Felipe Goycoechea, commander of the Santa Barbara company. Unlike the other three original ranchos, however, the Portezuelo was abandoned, apparently as early as 1810.

By what right did Governor Fages make these first three or four concessions of California ranch land, the absolute title to which had been vested in the King of Spain since Spanish occupancy in 1769? Certainly not under the authority given by Viceroy Bucareli in 1773 to the presidio commanders of San Diego and Monterey, which was both limited and temporary.

As if doubtful of his own authority to make allotments of tracts to settlers whether within or without pueblo boundaries, Fages referred the whole question to the Commandante General a month after he had given the first concessions of ranch land. From Galindo Navarro, whose office corresponded to that of our attorney general, came a legal opinion written October 27, 1785, in Chihuahua, Mexico. It was transmitted to Fages in 1786 by the Commandante General. Tracts of land outside of the four square leagues of pueblos could be granted for farms and cattle raising, Navarro found, citing the specific Laws of the Indies on which he based his opinion.⁴ No injury, however, was to be done to missions, pueblos, and Indian villages. Pasture lands in the allotted areas must remain "for the common advantage." One settler might have not more than three tracts and he would be obligated to use the land, that is, put men in possession, build a house, and keep cattle. Within a pueblo's four-square-league area, however, the governor had no power under the laws to grant land.

Supreme authority in New Spain, during the Spanish period, was vested in the Viceroy as representative of the King, with his seat of office in the city of Mexico. Under him and appointed by him were military chiefs, such as Pedro Fages, serving as governors in the outlying territories, such as California, who held extensive powers. Later, during the Mexican regime, the governors were not subject to the discipline of the Viceroy and the Commandante General but were answerable solely to the central government of Mexico.

Domínguez and his co-veterans, California's first rancheros, received no grants directly from the King of Spain

⁴ Book 4 of the *Recopilacion*, Title 12, Laws 1–13.

in whom the title to the land was vested. Instead, they secured provisional concessions, cattle-grazing permits— little more—from Governor Fages, who was the appointee of the Viceroy.

Popular talk of "Spanish grants" is often misinformed. It comes chiefly from descendants of first settlers and from writers of romantic fiction who like to think of a far-distant ruler taking kindly thought of Californians and signing beribboned documents that gave whole valleys to aristocratic men.

Viceregal authority over lands in New Spain dates back at least to October 15, 1754—fifteen years before the beginning of the occupancy by Spain of Alta California. By a royal regulation of that date, affirming the powers of viceroys, the necessity of applying to the King for confirmation of title to non-pueblo, non-presidio lands was abolished.[5]

Hence we shall find that the ranch or cattle-grazing concessions made in California before 1822—the beginning of the Mexican period—came from governors of the state, from military commanders of a district, such as Santa Barbara, and even from the Viceroy himself, as in the case of Mariano Castro's viceregal license in 1802 to occupy Las Animas or Sitio de la Brea (in Santa Clara County).

The transformation of soldiers into rancheros got well under way in Spanish California during the period that began in 1784 with the Fages concessions already mentioned and that ended in 1822 with those made by Governor Solá. The ranchos of these soldiers comprised some of the best valley and grazing land between the San Fran-

---

[5] Alfred Wheeler, *Land Titles in California* (San Francisco, 1852), quoting from the Laws of the Indies.

cisco Bay on the north and the Santa Ana River on the south.

Rancho San Antonio, for example, whose boundaries include Berkeley, Oakland, and Alameda, was granted in 1820 to Sergeant Luís Peralta. Peralta, who had come to California with the Anza expedition of 1776, became a corporal in the San Francisco company, headed the San José Mission guard, and led a number of punitive expeditions against non-Christian Indians. Peralta put his four sons in charge of San Antonio, and remained with the service until 1826.

Rancho Buena Vista on the Salinas River was occupied at least as early as 1795 by José María Soberanes, a soldier of the Portolá party, and his father-in-law, Joaquín Castro, of the San Francisco company. The Buena Vista was not far from the Monterey presidio's "rancho del rey" where the military pastured their horses, cattle, mules, and sheep. It was one of a group of six early and rather temporary private ranchos on the Salinas River near Monterey. Of the six, the names of the Buena Vista and Las Salinas appear in the list of ranchos the titles of which were finally confirmed.[6] The Buena Vista itself, long after the death of the first Soberanes and its abandonment by the family, was regranted to another soldier, José Mariano Estrada.

El Refugio Rancho, in the Santa Barbara area, was owned by soldiers; it was first granted either to Captain José Francisco Ortega or to his soldier son, José María Ortega. Ortega, senior, was the famous scout of the Portolá party and had a distinguished record as soldier and officer and as the founder and commander of Santa Barbara. The rancho was long in the Ortega family.

[6] The other four are: Bajada á Huerta Vieja; Cañada de Huerta Vieja; Mesa de la Pólvera; and Chupadero.

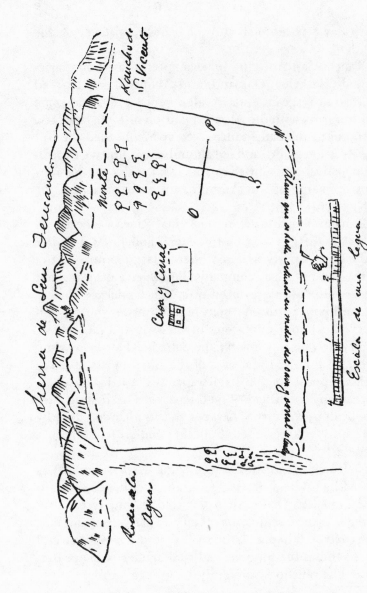

Figure 2. Diseño of Rancho San José de Buenos Ayres, Los Angeles County, embracing the Westwood area.

Rancho Santiago de Santa Ana, comprising ten square leagues in what is now Orange County, went to José Antonio Yorba and his nephew Pablo Peralta in the year 1810. Yorba was one of Fages' original Catalonian volunteers, retiring as a sergeant in 1797.

There were a number of other concessions to Spanish soldiers—and to some who may not have been military men. The vast Simi Rancho, most of it now in Ventura County, was granted Francisco Javier Pico, a soldier of the Santa Barbara company, and his two brothers, Patricio and Miguel. Adjoining the pueblo boundaries of Los Angeles, Rancho Los Felis—as it came to be called and which today includes Griffith Park—was given to Corporal Vicente Felis (Felix), and Rancho San Antonio—which today includes the site of Huntington Park and other modern cities—went to Corporal Antonio María Lugo.

How many rancho concessions were made during the Spanish period? At least thirty, if we add the references to various ranchos found in the works of historians Bancroft and Hittell or listed in claims made before the United States Land Commission. These include a number of ranchos that reverted because of abandonment by the ranchero owners. Among those abandoned were the Portezuelo, already mentioned; the Encino (or Reyes) Rancho, relinquished by Francisco Reyes to the missionary fathers who founded San Fernando Rey Mission in 1797, and not to be confused with the Encino of the Mexican period; and El Pilar, an indefinite tract along the San Mateo County coast, given in 1797 to José Dario Argüello.

No complete list of Spanish California land concessions is available. To make such a list would require detailed research on every land claim presented before the Board of Land Commissioners—and there were more than 800 of them—as well as those claims that never reached the Board. It is possible to make a fairly complete summing up, however, of those ranchos that originated in the Spanish period and that survived the Mexican with name intact—usually with a regranting and sometimes with intervening abandonment. Presented in approximate order of date, they include:

San Pedro, in Los Angeles County, Juan José Domínguez
San Rafael (originally La Zanja), in Los Angeles County, José María Verdugo
Los Nietos (originally La Zanja), in Los Angeles and Orange counties, Manuel Nieto
(This was broken into five ranchos during the Mexican period and granted as Santa Gertrudes, Los Coyotes, Los Alamitos, Los Cerritos and Las Bolsas.)
Buena Vista, in Monterey County, José María Soberanes and Joaquín Castro
Las Salinas, in Monterey County, Antonio Aceves and Antonio Romero
Los Felis, in Los Angeles County, Vicente Felis
Simi, in Ventura and Los Angeles counties, Francisco Javier Pico, Patricio Pico, and Miguel Pico
Las Pulgas, in San Mateo County, José Dario Argüello
El Refugio, in Santa Barbara County, José Francisco Ortega or José María Ortega
Las Virgenes, in Los Angeles County, Miguel Ortega
Las Animas (or La Brea), in Santa Clara County, Mariano Castro
El Conejo, in Ventura and Los Angeles counties, José Polanco and Ignacio Rodríguez
Topanga Malibu Sequit, in Los Angeles County, José Bartolomé Tapia
Santiago de Santa Ana, in Orange County, José Antonio Yorba and Pablo Peralta
San Ysidro, in Santa Clara County, Ygnacio Ortega

San Antonio, in Los Angeles County, Antonio María Lugo

La Ballona, in Los Angeles County
{
Agustín Machado
Ygnacio Machado
Felipe Talamantes
Tomás Talamantes
}

Vega del Rio del Pajaro, in Monterey County, Antonio María Castro

San Antonio, in Alameda County, Luis Peralta

Tularcitos, in Santa Clara and Alameda counties, José Higuera

Rincón de los Bueyes, in Los Angeles County, Bernardo Higuera and Cornelio López

Salsipuedes, in Santa Cruz County, Mariano Castro

Sausal Redondo, in Los Angeles County, Antonio Ygnacio Avila

Bolsa del Potrero y Moro Cojo, or La Sagrada Familia, in Monterey County, José Joaquín de la Torre

The list should probably include the San José de Buenos Ayres, whose grantee was Máximo Alanis, as well as the Rodeo de las Aguas, granted to María Rita Váldez. Both are in Los Angeles County, the former occupying the Westwood area, and the latter Beverly Hills. Alanis, a soldier who accompanied the party of Los Angeles settlers from Los Alamos in 1781, appears to have been in possession as early as 1820. Testimony before the Land Commission indicates that Sergeant Vicente Villa of "the Spanish army," husband of María Rita, was retired with a pension and that "when he left the service he went to live on" Rodeo de las Aguas. Possibly Santa Teresa, in Santa Clara County, should be included, for, when this rancho was granted by a Mexican governor in 1834, the grantee, Joaquín Bernal, a native of Spain, was ninety-four years old, had been in possession long enough to build four adobe houses and to have large flocks and herds and 78 children and grandchildren.

The first rancheros in California were veterans of the Spanish army of occupation. Most, if not all, of the holders of ranch concessions during the Spanish period were veterans. The rancho movement, however, did not fully get under way in California until the missions, with their vast land holdings, were secularized. Secularization took place during the 1830's, more than a decade after the passing of Spanish rule.

CHAPTER VI

Gifts of Land

WHEN Pío Pico, California's last Mexican governor and
one of the great landowners in the state, realized the in-
evitability of the American invasion, he is credited with
having made an extraordinary last-stand speech before a
military council in Monterey in 1846.

Here are Pico's words, or at least the words that have
been put in his mouth:

... We find ourselves suddenly threatened by hordes of
Yankee emigrants, who have already begun to flock into our
country, and whose progress we cannot arrest. Already have
the wagons of that perfidious people scaled the almost inaccessible summits of the Sierra Nevada, crossed the entire
continent, and penetrated the fruitful valley of the Sacramento. What that astonishing people will next undertake, I
cannot say; but in whatever enterprise they embark they will
be sure to prove successful. Already are these adventurous
land-voyagers spreading themselves far and wide over a
country which seems suited to their tastes. They are cultivating farms, establishing vineyards, erecting mills, sawing up
lumber, building workshops, and doing a thousand other

[59]

things which seem natural to them, but which Californians
neglect or despise . . .[1]

The perfidious Yankees came. They had been coming—
in small parties or as individuals—ever since the Jedediah
Smith party of trappers made the first American overland
expedition to California in 1826. Some of these men became citizens of Mexico and landowners. At the time of
the American conquest in 1846, toward which Californians were partly apathetic and, to an extent, sympa-
thetic, the white-occupied part of California—a very small
part, by the way—was a land of pueblos and ranchos.
The population in that year has been estimated to be
10,000, exclusive of Indians.

Established pueblos in 1846 were few in number:
Sonoma (founded under Mexican law in 1835 upon the
secularization of Mission San Francisco Solano), San
Francisco (Yerba Buena), Monterey, San José, Santa Barbara, Los Angeles, and San Diego. Four of these originated in presidios. The pueblo title to all seven was later
to be upheld by the United States. Branciforte, breathing
its last and presently to be succeeded by Santa Cruz, was
to make no claim before the United States Land Commission. Benicia and Sacramento were yet unborn. Townsmen in existing pueblos held lots granted them by
pueblo authorities under Mexican law.

New Helvetia, John Sutter's privately owned fortress
overlooking the Sacramento and American rivers had

---

[1] Pío Pico, as quoted by Joseph Warren Revere in *A Tour of Duty in
California* (New York, C. S. Francis and Company, 1849). Revere adds
that the speech may have been delivered by José Antonio Carrillo, whom
he refers to as reflecting Pico's views. See Theodore H. Hittell's *History of
California*, II, 397, and Bancroft's *History of California*, V, 138–266, which
indicate that Pico went no farther north than Santa Barbara to indulge
in declarations against Americans.

some of the physical aspects of a pueblo, with Sutter himself a combination of feudal lord and alcalde.

There were also a few villages of white families, or of both white and ex-neophyte families, that had sprung up out of the decay of secularized missions, such as San Juan de Castro at Mission San Juan Bautista, San Juan de Argüello at Mission San Juan Capistrano, together with San Luis Obispo and Carmelo. Some of the inhabitants held parcels of land distributed by commissioners appointed under Governor Figueroa's provisional rules for the secularization of the missions. There were a few purely Indian pueblos in the southern part of the state, too, such as Las Flores, San Dieguito, and San Pascual. None of these villages, white or Indian, were to present claims before the Land Commission, and whatever rights they had were swallowed up in rancho or other titles.

Most of California, however, was outside of pueblo areas at the time the Americans fulfilled Pío Pico's dire prophecy. And most of the good grazing land along the coast and the coastal rivers, along with a part of the San Joaquin and Sacramento valleys, was privately owned rancho land—land that had largely been the gift of the government to individual Mexican citizens. There were in Alta California in 1846 more than 500 ranchos, all but a handful of which had their origin in Mexican grants. Of the few that were of the Spanish period, ending in 1822, most had been confirmed to their original or later owners by new grants from Mexican authorities. The greater number of the ranchos of California had been carved out of former mission-controlled lands following the beginning, in 1834, of actual secularization of the missions.

The most northerly of the ranchos, and lying almost entirely in Shasta County, was that of San Buenaventura

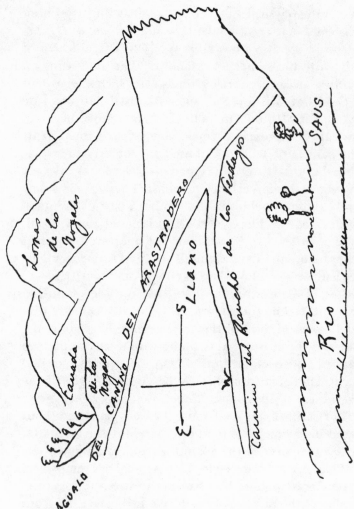

Figure 3. Diseño of Cañada de los Nogales, Los Angeles County.

along the Sacramento River, which was granted in 1844 to naturalized citizen Pierson B. Reading. Reading, a native of New Jersey, had come to California the year before with the Chiles-Walker party, entering into John Sutter's service as clerk and chief of trappers. His thick-walled adobe home still stands on the west bank of the Sacramento River near Cottonwood Creek. The cities of Redding (named after B. B. Redding, railroad land agent, and not ranchero P. B. Reading) and Anderson are today within the San Buenaventura's boundaries.

The most southerly rancho was the Otay, in San Diego County, close to the border. It was the property of Magdalena Estudillo, the daughter of José María Estudillo, Spanish captain of the San Diego company and founder of the Estudillo family in California. This rancho had been the site of an Indian ranchería, Otay Indians being among those who helped to destroy the first mission of San Diego in 1775.

The rancho map of California in the year 1846, when Mexican rule ended, shows rancheros owning much of the best land around the San Francisco Bay region, in what became the counties of Marin, Sonoma, Napa, Solano, Contra Costa, Alameda, and San Mateo. Coastal ranchos immediately north of San Francisco were limited to Marin and Sonoma counties. The entire coastal area from San Francisco to San Diego, however, was principally rancho land. In addition, and of more recent origin, was the thin line of ranchos following the Sacramento River up from John Sutter's Fort (established in 1839) and down along the Upper San Joaquin, or along tributary streams of these rivers. These "central valley" ranchos were held largely by men of Anglo-Saxon or other European origin who had been coming into California during the 'forties,

who had become naturalized to qualify for landownership, and who disregarded the Indian menace that had
held back native Spanish Californians from making use of
this land. Among them, in addition to Reading, were such
men as William B. Ide, William G. Chard, Albert G.
Toomes, Robert H. Thomas, Peter Lassen, William
Dickey, Edward A. Farwell, James Williams, William
Knight, Thomas M. Hardy, William A. Leidesdorff, and
John Bidwell. Elsewhere rancheros were predominantly
Spanish Californian: descendants of first soldiers and first
settlers, men of the Portolá and Anza expeditions and of
later parties of colonists. A few Yankee or European sea-
farers, trappers, merchants, and traders had been trickling
into California for many years and they also had settled
down to ranchero roles. These call to mind George Yount,
J. B. Chiles, William Pope, E. T. Bale, and John York,
who settled in Napa County, Abel Stearns, John Temple,
John Rowland, William Workman, Hugo Reid, Henry
Dalton, Isaac Williams, Benjamin D. Wilson, David W.
Alexander, and Francis Mellus, who found a prosperous
or pleasant way of life in Los Angeles County, and
shipmasters John Wilson, William G. Dana, Alpheus B.
Thompson, and Thomas M. Robbins, who turned readily
from seafaring to ranching. Christianized Indians, too,
held a number of the ranchos, north and south, for under
the law they were citizens and entitled to landowning
privileges.

The greater part of northern California, together with
vast mountain and desert areas throughout the whole
state—making up overwhelmingly the bulk of the state's
land area—remained Indian or unoccupied territory, unclaimed by white individuals. Almost none of what was to
become, with the Gold Rush, the Mother Lode country

of the lower western Sierra, was rancho land. An outstanding exception was the ten-square-league Rancho
Las Mariposas, in what is now Mariposa County, granted
in 1844 to Juan Bautista Alvarado and to become famous
through John Charles Frémont's later ownership. The
first claim to be filed with the Land Commission was Frémont's to Las Mariposas, over which there was much litigation.

The islands off the California shore should not be overlooked on the 1846 rancho map, for three of them in the
Santa Barbara and San Pedro channels were ranchos.
These were the islands of Santa Rosa, granted in 1843 to
José Antonio and Carlos Carrillo; Santa Cruz, granted in
1839 to Andrés Castillero; and Santa Catalina, granted in
1846 to Tomás M. Robbins.

Although private ownership of most of the ranchos
dates from the period following secularization of the missions (i.e., the 1830's and the 1840's), there was no interruption in the earlier granting of land concessions when
Spanish rule gave way to Mexican in 1822. Mexican
authorities, like the Spanish, continued to give vague
cattle-grazing permits and, when the land laws were really
clarified in 1828, to make actual grants of full title.

The first step toward clarification came on August 18,
1824, when the Mexican Congress established rules for
the colonization of national lands to stimulate land settlement and to satisfy the demands of Mexican promoters
of colony movements.[2] They promised security to foreigners who wished to establish themselves in Mexican
territory, but prohibited colonization of territory within
twenty leagues of the boundaries of a foreign nation or

---

[2] Halleck's Report in House Ex. Doc. No. 17, App. 4; John W. Dwinelle's
The Colonial History of San Francisco, Addenda XII.

within ten leagues of the seacoast unless previously approved by the supreme general executive power. They encouraged the entry of foreigners, but in the distribution of lands Mexican citizens were to be given preference. Prior promises made to "military persons," regarding lands, were to be carried out in the states. Disposal of vacant lands to military or court officers was permitted "the supreme authority." The area of land a person could own was limited to eleven square leagues (one of irrigable, four of farming, and six of pasture land). New colonists were prohibited from transferring possession "in mortmain"—that is, to the Church or other ecclesiastical corporations. Absentee ownership was forbidden.

To give effect to this Congressional act of 1824, specific rules and regulations for colonization of territories of the republic were enacted by the Mexican government on November 21, 1828.[3] Governors were given authority to grant vacant lands to "contractors (*empresarios*), families or private persons, whether Mexicans or foreigners, who may ask for them for the purpose of cultivating and inhabiting them." They outlined the steps to be taken by persons wanting lands, beginning with the petition to the governor and what it should contain and describing the land asked for by means of a map. Grants made to families and private persons were not to be held definitely valid without previous consent of the Territorial Deputation or of the supreme government, and grants to empresarios for colonization purposes called for final approval of the supreme government. The rules required the governor to issue a document, signed by him, "to serve as a title to the person interested," and the keeping of a record of petitions and grants, with the maps of the

---

[3] Halleck's Report, *loc. cit.*, App. 5; Dwinelle, *op. cit.*, Addenda XIV.

lands granted. Failure to cultivate or occupy the land granted, within a "proportionate time," would void the grant. The colonist was expected to prove cultivation or occupancy before the municipal authority in order that his right of ownership might be made secure and that he might dispose of his land freely.

Under these colonization laws of 1824 and 1828 and under governmental decrees in 1845 and 1846, authorizing the disposition of mission properties, more than 500 land grants were made. They were made between 1833 and 1846, that is, between the passage of the secularization act and American occupation.⁴

Few grants complied one hundred per cent with the letter of the law. Laxity in following details, such as the provision calling for a map describing the land sought, was prevalent. Little attention apparently was paid to the requirement regarding the type of land that should compose the eleven square leagues. Written approvals of the Territorial Assembly or of the supreme government often were not obtained. Although the United States Supreme Court held that restrictions against colonization of seacoast land were applicable only to foreign colonies, some confusion had existed during the Mexican period and

⁴ Regarding the disposition of hitherto undisposed mission estates, the Departmental Assembly on May 28, 1845, authorized the renting of some of the missions and the converting of others into pueblos. Governor Pío Pico on October 28, 1845, issued regulations for the sale and renting of certain missions. The Assembly on April 3, 1846, authorized the sale of the missions. On October 31, 1846—too late to be recognized as a valid act by the United States—the Assembly attempted to annul the sales of missions made by Governor Pico. In addition, the Mexican Minister of War and Marine had given the General Commander of the Californias on March 10, 1846, authority to take necessary steps for the defense of the nation—authority which Pico was to cite as legalizing the mission sales made by him. The United States Land Commission later upheld Pico's sales of the mission lands of San Diego, San Buenaventura, San Fernando, Soledad, and San Juan Bautista, but turned down his sales of San Gabriel and San Luis Rey.

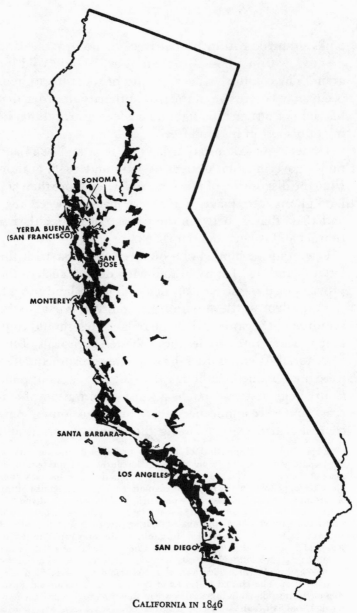

CALIFORNIA IN 1846

The black areas show the land included within the private land grants that were later confirmed by the United States. Pueblo and mission holdings were a part of the privately owned areas, but ranchos made up the bulk of them. In preparing this map the General Land Office's 1944 map of the state was used in determining land-grant boundaries.

before that ruling. Actually much of the seacoast was occupied by individuals under Spanish concessions years before the 1824 legislation, and Mexican governors continued into the year 1846 to grant such lands to its own citizens. In 1840 the Assembly had consulted the supreme government on coastal grants already made but no disapproval was expressed by the latter.[5] The United States Land Commission, functioning in the 1850's, and the courts to which appeals were taken displayed a liberal and fair attitude toward claimants and ordinarily confirmed the titles of persons who could prove possession and actual occupancy by themselves or predecessors in the Mexican period—regardless of whether or not the provisions of Mexican laws were followed religiously in obtaining Mexican grants. Patents were issued claimants by the United States (following confirmation by the Board of Land Commissioners, approval of the District or the Supreme Court, and approved government surveys) as final and perfect evidences of title. On the other hand, the commissioners or the courts were quick to throw out antedated or last-minute grants made in anticipation of American annexation, together with those made after July 7, 1846—the date Commodore John D. Sloat took possession of Monterey and the date arbitrarily assigned as the end of Mexican rule—as well as alleged grants, like the fantastic ones of José Y. Limantour, that were obviously fraudulent or forged.

A spot check of the rancho map of California in 1846 would show a few ranchos of less than 20 acres in size, such as the little rancho of Francisco Sales in the San Gabriel Valley of Los Angeles County, and others gigantic in area like the Ex-Mission de San Fernando, in the same county,

---

[5] Bancroft, *History of California*, VI, 531.

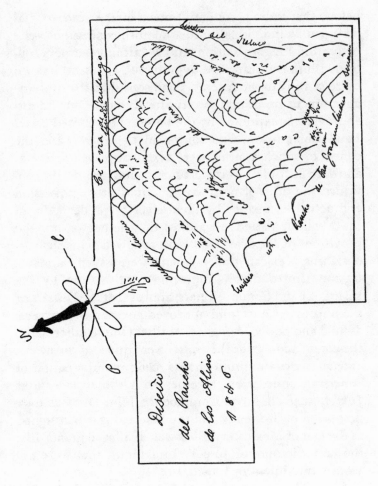

Figure 4. Diseño of Rancho Cañada de los Alisos, Orange County.

comprising more than 115,000 acres. It would disclose one man, the influential and wealthy José de la Guerra y Noriega of Santa Barbara claiming four ranchos—Simi, San Julian, El Conejo, and Las Posas—whose acreage totaled 215,857.88 acres. Even this vast land holding, however, is less than some twentieth-century holdings of California land. It would show substantial ownerships by members of such well-known Spanish Californian families as Avila, Alanis, Alvarado, Bernal, Carrillo, Castro, Domínguez, Estudillo, de la Guerra, Higuera, Ibarra, López, Lugo, Machado, Noriega, Ortega, Pacheco, Palomares, Peralta, Pico, Reyes, Ruiz, Sánchez, Sepúlveda, del Valle, Vallejo, Verdugo, and Yorba. It would show the Fort Ross (Russian) settlement included within the coastal four-square-league Rancho Muniz owned by Manuel Torres. It would show a scattering, north and south, of ranchos that had been granted by Mexican governors to Indians, for example, the Suisun in Sonoma County whose first owner was Christianized Francisco Solano, "chief of the tribes of the frontiers of Sonoma"; and the 126.26-acre rancho Huerta de Cuati in Los Angeles County, the property of Victoria Reid, Indian wife of the Scotsman Hugo Reid. The map would show Cayetano Juarez' Rancho Yokaya, in Mendocino County, the boundary of which on the north, east, and west, as described in early deeds, was "the country inhabited by the unchristianized Indians." It would reveal Captain John Wilson, who left the sea for the successful life of a California ranchero, as owner of 32,430-acre Rancho Cañada de los Osos Pecho y Islay, in San Luis Obispo County, and the possessor of a two-story adobe home in the "valley of the bears." It would show the Irish physician and Santa Barbara citizen Nicholas A. Den as owner of the coast rancho Los Dos Pueblos. The map would display Spanish names for most of the ranchos, yet it would also carry a substantial number bearing Indian labels: Cahuenga, Capay, Caslamayomi, Caymus, Cholami, Collayomi, Cosumnes, Cotate, Cucamonga, Cuyama, and Cujamaca, to name but a few.

Such was the California of ranchos that greeted William Carey Jones in 1849, when, representing the "perfidious people" of the United States and the United States Congress, he came to classify all grants and claims derived from Spanish and Mexican authorities.

CHAPTER VII

Chain of Title

A CHAIN OF TITLE is the sequence of ownership of a particular piece of land as shown by the public records of property transfers. These records are full of human interest, especially when they have to do with rancho lands that have had generations of owners from the pastoral age of California to the metropolitan present.

An example is Rancho San Pascual, the site of present-day Pasadena. Let us trace the chain of its ownership or title through the Spanish, Mexican, and American periods down to the present day. Not only will the changing laws of governments be reflected, but people long dead will come to life and testify how a Spanish Californian acquired a rancho, how he held, lost, or sold his title, how he and his successors lived, what most concerned them, how they got along with their neighbors, what interest rate they paid on their mortgages, the names of their children, what they provided for in their wills, what happened year by year to the land and its many owners, and what wars, droughts, booms, and busts did for or to them.

The story of Rancho San Pascual is only one of the stories of the five hundred and more ranchos that flourished on the river and pasture lands of California in the year 1846, when Mexican rule gave way to American. It is a story revealed in petitions, grants, deeds, mortgages, patents, court actions, in laws of nations, and in proceedings of federal, state, county, and municipal bodies, supplemented by the direct testimony of individuals found in public and private writings, records, and histories.

Before white people came to San Pascual there were, of course, Indians. They lived on the banks of a brook on the east side of Raymond Hill, at Los Robles Canyon in Oak Knoll, at the mouth of Millard Canyon, along the Arroyo Seco, especially at Garfias Springs, and no doubt in other places. Of their customs or laws regarding ownership of land we have no information, but something of their way of life, their villages or rancherías of stick-built huts, their rich language and involved beliefs, together with their reactions to Spanish invaders—beings with a "nasty white color and having ugly blue eyes"—is to be found in ranchero Hugo Reid's frank and illuminating essays that appeared in the Los Angeles *Star* during the year 1852. Reid, a Scotsman, had married an intelligent Indian woman, Victoria, who had been born in a ranchería and brought up as a neophyte of San Gabriel Mission. Part of the Indian phase, too, of San Pascual's story is told in the reports of those who have found Indian remains in the Pasadena area, referred to in local histories or accounts.

With the Spanish occupation of California the absolute title to the San Pascual area, as well as all other parts of the state, was vested, under the Laws of the Indies, in the King of Spain. The laws formulated in Spain by the Council of the Indies, through which the will of the King was carried out in America, regulated the affairs of the New World. When finally compiled, under the title of *Recopilación de Leyes de los Reynos de las Indias*, they were published in 1681 at Madrid, in a four-volume edition, by order of Charles II. Under the King the Indians were recognized as the theoretical owners of the territory they needed, but—to indulge in an understatement—the civilizing process to which they were subjected greatly reduced their land needs.

San Pascual land, with its Indian inhabitants, came under the jurisdiction of San Gabriel Mission, the first location of which, in 1771, was on the banks of the San Gabriel River near its passage through the southern hills of the valley. A few years later it was removed to its present place at the Indian village of Sibag-na. Near by lay the live oak forests, the good soil, and the streams of the Pasadena, the South Pasadena, and the San Marino areas over which, with other land, the mission was given jurisdiction.

The mission phase of San Pascual is part of the whole story of California, for the threefold plan of Spanish colonization provided for presidios, missions, and pueblos. We find the story of San Gabriel Mission and its missionaries interwoven in all the general histories of California, in the specific accounts of this mission, in the diaries of explorers, travelers, and trappers who visited San Gabriel, in interesting sidelights to be found in the archives of its nearest pueblo, Los Angeles, and in the transcripts of the United States Land Commission and district court proceedings involving the nearest ranchos: San Pascual, Santa

Anita, San Rafael, and San Francisquito. Secularization ended this phase, with secular administrator Colonel Nicolás Gutiérrez being placed in charge at San Gabriel in the year 1834. The laws and regulations which transformed this and other California missions into parish churches and made rich lands available to private ownership are to be found, among other places, in the much-quoted official reports of Henry W. Halleck and William Carey Jones, made in 1849 and 1850. During this mission period El Rincón de San Pascual—which was the full name given to the land bounded by the mission itself, the mountains, and the Arroyo Seco—served the interests of San Gabriel as a sheep and cattle ranch.

Even before secularization was a fact at least one far-seeing individual looked hopefully on San Pascual. He was sixty-three-year-old Spanish ex-artilleryman Juan Mariné (or Mariner), who had come to California in 1795 and had retired from the army in 1821 with the rank of lieutenant. He was a resident at Mission San Gabriel, and apparently a close friend of Father José Bernardo Sánchez, the popular and successful head of the mission. He was, perhaps, the same person as "Don J. M. M., an old Spaniard who had large commercial relations with the mission," referred to in Hugo Reid's essays on the Indians. These essays give an excellent picture of two men, Mariné and Sánchez, who loved good eating, hearty living, and practical joking.

Juan Mariné not only looked on San Pascual, he became its first owner—excepting, of course, the Indians and the King of Spain himself—and this happened soon after secularization of San Gabriel. The story of Mariné and of later claimants and owners may be found in United States Land Commission Cases 272 and 345, transcripts of which are a part of the court records in the office of the United States District Court in San Francisco. These Land Commission proceedings include copies of pertinent *expedientes* (land-grant files) obtained from the Mexican archives transferred in the 1850's from Monterey to the Surveyor General's Office in San Francisco. Throughout these documents there is inconsistency in descriptions and areas.

The Mariné story opens with a petition to the governor dated July 15, 1833, more than a month before secularization was decreed and a year or more before it was made effective. This was the first step required of a prospective ranch owner under the rules and regulations for colonization adopted by Mexico in 1828. Juan Mariné's petition reads:

I, Juan Mariner, a retired Lieutenant of Artillery of the Department of Mexico, now in Upper California and a resident of the Mission of San Gabriel, having had the misfortune to lose by the floods of the year 1831 an orchard in the Pueblo of Los Angeles, I went to the Mission of San Gabriel with the Rev. Father Sánchez that he might do me the favor of giving me a parcel of land for cultivation, build a house and keep there my livestock and he informed me that whenever the Indians agreed to it he would be ready, whereupon the (Indian) Alcaldes met and said it was all right and the tract would be given to me. The Rev. Father told them that it would not be for one or two years but forever and they answered that it was all right and they made preparations to measure the lands and give me the place named El Rincon de San Pascual to the extent of three leagues round about to keep my cattle where I drove it in the presence of the Sergeant stationed at said Mission as also the tract where the house is located together with the garden to the extent of one hundred steps in width by three hundred in length.

I ask and pray your Honor to grant me the place I solicit as a favor I hope to receive.

The governor of California was Figueroa. The law required him to make an investigation of the merits of this petition. Figueroa sent the petition to Father Tómas Estenaga of San Gabriel, successor to Sánchez on the latter's death in 1833. On the margin the governor wrote: "Let the Rev. Friar Tómas Estenaga Minister of this Mission make his report hereon." Estenaga, very coöperative, added: "There is no obstacle to the grant solicited by the petitioner, Juan Mariner, a retired Lieutenant of Artillery."

Going ahead with the investigation from Monterey, California's capital, the governor asked the ayuntamiento of Los Angeles which had jurisdiction over San Pascual to find out if San Pascual was within twenty leagues of the frontiers or ten leagues from the seacoast (limitations referred to in the colonization laws of 1824), and what sort of land it included, to get proof that the applicant, Mariné, was a Mexican citizen, to check his marital status, and whether he was a man who conducted himself well and had served in the army. Also, did the land applied for belong to any person, pueblo, or corporation and was it irrigable, arable, or pasture land? And, further, did Mariné have the cattle to stock San Pascual? The ayuntamiento made its report a month later:

In session of yesterday this Illustrious Ayuntamiento in conformity with the foregoing decree of the Hon. the Political Chief of the territory, ordered that a report be made stating that Don Juan Mariné a Spaniard by birth has the requisite qualifications required by law to be considered in his petition, for, besides the fact of his having resided about forty years in this territory, he has rendered various services in favor of the country, conducting himself honorably; that the land he solicits does not lie within the twenty leagues from the frontiers nor within the ten leagues from the littoral, but that it comprises irrigable, arable and pasture land and appertains to the Mission of San Gabriel and for the purposes that may be convenient.

I sign as president of the said corporation, together with the secretary thereof.

José Antonio Carrillo
Vicente Moraga, Secy.

The alcalde or mayor of Los Angeles contributed his share also:

In the Pueblo of Our Lady of Los Angeles, territory of Upper California, on the 8th day of January, 1834.

I, José Perez, Constitutional Alcalde, with the previous summons as ordered by the foregoing decree of the Hon. Political Chief, caused to appear before me and the assistant witnesses in default of a notary public, Don Juan Mariné who presented the qualified competent witnesses, citizens Maximo Alanis, Manuel Moreno and José Manuel Silvas and having questioned them according to the foresaid decree answered unanimously that they know Don Juan Mariné to be a native of the Province of Catalonia, Spain, married to a woman of this country by whom he had a large family; that his conduct during the forty years they have known him has been irreproachable; that most of that time they knew him to have served the nation in the army until he was retired with the grade of Lieutenant; that the lands he solicits appertain to the Mission of San Gabriel and is arable and pasture land, laying in the shape of a triangle extending on the South one league and one-half; that they know he has been in possession of it since the year 1833 and in proof of the truth of the foresaid witnesses signed the foregoing declaration with me and the assistant witnesses and as citizens Máximo Alanis and José Manuel Silvas knew not how to write each one made a cross.

With the petition and these reports in front of him, as one document, Governor Figueroa on May 6, 1834, declared Don Juan Mariné the "owner in fee of the land

known by the name of Rincon de San Pascual, bounded
by the Mission of San Gabriel, the Sierra and Arroyo
Seco, subject to the conditions that may be stipulated."
He ordered a title to be issued and the record to be sent
the Territorial Deputation for its approval.

The formal grant of title was in these words:

> José Figueroa, General of Brigade of the Mexican Repub-
> lic, Commandante General, Inspector and Superior Chief
> of Upper California:

> Whereas, Don Juan Mariner, a meritorious Lieutenant,
> has solicited for his personal benefit and that of his family
> the tract of land known by the name of Rincon de San Pas-
> cual, bounded by the Mission of San Gabriel, the Sierra and
> Arroyo Seco; the proper proceedings and investigations hav-
> ing previously been had agreeably to the provisions of the
> laws and regulations in virtue of the authority on me con-
> ferred in the name of the Mexican Nation I have thought
> proper by a decree of the 6th May last to grant to the fore-
> said Don Juan Mariner the above mentioned tract of land
> of El Rincon de San Pascual, declaring it his property by the
> present letters, understanding the said concession in entire
> conformity with the provisions of the laws subject to the
> approval or disapproval of the Exct, the Territorial Deputa-
> tion and of the Supreme Government, and under the follow-
> ing conditions:

> 1st. That he will submit to the conditions that may be stip-
> ulated by the regulations to be framed for the distribution of
> vacant lands and that in the mean time neither the grantee
> nor his heirs shall divide nor alienate the land hereby granted
> to him nor subject it to rent, entail, bond, mortgage, nor other
> encumbrance even though it were for a charitable cause, nor
> convey it in mortmain.

> 2nd. He may enclose it without detriment to the crossways,
> roads and servitudes. He will enjoy it freely and exclusively,
> putting it to the use or cultivation that may suit him best,
> but before the end of one year at the furtherest he shall build
> a house and it shall be inhabited.

3rd. When the ownership shall have been confirmed to him he will request the proper magistrate to give him the juridical possession in virtue of this title whereby the boundaries shall be marked out, at the limits whereof he shall set besides the land marks, some fruit or forest trees of some utility.

4th. The land of which donation is hereby made to him is of the extent of one-half (sitio de ganado mayor) square leagues, little more or less, as explained by the map annexed to the record of proceedings. The magistrate who may give the possession will cause it to be measured agreeably to the ordinance for the marking of boundaries, the surplus (sobrante) which may result in favor of the nation remaining for convenient purposes.

5th. If he contravene these conditions he shall forfeit his right to the land and it shall be open to denouncement by another party.

In consequence I order that the present serving as his title and holding it as firm and valid it be recorded in the corresponding book and be delivered to the interested party for his security and further purposes.

Given in Monterey on the 18th February, 1835.

> José Figueroa
> Agustín V. Zamorano, Secretary.

There is this entry, too:

This title is recorded in the book of grants of land leaf 63, No. 61 on file in the secretary's office under my charge.

Monterey, February 18th, 1835.

> Zamorano.

The Territorial Deputation, California's Assembly, took a few months to act, but on August 27, 1835, referred the matter to its committee on vacant land. Juan Castro, who headed this committee, acted promptly and the next day gave approval to Citizen Mariné's concession. The deputation's approval came on August 29, 1835, the notation being: "In session of this day ... the Deputation approved the foregoing opinion and it was agreed that the record of proceedings be forwarded to the Superior Political Chief for the conclusion thereof."

The record of Mariné's acquisition of Rancho San Pascual, beginning with his petition and ending with the final approval of the Assembly, made up his land-grant file. It was given the number of 211 in the Jimeno Index at Monterey, and a copy appears in the proceedings of Land Commission Case No. 272 and the United States District Court (Southern Division) Case No. 116.

Juan Mariné had still to be officially given possession of the property, but this matter was a local affair to be taken care of by the mayor of Los Angeles and assistants. It was a job for chainbearers and amateur surveyors proceeding on horseback around the boundaries of the rancho, using a cord 100-varas long to each end of which was fastened a wooden stake, and placing proper landmarks as they went.

Shortly before Mariné had set in motion the machinery for getting his rancho he married a widow, Eulalia Pérez de Guillen, elderly nurse and midwife at San Gabriel, a woman destined to outlive Mariné and to become famous for her age. It was not his first marriage, for the Land Commission proceedings show his first wife to have been María Antonio Sepúlveda by whom he had six children. The second marriage to Eulalia, we may well believe, was a match made by practical-minded Father Sánchez. By it, San Gabriel could satisfy its obligations to the hard working Eulalia—and Eulalia came to believe that Father Sánchez gave the San Pascual to her. "When I married him," she said in later reminiscing about her marriage to Mariné, "I was a very old woman"—nearly sixty, probably—

"but strong and active, with scarcely a gray hair. Nevertheless, I never had any children by him."

Juan Mariné died in 1838. His widow retained the house and garden at San Gabriel, but his son Fruto, who was a soldier, sold his interest in the rancho to José Pérez, Eulalia's cousin, for six horses and ten head of cattle. The sale took place on April 1, 1839, Fruto going before the alcalde of Los Angeles, making known his purposes, in the presence of witnesses, and stating that his brothers had consented to the transaction, and acknowledging receipt of the horses and cattle. The deed was drawn up as evidence and was filed with the alcalde who also acted as recorder. An English translation of this deed may be seen today in the office of the recorder of Los Angeles County (Book A).

But Mariné, it seems, had been really no ranchero at all. He had failed—and his heirs failed—to use and cultivate San Pascual, though Governor Figueroa provided for this in the grant itself. The land laws of 1828 provided that failure to occupy or cultivate land voided a grant, and the fifth stipulation in the deed to Mariné said: "If he contravenes these conditions he shall forfeit his right to the land and it shall be open to denouncement by another party."

And so it happened. On April 10, 1840, Mariné's Rincon de San Pascual was "denounced" by José Pérez and his friend Enrique Sepúlveda. Their petition to the governor, asking for this land and vacant land adjoining, accompanied by a *diseño* or map, was transmitted to Juan Bandini, then administrator of the mission. Pérez and Sepúlveda claimed that the land had been abandoned for the past four years.

Bandini reported the property to be "vacant sobrantes

(surplus lands) for the benefit of the nation," and the prefect stated that the Mariné heirs had not met the government's requirements.

Accordingly, on September 24, 1840, Governor Alvarado made a provisional grant of Rancho San Pascual to Pérez and Sepúlveda on condition that they would not obstruct the crossways and roads and would obey the rules which San Gabriel might adopt with respect to its "town limits."

The new owners took possession, with their horses and cattle. Each built a small house near the Arroyo Seco.

Then, for a second time El Rincon de San Pascual was to be abandoned by its owners and "denounced" by other landseekers.

"I was on the place in the year 1840 or 1841," said Abel Stearns, a witness for the new applicant, Manuel Garfias. "Sepúlveda and Pérez had each a small house on the land which was occupied. They had stock on the place. Sepúlveda I recollect had a pretty good stock of horses and mares and a small stock of cattle. Pérez I think had stock there. The occupation of Pérez continued until he died, which was, I think, in 1841. Sepúlveda I think occupied it until his death which was I believe in 1843 . . ."

At Pérez' death his cattle and horses were sent to the ranch of Antonio María Lugo, the widow's father. Sepúlveda's animals were killed, stolen, or scattered, "all of which," he explained, "made me give up the desire to stock and cultivate the place."

Garfias, a young officer in the Mexican army, paid $70 to Sepúlveda and $100 to the widow of Pérez to compensate them for the two adobe houses. On November 28, 1843, he received the formal grant from Governor Micheltorena and took possession.

A year before the signing of the Treaty of Guadalupe Hidalgo, by which California was ceded to the United States, the Pasadena area figured slightly in the contest between American troops and Mexican. After being defeated at the Battle of La Mesa (January 9, 1847), the Californians under General Flores withdrew to Rancho San Pascual and to the south slope of Raymond Hill. Here was a stream of water, an oak grove and a building (now called the Flores Adobe). Sentinel horsemen were posted on top of Raymond Hill to watch for the coming of the United States troops. The Americans, however, ignored them; instead of marching to Pasadena they went into Los Angeles with flags flying and took formal possession.

The transition to American rule was an easy one, since local government was unaffected for the time being, and since local officials continued in office.

When the three members of the Board of United States Land Commissioners, Alpheus Felch, Thompson Campbell and R. Augustus Thompson, arrived in Los Angeles in August of 1852, they were greeted most warmly, especially by those who expected to file land claims. Manuel Garfias gave a grand ball in their honor at his Main and First Street adobe residence in Los Angeles.

When Garfias filed his claim to San Pascual on September 16, 1852 (Land Commission Case No. 345), he accompanied it with a wealth of evidence and followed this up with the depositions of such eminent southlanders as Pío Pico, José Antonio Carrillo, Manuel Domínguez, Antonio F. Coronel, Ygnacio del Valle, Fernando Sepúlveda, Agustín Olvera, Abel Stearns, and José del Carmen Lugo.

The claim was approved April 25, 1854, Thompson delivering the opinion. Confirmation by the district court (Case 173, Southern District) came March 6, 1856. The survey, when completed, included 13,693.93 acres in the rancho. On April 3, 1863, the United States patent was issued. Abraham Lincoln's signature appeared on this document, which was recorded in Book 1, Page 14 of Patents, County Recorder's Office, Los Angeles. The Recorder's Office, it might be noted, was part of the system of American county and town governments organized by the legislature in 1850, as provided for by the constitution of California adopted in 1849.

Meanwhile, Garfias built an adobe house not far from the springs where the Indians once had a village. It became famous as a country place, a favorite spot for the Los Angeles friends of the owner. Judge Benjamin S. Eaton, coming to San Pascual Rancho in 1858, visited at the "Garfias hacienda." He described it as one of the finest country establishments in southern California. "It was a one and a half story adobe building, with walls two feet thick, all nicely plastered inside and out, and had an ample corridor extending all around. It had board floors, and boasted of green blinds—a rare thing in those days. This structure cost $5,000—in fact, it cost Garfias his ranch, for he had to borrow money to build it."

The walls of the Garfias adobe were pulled down during the boom of the 'eighties to make way for a subdivision. The ancient oak tree, known today as Cathedral Oak, which it faced still grows near the edge of the arroyo.

San Pascual was not the best of cattle ranges and when dry years came the fortunes of Manuel Garfias suffered. Then, too, Garfias liked politics better than ranching; he liked it better than serving in the army under Flores. While he acted as the county treasurer of Los Angeles in 1850–1851, his mother-in-law Doña Encarnación Sepúlveda de Avila, ran the ranch. Finally his borrowings, at the usual ruinous rates of interest, forced him to sacrifice his property.

In January, 1859, Garfias deeded the ranch to Benjamin D. Wilson, the disclosed consideration being $1,800. The following year, in May, Wilson gave John S. Griffin a half interest for $4,000.

Benjamin D. Wilson—Don Benito—after whom a mountain, a canyon, a lake, a ditch, a trail, an avenue, and a school were named, had come to Los Angeles with trappers in 1841. In 1852 he bought what was known as the Lake Vineyard property, adjoining San Pascual, where he built his home near the "Old Mill." Dr. John S. Griffin had come as chief medical officer with the American Army.

From time to time various parts of the ranch were sold and in 1873 Wilson and Griffin partitioned the unsold section between them. Griffin, who wished to sell out to the "Indiana Colony," took approximately four thousand acres. Wilson, who wanted to hold on, took sixteen hundred acres. The Griffin land included the original site of Pasadena.[1]

One fall day in 1873, Judge Eaton had taken a visitor from Indiana to the San Pascual Ranch. They drove from Los Angeles, following the Arroyo Seco, stopping at the Garfias adobe and then on to "Fair Oaks," Eaton's home. The pleasant valley and the luminous mountains captivated the Judge's guest, who was D. M. Berry, purchasing agent for the California Colony of Indiana. This organization of Indiana people, hopeful of emigrating to California, had grown out of a meeting of friends at Dr. T. B. Elliott's home in Indianapolis one cold Sunday during

[1] For Garfias-Wilson-Griffin deeds, see Book 4, p. 310; Book 5, p. 79; Book 27, p. 229, of Deeds, County Recorder's Office, Los Angeles.

the winter of 1872–1873. Berry had been sent on to spy out the promised land.

When at last Berry saw the San Pascual Ranch, after weary months of colony-site hunting, he knew he need go no farther. Meanwhile the panic of 1873 had nearly wrecked his original Indiana group. So, to buy and colonize San Pascual land, he formed a new organization in Los Angeles, the San Gabriel Orange Grove Association, most of the stockholders of which were not Hoosiers. Before the end of the year incorporation was completed, as shown by articles of incorporation filed in the County Clerk's office. Capital stock in the amount of $25,000, divided into shares of $250 each, was subscribed by those eager to settle on the rancho.

On December 26, 1873, John S. Griffin made a deed of his four thousand acres to Thomas F. Croft, one of the directors of the new corporation, and three days later Croft gave title to the San Gabriel Orange Grove Association. The consideration passing to Griffin was $25,000.[2]

Since buying Griffin's land, the association had surveyed and platted fifteen hundred acres lying west of what is now Fair Oaks Avenue, each colonist to get fifteen acres for each share of stock. (Two years more were to pass before B. D. Wilson's holdings, lying east of the Avenue, would be subdivided.) The lots ranged on both sides of Orange Grove Avenue, which was given its name by Calvin Fletcher.

By ten o'clock on the morning of January 27, 1874, buggies began to arrive on the plain that was to be Pasadena. In the buggies were men, women, children, and

---

[2] The Croft deeds are recorded in Book 27, pp. 251 and 267, of Deeds, County Recorder's Office, Los Angeles.

picnic baskets. The hills were green and flowers were out, for there had been early rains. After lunch, on that important January day in 1874, there was a roll call of subdividers. Then the lots were chosen and assigned.

Cultivation began at once. By the end of May the colony had houses, a reservoir to hold 3,000,000 gallons of water, an irrigating system, 80 acres of grain raised for hay, 100,000 grape cuttings set out, 10,000 small trees purchased for nursery planting, and a large area of land prepared for corn.

Apparently no colonist thought of drawing upon local terms in christening the village. So "Indiana Colony" gave way to "Pasadena" at a meeting of the San Gabriel Orange Grove Association held April 22, 1875. "Pasadena," coined out of the Chippewa language, was offered by Dr. T. B. Elliott. Its meaning is "valley between hills."[3]

Such is the story of Rancho San Pascual and its transformation into a city. If continued to the present moment, it would include the life stories of every owner of every parcel of land in Pasadena. The story as presented has been told largely from original sources, and in chronological order. The professional title searcher, however, asked to "search" the title to a piece of Pasadena land, would reverse this procedure. He would start with a lot in a particular block in a particular Pasadena subdivision. Beginning with the deed to the present owner of that lot, he would work backward, examining every recorded deed and every recorded or filed document or proceeding relating to it. Soon, he would be dealing with land before its present subdivision, in time he might come across a conveyance from the San Gabriel Orange Grove Associa-

---

[3] Phil Townsend Hanna, *The Dictionary of California Land Names* (Los Angeles, 1946).

tion itself, and, further back, a deed from John S. Griffin, one from Benjamin D. Wilson, and another from Manuel Garfias in whose name the title to all of Rancho San Pascual was vested. He would find the recorded United States patent confirming Garfias' title, and, if he were bent on rolling back local history, he would dig into all the Land Commission and district court proceedings relating to this rancho, as well as the records of the Mexican and Spanish periods—local and state—and not overlook the supplementary and illuminating items to be furnished by histories and personal accounts. An insurer of land titles, however, would have no occasion to go back of the Garfias patent, since United States patents in confirmation of Spanish or Mexican titles are today incontestable.

San Pascual is only one rancho. Probably every other rancho in California would have a revealing, human-interest story if its chain of title were prepared and the source materials studied.

CHAPTER VIII

The Land Commission

TWENTY DAYS out of Panama, the steamship *Oregon* arrived in the pleasant port of Monterey, California, one September night in 1849. It brought lawyer William Carey Jones, confidential agent of the United States government.

Facing its small bay, but not far from ocean surf, Monterey at the time of Jones' visit was a village of sandy streets and lanes, of thick-walled adobe houses—many of them spacious—of gaily dressed Spanish-speaking people, a few Americans mixed among them, of men on horseback riding vaquero style, of guitars at night, and in the air the smell of pine trees and the sea.

Jones, son-in-law of Senator Thomas Hart Benton, had been chosen for this journey to newly annexed California because he was adept in the Spanish language and well acquainted with Spanish colonial titles. He was traveling on an expense account of $2,500. He carried with him the detailed instructions of Commissioner of the General

Land Office Butterfield, others from Secretary of the Interior Ewing and the latter's best wishes for a pleasant voyage, health, and success in what the latter called an "arduous undertaking."

Jones came to California to examine the records of land titles. He had been told to classify all grants or claims derived from Spanish and Mexican authorities and to list separately those originating during the period of the late Mexican War. He was to collect the legal forms—from petition to grant—that had been used by Californians and to prepare a table of land measurements. He was instructed to investigate mission lands and their source of title, to report on mining titles, to check on claims to islands, and to look into Indian rights. Jones was to get reliable information about the whole land-holding system of the former governments of California, to keep a journal and an account of personal expenses, and, to get the report in before the end of the next session of Congress.

When Jones stepped ashore in Monterey he found a convention in session, with delegates from all districts of California at work on California's first constitution. That fact did not prevent him from getting under way with his research. On the order of General Riley of the United States Army, Military Governor of California, the archives were thrown open to him. He found the records of land titles imperfect and in confusion. Those records prior to 1839 seemed to be missing, and no book had been started for 1846. Perhaps the records of Los Angeles would supply the deficiencies. What did impress him, though, was the large size of the individual grants allowed under Mexican law—as much as eleven square leagues of land, nearly 50,000 acres—which he felt would call for a liberal attitude on the part of Congress.

Before leaving Washington, Jones had had time to make a hurried reading of the report, made early in the year by H. W. Halleck, California's Secretary of State (afterward General Halleck of Civil War fame), on the Spanish and Mexican laws relating to land and mission properties in California. This report, with W. E. P. Hartnell's translations attached, was the pioneer work in the field that was to be more fully explored by Jones. Halleck, incidentally, was participating actively in the convention debates on the constitution at the time of Jones' Monterey visit.

Jones continued his investigations in San Francisco, San Jose, Los Angeles, San Diego, and Mexico City, staying in the last place two weeks. Returning to Washington he completed his report on April 10, 1850, and presented it to Secretary Ewing. President Millard Fillmore, to whom it was transmitted, sent it to Congress which—after the admission of California into the Union on September 9, 1850—would be considering legislation for the settlement of private land claims in the state.

Remarkable in scope and detail, as well as being a model of clarity and direct writing, the Jones report is a landmark in the history of land titles in California. It had its effect on the legislation Congress passed, and its liberal viewpoint found continuing expression in later court decrees ruling upon the ownership of California land.

As for grants or claims derived from the government of Spain, the Jones report found the chief local authority to grant lands in the province of California had been, ex officio, the military commandant, who was likewise the governor of the province. He had authority by virtue of his office and also under the Viceroy's instructions of 1773. The principal recipients of grants were officers and soldiers upon their retirement from service. The Viceroy of New Spain also had authority to make grants and sometimes exercised it. It was pursuant to his order that presidios, missions, and pueblos had been established. Spanish grants or claims had been respected by the Mexican government, many holders taking the precaution to have them renewed under Mexican law.

Jones found that grants of land during the Mexican period, except those of pueblo lots and perhaps some north of the bay of San Francisco, had been made by the different political governors. The great majority were made after January, 1832, under the Mexican colonization law of 1824 and the regulations adopted in pursuance of that law in 1828.

The report discussed in detail how these grants were made. Anyone desiring a grant presented a petition to the governor, stating his name, age, country, and vocation, the quantity and, as nearly as possible, the description of the land. The petition was accompanied by a crude map or diseño. The next step was for the governor to make a marginal notation on the petition directing the prefect or the local officer to examine and report whether the land was vacant and could be granted without injury to third persons or the public. This official's reply, called the *informe,* was written upon, or attached to, the petition and the whole returned to the governor. If satisfactory, the governor issued the formal grant. The original petition and informe, together with a copy of the grant, were filed in the archives by the secretary of the government. The original grant was delivered to the grantee. The filed papers were attached so as to form one document constituting the evidence of title and called the *expediente.* The last step was to obtain approval of the grant by the Territorial Deputation or Departmental Assembly. The governor took care of this matter by communicating with the legislative body, his communication being referred to a committee which would make its report later. If the legislative body did not concur, it was the governor's duty to appeal to the supreme government.

As for mission-held land, Jones reported: "The missionaries there [in California] had never any other rights than to the occupation and use of the lands for the purpose of the missions and at the pleasure of the government. That is shown by the history and principles of their foundation, by the laws in relation to them, by the constant practice of the government towards them, and by the rules of the Franciscan order which forbid its members to possess property."

The report also found that, under the Laws of the Indies the pueblos had been entitled to four square leagues of land. It pointed out, too, that Spanish colonial laws recognized the rights of Christianized Indians to occupy and use lands needed for habitations, tillage, and pasturage of flocks. Jones favored a continued observance of this principle. His report found only one "grant of gold mines," that by Governor Micheltorena to Don Juan Bautista Alvarado in February, 1844, of the Mariposas. It did not find in Mexican laws any reservation of mines of gold, silver, quicksilver, or other metal or mineral. It pointed out that Alcatraz Island was indispensable to the United States government, though purportedly granted to Francis P. Temple of Los Angeles. The report expressed the view that it would not be hard to detect fraudulent last-minute Mexican grants, and concluded with the opinion that the grants of California were "mostly perfect titles."

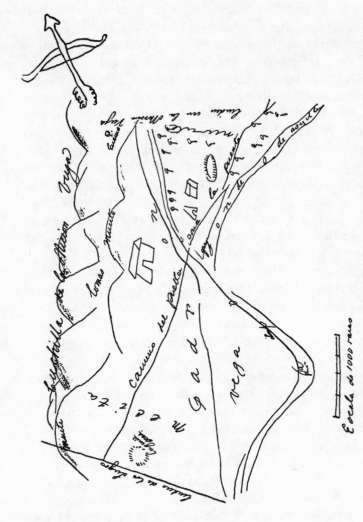

Figure 5. Diseño of Rancho La Merced, Los Angeles County.

Thirty-three papers accompanied and were a part of this report: copies of laws, decrees, forms, letters, regulations, proclamations, an early map of San Francisco, and a list of the private land grants in California found in the archives at Monterey.[1] This simply written Jones report showed a definitely friendly attitude toward Californians and helped to lay the basis for tolerance and understanding in meeting the claims of those who were in possession of the land of California.

It is interesting to compare the Jones report with the earlier one of Secretary of State Halleck which had been turned over to Governor Mason on March 1, 1849.[2]

Halleck pioneered in collecting and examining the Spanish and Mexican material at Monterey bearing upon land titles. He summarized his own report by saying that it covered the laws and regulations governing the granting or selling of public lands in California, the laws and regulations respecting the lands and other property belonging to the missions of California, and the titles of lands in California which might be required for fortifications, arsenals, or other military structures for the use of the general government of the United States. Halleck sketched briefly the history of land titles in California, stating that in many cases the laws had not been complied with in obtaining grants. Grants made after November 21, 1828, were invalid, he said, unless approved by the territorial legislature or by the supreme government of Mexico. So, too, grants of land within ten leagues of the seacoast or within twenty leagues of the boundaries of any foreign power, as well as grants that exceeded the specified areas for specified kinds of lands. He pointed

[1] Senate Ex. Doc. No. 18, 31st Cong., 1st sess., 1850.
[2] House Ex. Doc. No. 17, 31st Cong., 1st sess., 1850.

out the indefiniteness of the boundaries of a large number of land grants. He called attention to the probability that Pío Pico antedated some grants made after the United States had taken possession and to possible frauds and irregularities in the sale of pueblo lands. Halleck went into the history of the secularization of the missions, pointing out some of the chaotic conditions existing at the time of his report. Briefly, too, he discussed the title situation at San Diego, Monterey, San Francisco, Alcatraz Island, Angel Island, and other points where it might be desirable to establish military posts or fortifications. Attached to the report were assembled documents illustrating or bearing upon the statements made.

Halleck's report was and is valuable largely as a pioneering document. It emphasized and magnified title defects and title problems. Had the Land Commission or the courts adopted the skeptical and cautious spirit shown by Halleck, it seems certain that the landowners of California would have suffered even more delays and disappointments, if possible, than they actually did.

Both Halleck and Jones played a large part later as attorneys in court contests involving California titles. Between 1854 and 1860 the former was a member of the San Francisco law firm of Halleck, Peachy and Williams, taking part as counselor in many of the land suits and building a reputation also as an authority on military, mining, and international law. Jones likewise appeared as attorney for many California land claimants and had already acted as counsel for his brother-in-law, John C. Frémont, in the latter's court-martial in Washington. His son, also named William Carey Jones, attained distinction as dean of the School of Jurisprudence at the University of California.

California's first Senators, John C. Frémont and William M. Gwin, made their presence felt in the United States Senate soon after they were sworn in as members following California's admission into the Union. Frémont offered a bill for the settlement of private land claims in his state. Gwin offered a substitute, and Benton of Missouri offered an amendment to the substitute.

"Our titles in California are *equities*," Gwin stated, in debate with Benton. "We call upon you to examine them in a liberal and beneficial spirit, and confirm all that are just. We ask the interposition of a board to collect the evidence, and then the right to bring our titles before our own court. Then, as a final resort, and forever to settle the question, we claim a right of appeal to that power at Washington 'which has neither guards, nor palaces, nor treasure.' "[3]

Gwin, whose recommendations were to prevail, probably voiced the opinions of the average American who regarded California as a fabulous region that should be open to land-hungry Americans and who looked with suspicion upon the huge size of the California ranchos. Gwin believed land titles in California were vague. Benton, echoing Jones' opinion, held they were perfect. Gwin wanted the courts to pass upon the claims of Californians to land. Benton would have established a recorder as keeper of the archives and of all evidences of land titles; his duty—except where forgery was suspected—being to examine all claims, with the help of the United States District Attorney. Benton favored what he thought would be a simple system, fair to Californians. He foresaw many of the hardships that landowners were later to suffer under the Gwin measure.

---

[3] *Speeches of Mr. Gwin in the Senate of the United States on Private Land Titles in the State of California* (Washington, 1851).

The Gwin bill passed the Senate and the House, becoming the Act of March 3, 1851.[4] It threw the burden of proof on every Californian who claimed land—in spite of Articles VIII and IX of the Treaty of Guadalupe Hidalgo which specifically promised full and complete protection of all property rights of Mexicans.[5]

The Act of 1851 provided for a commission of three members, to be appointed by the President and to function for three years. (This period was twice extended by Congress so that the commission had a five-year life.) Provision was made for a secretary, skilled in the Spanish and English languages, to be appointed by the commissioners and to act as interpreter and to keep a record of the proceedings. Clerks not to exceed five in number were also to be appointed by the commissioners. Furthermore the President was empowered to appoint an agent "learned in the law and skilled in the Spanish and English languages," to represent the public interests.

The Act provided that "each and every person claiming lands in California by virtue of any right or title derived from the Spanish or Mexican government, shall present the same to the said commissioners when sitting as a board, together with such documentary evidence and testimony of witnesses as the said claimant relies upon in support of such claims." The commissioners were to proceed promptly to examine the evidence "and to decide upon the validity of the said claim, and, within thirty days after such decision is rendered, to certify the same, with the reasons on which it is founded, to the district attorney of the United States in and for the district in which such decision shall be rendered."

---

[4] 9 *Stat.* 631.
[5] See below, Appendix I.

In the event of either rejection or confirmation of a claim by the board, the claimant could petition the District Court for a review. (Later the appeal was made automatic.) The petition was to be accompanied by a full statement of the claim and a transcript of the commissioners' report. If the District Court's decision was against the claimant, he could ask for an appeal to the Supreme Court of the United States.

Commissioners and courts were to be governed by the Treaty of Guadalupe Hidalgo, the law of nations, the laws, usages, and customs of the government from which the claim was derived, the principles of equity, and the decisions of the Supreme Court of the United States, so far as they were applicable.

All lands the claims for which should be finally rejected by the commissioners or finally held to be invalid by the courts, and all lands the claims to which should not have been presented to the commissioners within two years, would be considered as part of the public domain of the United States. For all claims finally confirmed, on the other hand, a patent from the United States was to be issued upon the claimant's presenting to the General Land Office an authentic certificate of such confirmation and a survey duly certified and approved by the Surveyor General of California.

The act provided that the "corporate authorities" of any city, town, or village established under the Spanish or Mexican government or existing on July 7, 1846, or at the date of the act, were to present the claims to the land embraced within the limits of such city, town, or village, and not the individual holders of granted lots. Proof of the existence on July 7, 1846, of a city, town, or village was to be prima facie evidence of a grant.

Final decrees by the commissioners or by the courts and any patents issued under the act were to be conclusive between the United States and the claimants, but were not to affect the interests of "third persons."

The commissioners were also given the duty of reporting to the Secretary of the Interior on the tenure by which the mission lands were held, and "those held by civilized Indians, and those who are engaged in agriculture or labor of any kind, and also those which are occupied and cultivated by Pueblos or Rancheros Indians."

The board began its work in San Francisco in January, 1852, though the first decision was not reached till August. Early claims filed included those for Las Mariposas (by John C. Frémont), Suisun (by Archibald Ritchie), San Antonio in Alameda County (by Domingo and Vicente Peralta), Nipoma (by William G. Dana) and Las Pulgas (by María de la Soledad, *et al.*). The original board appointed by President Fillmore was composed of Harry I. Thornton, James Wilson, and Hiland Hall. In March, 1853, President Pierce appointed a new board: Alpheus Felch, Thompson Campbell, and R. A. Thompson. When Campbell resigned in the following year, his successor was S. B. Farwell. The first secretary was J. B. Carr, but, beginning in January, 1852, George Fisher held the secretaryship to the end. Law agents were, in succession, George W. Cooley, V. E. Howard, and John H. McKune. Among the leading law firms employed by claimants were Halleck, Peachy and Billings; Clarke, Taylor and Beckh; Jones, Tompkins and Strode; and Crosby and Rose.[6] All the sessions of the board were held at San

---

[6] An extensive and important collection of legal briefs, opinions, depositions, arguments, and pamphlets bearing on land titles and the Land Commission—originating apparently in the law library of the firm of Halleck, Peachy and Billings—are bound together in the 19 volumes making up Henry E. Will's *California Titles*, deposited in The Huntington Library, San Marino, California.

Francisco, except for one term at Los Angeles in the autumn of 1852. This brief jaunt to Los Angeles—the center of a district with an economy based largely on existing grants—caused the Los Angeles *Star* to urge claimants to present their cases as early as possible. Previously its editors had denounced the whole process as one certain to keep all titles in litigation. Its issue of August 28, 1852, carried advertisements of the lawyers who followed the board south.

Up and down California, during the five years of the board's activities, Californians gathered up all the papers they could to prove to the gentlemen of the board that they owned the land they had been living on for so many years. They looked into their leather trunks for original grants from Mexican governors. They called upon their friends and relatives to testify to long residence and to the number of their cattle. They went to Yankee lawyers for help. They sent to the Surveyor General's Office in San Francisco for copies of the archives files relating to particular ranchos. They made journeys and drew upon their slender fund of cash. They sometimes mortgaged their lands and their futures or conveyed "undivided" interests to their attorneys. Town officials bestirred themselves to prove pueblo titles. Mission claimants did likewise. Indians, quite unaware of what was happening, did nothing about the lands they were occupying.

The hard-working and fair-minded commission continued in existence until March, 1856. Under the Act of 1851 appeals might be taken to the courts of the United States from the board's decisions, but under the Act of August 31, 1852, appeals were automatically taken to the United States District Court. Thereafter board *decisions* obviously were less important. The great majority of the

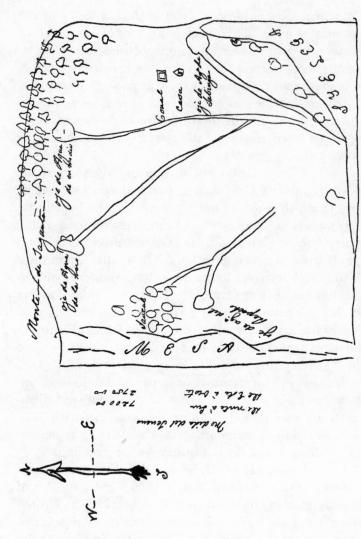

Figure 6. Diseño of Rancho Tajauta, Los Angeles County.

claims, after being passed upon by the board and the courts, were confirmed. Some claims were withdrawn; others were rejected for fraud or for serious defect. Grants made after July 7, 1846, the date Commodore John D. Sloat took possession of Monterey, were held invalid by the Supreme Court. The board and the courts took a liberal attitude and were ready to overlook a claimant's failure to have followed the details of Mexican law in obtaining his grant or inability to find all the papers to prove he had. They were interested largely in proof of possession and use of land.

J. N. Bowman, conducting recent and extensive research into the proceedings of the Land Commission, of the United States District Court, and of other courts to which appeals were carried, revises the data contained in Judge Ogden Hoffman's much quoted *Report of Land Cases* (1862), and has this general statement on claims:

The total number of private land grant cases in California as determined finally by the board, the District Court, the Circuit Court, the Court of Appeals, the Supreme Court, and Congress, was 848. This means claims filed, it does not mean the number of grants or granted pieces of land. For the rancho Napa of four leagues 56 claims were presented and one board case included 23 separate claims. Two cases were claimed before Congress, one was confirmed and the other rejected.[7]

Taking the 813 cases listed by Hoffman, and without the benefit of Bowman's revisions, William W. Morrow in

---

[7] Quoted from "Index of California Private Land Grants and Private Land Grant Papers," 1942. manuscript volumes in Doctor Bowman's possession in Berkeley, California. His manuscript "Private Land Cases" (1941), which is a revision of the Hoffman index and which is an index of the cases in the Minutes and in the Decree books of the United States District Courts, as well as an index of maps, in the custody of the clerk of the United States District Court in San Francisco, is on file in the Bancroft Library, Berkeley. Another copy is in the office of the clerk of the United States District Court, San Francisco.

his *Spanish and Mexican Private Land Grants* (1923) broke them down into 604 finally confirmed, 190 finally rejected, and 19 withdrawn. "The 813 is the number of the cases of the board," comments Bowman, "but one of them was a clerical error, two were preëmption claims and another made no claim to any Spanish or Mexican origin. This leaves 809 cases of the board. Now all but 19 of the board cases were appealed to the District Court, so the final decision was with the higher bodies—District Court, Circuit Court, Circuit Court of Appeals, and the United States Supreme Court. Of the 19 cases, 16 were carried by other cases relative to the same grant; so only three cases involving three pieces of land granted were decided by the board."

After a claim had been confirmed, and the official survey by the Surveyor General of California approved, a patent by the United States was issued to the successful claimant. Lands for which claims were finally rejected or not presented were to be considered henceforth as part of the public domain.

Seventeen years was the average length of time that the California landowner had to wait for his patent after filing his petition, according to Bowman. Delays were caused by extended litigation, by unnecessary appeals by government attorneys, and by the difficulties in getting approved surveys. Meanwhile—and as a result of these delays—rancho land was not salable, squatters came in like locusts, and the owners' funds and resources went to lawyers and lenders. Most claimants were bankrupted in the process of getting clear titles. Some chose to sell out to speculators and sharpers. It was a ruinous period for Spanish Californians. Apparently the Treaty of Guadalupe Hidalgo was not taken literally by the United States.

Delay in settling survey questions—perhaps the greatest obstacle of the land claimant—caused Congress to pass the Act of June 14, 1860, under which the District Court, upon application, could order into court the survey of a private land claim, for examination and adjudication.[8] Previously the General Land Office had handled these questions. The slow methods used by this office were responsible for the establishment of the new procedure which, though coming late, proved helpful to claimants.

The Act of 1860 not only reduced delay, but by bringing interested persons before the court did away with disputes arising from independently made and sometimes overlapping governmental surveys. Furthermore it gave assurance that the title of the patentee and of his successors would be free from the claims of "third persons," mentioned in the Act of 1851. The absence of such procedure earlier had resulted in litigation over conflicting claims and even over conflicting patents.

Bearing on the conclusiveness of federal patents is the Act of March 3, 1891. This act requires that suits by the United States to vacate and annul any patent already issued must be brought within five years from the passage of the act and, as to any patent thereafter issued, within six years after the date the patent was issued. Also in point is California's statute of limitations barring an action to recover real property unless the plaintiff or his predecessor has been in possession within five years before the commencement of the action. Furthermore, five years of adverse possession at any time since the passage by the California legislature of the Act of April 18, 1863, bars an action by the holder of an unconfirmed title of Spanish or Mexican origin.[9]

---

[8] 12 *Stat.* 33.   [9] *Statutes* 1863, p. 325.

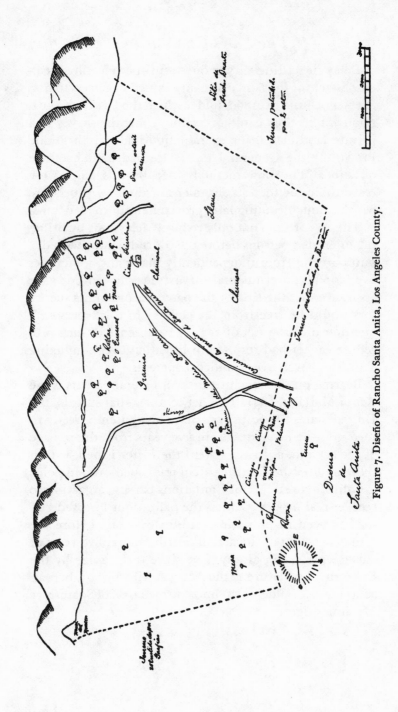

Figure 7. Diseño of Rancho Santa Anita, Los Angeles County.

Historians and lawyers like to argue over the wisdom and justice of the procedure set up by the Act of 1851 to pass upon the validity of Spanish and Mexican land grants in California. The former, confronted with the injustice that resulted, feel that a simpler, quicker system for separating good titles from bad could have been established. The latter, who benefited most from long-drawn-out litigation, point out that, in the United States, courts—and not recorders or registrars—have the final word in controversies and that the vagueness and defects in Spanish and Mexican records, titles, and surveys made inevitable long court battles over desirable land. Lawyers like William W. Morrow have said that condemnation of the whole procedure comes only from those not familiar with the situation. Regardless of whether the Frémont, the Gwin, or any other measure was adopted, California landowners were due to have years of trouble. As proof of this statement, the attacks on land titles, always beaten off, have continued to the present day. To those commentators who so casually state that the United States should have "bought" all the privately owned land in California to make it part of the public domain, it is enough to say that this would have been contrary to the Treaty of Guadalupe Hidalgo as well as highhanded.

Doubtless short cuts in procedure could have been adopted early in the 1850's—as was done finally in 1860—with the result that some of the ranchos might have been broken up quickly and sold at existing low prices. This would have staved off much of the later litigation, reduced squatterism, and eased the demand for cheap land—a contention well stated by Elisha Oscar Crosby, an attorney who handled many of the claims before the Land Commission.[10] Such observations are easily made in retrospect.

---

[10] *Memoirs of Elisha Oscar Crosby* (The Huntington Library, 1945).

CHAPTER IX

Shotgun Titles

EVERY AMERICAN is a squatter at heart—or so it seems if we think of the tide of adventurous men that began moving west at the close of the Revolutionary War, men impatient of governmental authority and as contemptuous of the rights of Indians as of wild animals, men who believed land should be free as air. This tide finally reached the westernmost boundary of California.

Squatterism is as old as our country. George Washington in 1784 was making entries in his diary about his experiences with squatters on lands he owned west of the Alleghenies. The squatter movement that began in the eastern states continued steadily west and farther west, greatly influencing the land policies of the government. It found its climax, but hardly its conclusion, when gold-hungry pioneers looked enviously and graspingly on the vast ranchos held by Californians under Mexican laws. Squatterism in California has never entirely died out, although shotguns gave way to lawyers. In recent years,

with California rancho titles all settled, we still find mild
flare-ups of the squatter spirit, for the desire to settle upon
the good lands held by another person dies hard. Who
does not want to get something for nothing!

Even before California became a part of the Union—
September 9, 1850—the wagons of the immigrants were
moving in and coming to a stop on the good valley lands
of the rancheros. Squatters began early to organize into
armed bands to get what they wanted. Some were interested in ranches. Some began staking out, or helping
themselves to, lots on the outskirts of growing towns like
San Francisco and Sacramento.

Many years were to elapse before a land commission,
authorized under Act of Congress in 1851, and the courts
to which its decisions could be appealed, could pass upon
all of the 800 and more private land claims in California.
Meanwhile adventurous American immigrants, who believed—as in the popular song—that "Uncle Sam is rich
enough to give us all a farm," found on their arrival that
all the best land in California, or at least the most usable,
was included in enormous grants made by the Mexican
regime. To many of these "North American adventurers,"
as native Californians liked to refer to them, the great
landowners were merely monopolists who, like the Indians, were obstructing the path or progress of civilization. After all, California had been captured, as well as
bought, from Mexico.

No doubt some of these newcomers brought with them
the honest notion that this teritory obtained from Mexico
was inevitably public land and that they, therefore, had
the right to preëmpt and settle upon lands in California
as freely as they had been doing upon any part of the
public domain in other states. When they found the best

areas claimed under Mexican titles or held by speculators who had bought them up, clashes were inevitable. Hardly any part of inhabited California was free from violence. The story of squatterism in California is just one chapter in the story of mob law in America.

Beginning in 1849 and 1850 swarms of squatters settled on every available spot in or about San Francisco, whether claimed or not. They fenced in the sand hills. Soldiers had to be despatched from the presidio to destroy the tents and shanties of squatters who had helped themselves to the land of the government reserve at Rincon Point, the government having just given its lease for this area to Theodore Shillaber. Union Square was fenced in by one "settler" who had to be disarmed when the street commissioner attempted to remove the fence. By midsummer of 1853 squatters had swarmed over the land deeded by Samuel Brannan for the Odd Fellows' cemetery. Ten men on each side fought a battle over a lot at Mission and Third streets, two being killed and five wounded. By 1854 property owners whose titles were derived from the city were hiring special police to protect their lots. Squatters became bolder and entrenched themselves on a lot at the west corner of Howard and First streets. Here they planted the galley from a sailing vessel as a fortress—Fort Larkin, they called it—and defied attempts to expel them. Possession was regarded as the best title. There were many battles along the water front over submerged areas and "water lots" fenced in by the driving of piles.

In San Francisco, where the pueblo title to four square leagues was not to be confirmed until 1865, squatting was inevitable and perhaps logical. It even became a trade. Men squatted for themselves and for hire, and did this over a twenty-year period. Squatting implements consisted of blankets and firearms. In the long run the city of San Francisco was forced to recognize the claims of squatters in certain large areas and, under the Van Nuys and later ordinances, to issue city deeds on the strength of possession. Many a real estate fortune in San Francisco, and the rise of many a prominent San Francisco family, dates from this municipal recognition of possessory rights.

Sacramento, the gold-rush city, was the scene of the most violent of the squatter riots. The original city had been laid out by John A. Sutter on part of the eleven square leagues granted him in 1841 by Mexican Governor Alvarado, the title to which later was upheld as valid by the United States. Sacramento was first a tent city, but by 1849 substantial buildings were going up. On the vacant lots owned by purchasers from Sutter several thousand immigrants had squatted, disregarding the wishes and orders of owners and city authorities. By December public meetings of squatters were being held, with speakers to harangue them in increasingly violent language. The people of Sacramento became divided into those who sided with the squatters and those—like Samuel Brannan and city officials—who were on the side of law, order, and Sutter's title. On June 21, 1850, Sutterites demolished a squatter's house and the next day raided other squatter-held lots, destroying houses and pulling down fences. On July 1 the squatters, in a meeting to raise money and to hire lawyers to fight suits brought to enforce the Sutter title, were told by Chairman Charles Robinson that every man had a sacred right to a homestead and a sacred duty to defend it. As for himself, Robinson believed it as easy to squat on 160 acres as on one acre, and as easy to defend it. James McClatchy was of Robinson's mind and at the next meeting—when it was announced that four lawyers had been hired—said: "Let us put up all the fences pulled down and also put up all the men who pull them down."[1]

On August 13 the climax was reached when McClatchy and Michael Moran were arrested and put in the prison ship. They were charged with resisting or attempting to resist the sheriff in the execution of a judgment of forcible entry and detainer by the county court against some of the squatters. The next morning thirty armed squatters, under the leadership of John Maloney marched toward the prison ship. Calling upon the citizens of Sacramento to take up arms for the defense of the laws, Mayor Harden Bigelow led an armed group of citizens to the water front. But the squatter army, led by Maloney carrying a drawn sword, made no attempt to release the prisoners on the ship. Instead, they marched up J Street, followed by a jeering, hooting crowd.

At Fourth Street the squatters halted and turned around. Mayor Bigelow and Sheriff Joseph McKinney, riding up, told the squatters to lay down arms and surrender. Maloney then gave the order: "Shoot the Mayor! Shoot the Mayor!" The squatters fired and their fire was returned. The Mayor fell, wounded, from his horse (and two months later was to die as an aftermath of his wound), City Assessor J. M. Woodland was killed, as were three squatters—including Maloney—and both sides counted several wounded. The battle was continued the next day when the sheriff and his party entered a saloon where eight or ten squatters were awaiting them. On both sides there were killed and wounded, among those killed being the sheriff himself.

Though this uprising at Sacramento surpassed others

---

[1] Hittell, *History of California*, III, 673–674.

in violence and was condemned throughout the state, the claims of the squatters there were not different from those of squatters elsewhere. In complete disregard of the rights of the Peralta family, squatters in 1850 rushed on Rancho San Antonio and laid out Oakland. It was many years before deeds and compromises cleared Oakland's title from squatter taint. So large was the squatter population in California that politicians began bidding for their vote. Governor John Bigler, in his message to the legislature on January 4, 1854, called for legislation on their behalf and referred to the squatters as "bona-fide settlers." He believed that compensation should be given anyone who had been evicted after putting up a house on land he thought belonged to the government. He also thought the government should not charge $1.25 per acre to California settlers on the public domain when it was giving away land in Oregon. Finally, in 1856, the legislature passed a law providing that all lands in the state were to be regarded as public until the legal title should be shown to have passed to private parties. This extraordinary statute was held unconstitutional by the Supreme Court. Its passage, however, showed that squatters were a power in the land. There were squatter governors, squatter legislators, squatter courts, and squatter judges.

The squatter troubles of the 'fifties, 'sixties, and 'seventies occurred primarily because so many land titles had not yet been confirmed by the Land Commission or, if confirmed, were still in the courts on appeal or were awaiting governmental survey before a patent could be issued. Everywhere the original California rancheros, or their successors, were harassed by squatters and often impoverished by the expense of fighting claims. With an uncertain title, too, a ranchero found it hard to sell and

Photo, Title Insurance and Trust Company, Los Angeles

THE YGNACIO MARTÍNEZ ADOBE
RANCHO EL PINOLE, CONTRA COSTA COUNTY

Photo, Title Insurance and Trust Company, Los Angeles

THE RAIMUNDO YORBA ADOBE
RANCHO RINCÓN, SAN BERNARDINO COUNTY

Photo, Title Insurance and Trust Company, Los Angeles

**NEW ALMADEN MINING CAMP
SANTA CLARA COUNTY**

Photo, Title Insurance and Trust Company, Los Angeles

STORE AT NEW ALMADEN

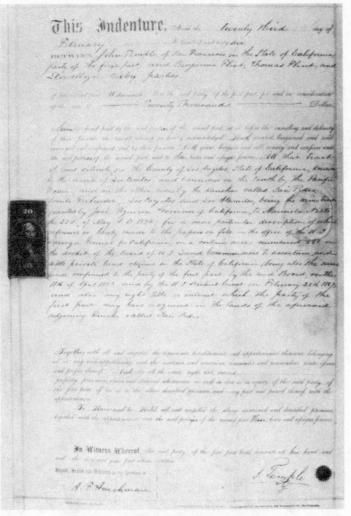

JOHN TEMPLE'S CONVEYANCE OF RANCHO
LOS CERRITOS, 1866

BODEGA COAST, BY EDWARD WESTON

TOMATO FIELD, MONTEREY COUNTY
BY EDWARD WESTON

OWENS VALLEY, BY EDWARD WESTON

Photo, Title Insurance and Trust Company, Los Angeles

FOOTHILL SCENE, SOUTHERN CALIFORNIA

Photo, Society of California Pioneers, San Francisco

SAN FRANCISCO WATER LOTS, 1856

Photo, Title Insurance and Trust Company, Los Angeles

OIL WELLS AT SUMMERLAND, SANTA BARBARA COUNTY

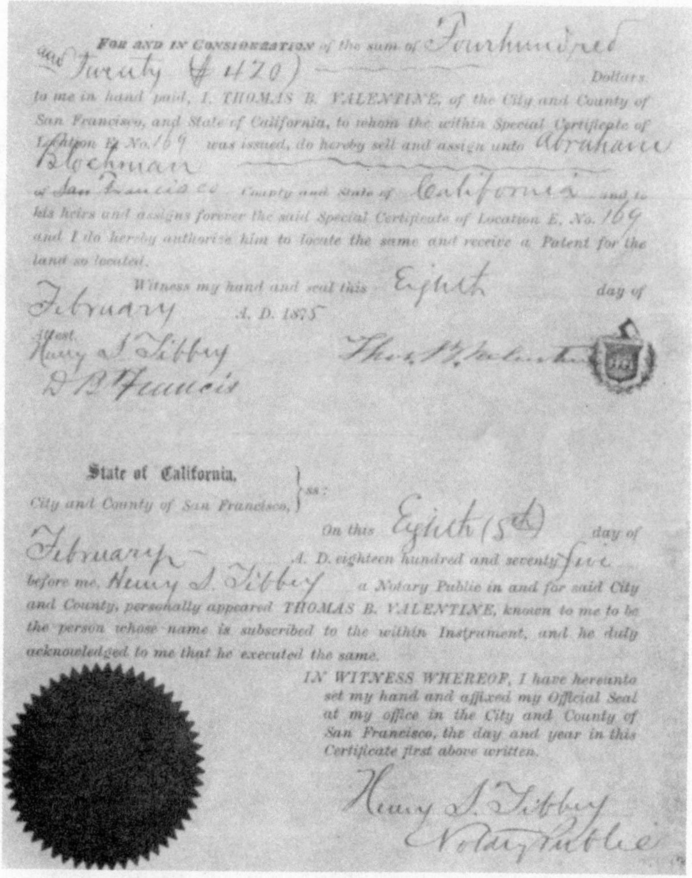

For and in Consideration of the sum of Fourhundred and Twenty ($420) Dollars to me in hand paid, I, THOMAS B. VALENTINE, of the City and County of San Francisco, and State of California, to whom the within Special Certificate of Location E. No. 169 was issued, do hereby sell and assign unto Abraham Blochman of San Francisco County and State of California and to his heirs and assigns forever the said Special Certificate of Location E. No. 169 and I do hereby authorize him to locate the same and receive a Patent for the land so located.

Witness my hand and seal this Eighth day of February A. D. 1875

Attest. Henry S. Tibbey
D B Francis

Thos. B. Valentine

State of California,
City and County of San Francisco, } ss:

On this Eighth (8th) day of February A. D. eighteen hundred and seventy five before me, Henry S. Tibbey a Notary Public in and for said City and County, personally appeared THOMAS B. VALENTINE, known to me to be the person whose name is subscribed to the within Instrument, and he duly acknowledged to me that he executed the same.

IN WITNESS WHEREOF, I have hereunto set my hand and affixed my Official Seal at my office in the City and County of San Francisco, the day and year in this Certificate first above written.

Henry S. Tibbey
Notary Public

TRANSFER OF VALENTINE LAND SCRIP, 1875

Photo, Title Insurance and Trust Company, Los Angeles

SAN LUIS OBISPO, ABOUT 1890

Photo, Title Insurance and Trust Company, Los Angeles

CLAREMONT AND MT. SAN ANTONIO, ABOUT 1907

convey even though there was a settler buyer who could well use part of a huge acreage. When valuable land was involved, such as the so-called Suscol grant in Solano and Napa counties, the rejection of the title of its claimant by the Land Commission or by the courts resulted in a rush to it by squatters. Or, when the government's survey excluded valuable land from the boundaries of the area claimed—as in the case of the Sobrante grant in Contra Costa County or the Azusa de Dalton and adjoining Dalton grants in Los Angeles County—squatters swarmed in upon the excluded parts.

Even after a title had been perfected and the United States had issued its patent, the rancho was not always free from the harassment of squatters whose lawyers would undertake to prove that some requirement of Mexican law had not been fulfilled by original owners or that the government survey took in too much territory, and that, therefore, the land was public domain. This kind of attack—though never successful, since the Supreme Court holds that a United States patent issued in confirmation of an earlier Spanish or Mexican title is binding and conclusive as against squatter claims—has continued, although in an ever-diminishing degree, almost to the present time. Hence, the story of squatting is a continuous one throughout California's history, violent in its early phases, but tending toward court battles in its later phases. As the large ranchos were broken up, squatters found less and less to excite their cupidity, and squatterism as a political issue eventually died out. California's titles today do not originate in squatter claims, but the pressure of squatters on government and individuals, as happened in San Francisco and Oakland, compelled compromises that were partial victories for squatters.

A check of the county histories of the state and of the volumes on local history reveals an extraordinary story of squatter violence in California throughout the 'fifties, 'sixties, and 'seventies.

In May, 1853, Jack Powers, who was a squatter on land of Nicholas Den near Santa Barbara, barricaded himself with fifteen of his friends behind logs and wagons and defied the sheriff's attempt to oust him. They were armed with revolvers, rifles, and shotguns and were supplied with liquor and food. In the battle that developed there were killed and wounded on both sides.

Trespassers and squatters roamed and mined at will along the creek beds of John Charles Frémont's ore-rich Mariposas grant, and when the final survey showed valuable mines included within the rancho's boundaries, Frémont's settlement became an armed camp. Miners attempted to seize the mines they had worked. Bloodshed and riots followed.

Two hundred squatters along the Russian River near Healdsburg in Sonoma County banded together for defensive and aggressive action. Fifty armed men attacked a government surveyor, tore up his papers, and threatened his life if he did not stop surveying and go home. They forced one Spanish Californian landowner to release his title to certain land and to get out. They threatened to burn Healdsburg to the ground, but a rally of citizens caused the "free land" men to retire.

John Bidwell rid himself of squatters on his Rancho Chico in Butte County by buying out some of them and bringing suits of ejectment against others.

The "battle of Waterloo" took place November 9, 1861, eight miles north of Stockton at a place called Waterloo, when a squatter named John Balkwill turned his house into a fort and successfully defended it against the owner who attacked with a nine-pound cannon.

Thomas More, owner of Rancho Sespe—six-league rancho in the Santa Clara Valley of the present Ventura County—was murdered on March 23, 1877, by F. A. Sprague, leader of a band of seven masked men. Sprague, a former Baptist minister, was the leader of the Sespe Settlers League and had filed preëmption claim to part of the original Sespe grant. This league had warned More in the Santa Barbara and Ventura newspapers not to interfere with any settler upon land in the Santa Clara Valley between Santa Paula Creek and Piru Creek.[2]

Employees and tenants of Henry Dalton filed homestead and preëmption claims on land excluded by Henry Hancock's survey of Ranchos Azusa de Dalton, San José, and Addition to San José, in Los Angeles County. A settlement of shacks sprang up known as Azusa Four Corners. Dalton was unable to have these settlers ejected, since the Hancock survey was the government's official survey, and endured twenty-nine years of futile legislation trying to recover the land. This legislation cost him so much that he lost the rest of his land through foreclosure.[3]

The most publicized conflict of squatters with the Mormon owners of Rancho San Bernardino was that involving "Apostate" Jerome Benson who had taken up land on the Santa Ana River which he assumed to be outside rancho boundaries. He disregarded notices that he was trespassing. The court decided against Benson, but Benson surrounded himself with friends who were anti-Mormon and fortified his place with a Fourth of July cannon. "Fort Benson" was maintained for a year but was aban-

[2] Robert Cleland, *The Place Called Sespe* (Chicago, 1940).

[3] C. C. Baker, "Don Enrique Dalton of the Azusa," Historical Society of Southern California, *Annual Publication*, 1917.

doned when the government survey proved it a part of the rancho. Benson was paid the value of his improvements.[4]

Mountain areas were not free from squatters nor were offshore islands. John M. James, for example, cut timber over the Crestline and Skyland region in the San Bernardino Mountains. Several squatters bequeathed their names to canyons in the San Gabriel Mountains. Santa Catalina Island was a favorite spot for squatters both before and after Tómas Robbins received his grant from Governor Pío Pico.[5]

With the settlement of titles and the breakup of ranchos, squatterism languished. But it took on a new lease of life and a new phase in southern California with the advent in 1897 of the Land Settlers League—sometimes termed the "Land Suckers League"— headquarters in Los Angeles. Henceforth squatting was to be promoter induced. Credulous members were persuaded to join the League on the representation that the title to certain Spanish or Mexican grants could be successfully contested and the land then thrown open to settlement. They paid fifty dollars down and dues of fifty cents a month and, about two hundred of them received conditional deeds of quarter sections of land in the pleasant San Fernando Valley. These deeds involved several subdivisions in Rancho Ex-Mission de San Fernando, the title to which rancho had been confirmed by the Board of United States Land Commissioners in 1855 and a government patent issued in 1873.[6] Only the promoters profited, for the United States Supreme Court upheld the finality of this patent.[7]

[4] George William Beattie and Helen Pruitt Beattie, *Heritage of the Valley* (Pasadena, 1939).

[5] W. W. Robinson, *The Island of Santa Catalina* (Los Angeles, 1941).

[6] See Los Angeles *Times,* October and November, 1897.

[7] 180 U.S. 72.

The pattern of promotion laid down by the Land Settlers League, was followed in the 1920's by a Homesteaders Association which induced "homesteaders"—so called—to file applications in the United States Land Office at Los Angeles for land, not only in the San Fernando Valley but in Rancho Lomas de Santiago (the Irvine Ranch), Orange County, and in Rancho Los Palos Verdes, in Rancho Topanga Malibu Sequit, Los Angeles County, and other places. The Association charged a filing fee plus a legal retainer fee varying from one hundred to one thousand dollars. Prospective applicants, who yearned for land that others had improved, were taken out and shown bearing orchards, vineyards, productive farms, and modern dwellings, even towns with buildings of brick. They were informed that through appropriate action of Congress or the courts the titles of the present occupants would be held invalid, that the land would then be subject to homestead entry, and that their applications would take priority.

So active were the promoters with their charge that California rancho titles were invalid or clouded and so numerous were the city-bred "homesteaders," that the Committee on Public Lands and Surveys was directed by the United States Senate to investigate charges and reports that vast tracts of land within the area ceded to the United States by Mexico were fraudulently held by private interests. The Committee conducted hearings in Los Angeles, beginning in April, 1929, and in Washington, D.C. The hearings in Los Angeles were before subcommitteemen Senator Gerald P. Nye of North Dakota, Senator Sam G. Brattan of New Mexico, and Senator Porter H. Dale of Vermont. They revealed that since 1922 about 800 "homesteaders" had expended $300,000 and had kept a number of attorneys with sizable staffs busy during that time. Parts of about 175,000 acres of land which had long been the undisputed property of their owners were being "homesteaded." The filings usually were for 160 acres, but sometimes for 80 or 40 acres. It was the rejection of these filings by the local land office and the appeal to the United States Land Commissioner in Washington, D.C., then to the Department of the Interior, and finally to the Attorney General, that had brought about the Senate investigation.

In the eight-page report issued by the Committee, March 15, 1932, the work of the Board of Land Commissioners is summarized.[8] The Supreme Court has been called on many times, the report points out, to review the Act of March 3, 1851, under which the board acted. In these cited cases it has been held over and over again that an adjudication of the board, when not appealed from, or the decree of the court, in the event of an appeal, is conclusive. All further inquiry is ended. This would be true even if it could be shown that a particular grant had been obtained through fraud. The case of United States *v.* Throckmorton (98 U.S. 61) is cited in point. In addition, the report explains that the validity of a patent cannot be questioned even if it should have included land in excess of that originally granted, for the patent was issued in conformity with the act's requirements—which included a survey of the granted land. Furthermore, if any rancho land were to be restored to the public domain, it would be the policy of the Department of the Interior to give a preference right to acquire this land to the person in possession who is asserting claim or color of title. Finally, the Committee finds the grants in question to be valid, with no evidence of fraud, the patents to be binding, and the

---

[8] Senate Report No. 426, 72d Cong., 1st sess., 1932.

attacks upon the titles made "by persons seeking to profit financially at the expense of well intentioned but grossly misled applicants for homestead entry."

Since every American seems to be a squatter at heart, court decrees and Senate reports do not entirely kill the urge to get something for nothing—nor the fundamental need for a place to live. Consider the case of the hapless 300,000 migrants from the "Dust Bowl" who in the early 'thirties poured into California in broken-down cars. Stranded in the San Joaquin Valley, they put their cook-stoves, iron washtubs, bedsprings, and mattresses upon "vacant" land and established squatter camps that were notoriously filthy. For several years these indigents and jobless squatters were a major state and national issue. The housing shortage at the end of World War II brought about a renewal of squatter activity, though to a minor extent. Consider, too, the group of men who a few years ago pitched tents along the Santa Monica shore in the hope that a benevolent government would tell them that the coastal strip lay outside original rancho boundaries and was therefore open to settlement. Consider the holders of various kinds of valid "scrip"—government-issued rights to "locate," such as the high-priced Valentine scrip—who wander about year in and year out, like the never-give-up desert prospectors, looking for a piece of "unclaimed public land" valuable enough to claim. Consider the "swivel-chair squatters," or "claim jumpers," living in cities close to the Pacific, who filed nearly two hundred applications for federal oil leases covering segments of oil-rich, submerged, offshore land, frequently in conflict with one another, hoping, if it should be held to be part of the public domain, that they would supplant present claimants.

Yes, every American seems instinctively a squatter, but modern squatterism has come a long way from the time when men of adventure were moving into California in the late 1840's and early 1850's, pioneers who were carving a destiny for themselves and California.

CHAPTER X

Titles in El Dorado

NINETY-FOUR-YEAR-OLD Luís Peralta, owner of Rancho
San Antonio—site of Berkeley, Oakland and Alameda—
one day called his sons together. James W. Marshall had
discovered a few flakes of gold at Coloma on the South
Fork of the American River and practically every man in
California was rushing to the streams and canyons of the
Sierra Nevada. Peralta wanted to caution the men of his
own family.

"My sons," said the old ranchero, "God has given this
gold to the Americans. Had he desired us to have it, he
would have given it to us ere now. Therefore go not after
it, but let others go. Plant your lands, and reap; these be
your best gold-fields, for all must eat while they live."[1]

Few Californians, whether native-born or immigrant,
were of the mind of this wise patriarch who had come to
Alta California as a Spanish soldier in the century preceding. Accordingly, pueblos and ranchos were quickly

---

[1] Bancroft, *History of California*, VI, 65–66.

depopulated. From San Francisco, where sailors abandoned their ships, to San Diego, the southernmost town, the story was the same. In the southern part of the state, as in the central, rancheros had become miners, and, in their absence, Indians were driving horses off to the mountains. From the vicinity of Monterey, the capital, a thousand men are said to have left for the mining areas within one week. The government in Monterey was stricken, soldiers deserted, and Military Governor Mason was reduced to peeling his own onions and cooking his own dinners.

By the close of 1848, four-fifths of California's able-bodied men, whether Californians or imported, had become gold miners. Mining was in progress throughout a two-hundred-mile stretch along the axis of the Sierra Nevada, extending north from the scene of discovery at Coloma, which was in the John Sutter domain. Pierson B. Reading, owner of the most northerly of the ranchos, was at work with a force of his Indians on Clear Creek in Shasta County. John Bidwell, another ranchero, was mining along the North Fork of the Feather River at the rich placer which became known as Bidwell Bar. Mormon settlers were among the earliest and most active of the miners. As the influx of newcomers to the gold area continued, the streams and rivers for thirty miles on either side of Coloma were taken over by wielders of pick, knife, and pan. Then rivers farther away were sought out. By June of 1848 the miners had numbered 2,000, half of whom were panning for gold on the branches of the American River. Indians were hired to mine, but presently, tiring of being exploited, many of them went into business for themselves. By October perhaps 9,000 men were actually hunting the yellow metal in the gulches and along the creeks of the Sierra Nevada. Experienced Mexican miners from Sonora, Mexico, had come north and founded the California mining camp of Sonora. They gave the "Mother Lode" its name.

By the end of 1848 all of America was gold crazy, and thousands of America's most energetic young men were on the way to the California gold fields. They were singing:

> Oh! California, that's the land for me!
> I'm bound for the Sacramento,
> With the washbowl on my knee!

Meanwhile San Francisco, Sacramento, and Stockton were taking form as cities that existed solely to supply the miners of California. Los Angeles, heart of the cattle country, was sending herds of cattle north to supply the expanding demand for beef. By the spring of 1853 the state's population was 300,000, more than $260,000,000 had been dug from the gold fields, and many a mining camp had become a substantial town. The constant rush to new fields had opened distant regions to settlement.

The gold fever did not burn out in the 1850's, though certain phases began to subside. Placer digging was followed by quartz crushing, and hydraulic mining started in 1855. There were recurrent miners' stampedes; for example, the stampede to Santa Catalina Island as late as 1863–1864, after the Gold Rush of the north had ebbed southward via the Kern River rush of the middle 1850's and the Los Angeles County placer excitement of 1858–1862—in the San Gabriel, Santa Anita, and San Francisquito canyons. California is today a great gold-mining state, on a large and small scale, and individual prospectors still go forth for recreation if not for profit. Eldorado County itself—scene of the gold discovery at Coloma and center of early Gold-Rush activity—has today mines of gold, copper, slate, limestone, and other materials that produce $3,500,000 annually.

When miners were few in number—as in the early days after the discovery in 1848—they could move about over a large field and, without dispute, help themselves to the cream of what they found and move on to new fields. But as soon as miners began to assemble in any number along the streams and in the canyons the need for law and order became apparent. Late comers and less fortunate miners demanded equal rights with others. Mining activities were largely on public land, for the ranchos rarely extended into mountain regions. There was no legal machinery in existence, territorial or federal, that covered mining on public lands or that could protect a miner in his discovery. Mexican mining procedure did not apply, and as early as February 12, 1848, Governor Mason had issued an order from Monterey purporting to abolish "Mexican laws and customs now prevailing in California, relative to the 'denouncement' of mines."[2]

Miners' camp meetings called to adopt rules governing mining and mining titles were the answer to an anarchistic situation. They grew out of necessity and experience, though they have antecedents in European and Spanish-American mining practice. Camp-meeting rules became logically the laws of the district and in time the mining laws of the nation, as well as the basis for mining jurisprudence in many other countries.

The size of claims, how to mark them, the registering of claims, the appointment of a recorder, what constituted abandonment, the boundaries of the camp—and later of the district—the settlement of disputes—these

---

[2] House Ex. Doc. No. 17, pp. 476–477.

matters were what miners talked about in their camp meetings. The will of the majority was accepted. Rules were put in writing. The miners abided by them. Later disputes were settled by the recorder, the alcalde, an appointed committee, or the camp meeting itself.

In some camps or districts the claims were limited to ten feet square. In others fifty feet was allowed, in poorer districts one hundred or more feet. Size was governed by richness of the locality, its extent, the number of miners, and the difficulty of working the ground. The discoverer usually was allowed first choice or two claims. Claims were registered with the recorder, at a fee of fifty cents or one dollar. Stakes, ditches, and notices marked the claims. To hold a claim a miner had to do a certain amount of work upon it. In time the transfer of claims became a practice—like the conveying of real estate. At first, verbal transfers, if accompanied by actual transfer of possession, were sufficient and so recognized by the California courts. Later, after 1860, they had to be in writing.

The source of title—universally recognized by miners' camps—was discovery and appropriation. Continued possession of a claim was dependent upon its development by work being done upon it. These fundamentals are a part of present-day mining law. To them federal legislation added the right of a miner to obtain, not merely a possessory title, but full and permanent ownership of the land itself, to be evidenced by a patent issued by the United States.

The early title situation in the gold fields of California, when camp law was mining law, has been the subject of philosophic comment by many writers. Henry George saw the miners being thrown back upon first principles.

It was by common consent declared that this gold-bearing land should remain common property... The title to the land remained in the government, and no individual could acquire more than a possessory claim. The miners in each district fixed the amount of ground an individual could take and the amount of work that must be done to constitute use. If this work were not done, any one could re-locate the ground. Thus, no one was allowed to forestall or to lock up natural resources... One man might strike an enormously rich deposit and others might vainly prospect for months and years, but all had an equal chance. No one was allowed to play the dog in the manger with the bounty of the Creator... With the decadence of placer mining in California, the accustomed idea of private property finally prevailed in the passage of a law permitting the patenting of mineral lands.[3]

There were probably more than five hundred placer camps in California during the flush period.[4]

A typical set of mining regulations were those adopted by the miners of the Rock Ditch and Mining District at a meeting held December 1, 1853. They provided:

I. This district shall be bounded by the Fordyce and Booth Rock Creek Districts on two sides, the Spout Spring Ravine on the lower sides, and the south branch of Rock Creek on the other.

II. All claims shall be one hundred feet front, running into the mountain to such depth as the parties locating may desire.

III. That it is necessary to thoroughly prospect the said ground, and that the prospecting of one claim will test the whole. All persons holding claims are requested to assist in running in a cut—to be commenced so soon as it rains, and all persons who may assist in the cut shall be entitled to one claim extra as discoverers.

IV. All claims not represented in the cut shall have two full days' work in six done on them, or otherwise are subject to forfeiture.

---

[3] Henry George, *Progress and Poverty*, chap. v.

[4] Charles Howard Shinn, *Mining Camps, A Study in American Frontier Government* (New York, Charles Scribner Sons, 1885).

V. Where claims are not workable for want of water, a notice shall be placed on them and renewed every thirty days.

VI. John Wharton, Sr., was duly elected recorder of said district, and all claims shall be duly recorded within three days from day of location or transfer.[5]

The notices that miners posted on their claims were often intentionally or unintentionally humorous.

Notis: To all and everybody. This is my claim, fifty feet on the gulch, cordin' to Clear Creek District Law, backed up by shot-gun amendments. (Signed) Thomas Hall.

Clame Notise. Jim Brown of Missoury takes this ground, jumpers will be shot.[6]

Race restrictions were included in the laws of some mining districts. The regulations of the Columbia District, for example, provided that "neither Asiatics nor South-Sea Islanders shall be allowed to mine in this district, either for themselves or for others." The gold rush had brought the races of the world to California. American miners, though themselves newcomers and conquerors, had no wish to share the wealth of the foothills with "foreigners"—particularly with Spanish Americans and Asiatics. There were thousands of Mexicans, Chilenos, and Chinese to offer competition to citizens of the United States. Sandwich Islanders (Hawaiians) were numerous and objectionable to the American 'forty-niner. The native Indians were detested. Foreign miners, when not excluded by race restrictions, were taxed. No one bothered to legislate against Indians, and when they got in the way of American miners they were, in hundreds of instances, hunted down and shot.

The California Legislature acknowledged as early as

----

[5] Bancroft, *California Inter Pocula,* pp. 240–241.

[6] Shinn, *op. cit.*

1851 that the miners themselves had perfected a practical working system. Jurisdiction in actions involving mining claims was conferred upon the local justices of the peace. The proceedings of miners' meetings were recognized by the courts so far as they were not inconsistent with the laws and constitution of the state.

By 1861 Colorado, Illinois, Nevada, Idaho, and Arizona were following the usages and laws of California miners.

Said Chief Justice Chase in 1865, in one of his decisions: "A special kind of law, a sort of common law of the miners, the off-spring of a nation's irrepressible march—lawless in some senses, yet clothed with dignity by a conception of the immense social results mingled with the fortunes of these bold investigators—has sprung up on the Pacific Coast."[7]

In the following year, on May 28, 1866, the Conness Committee, reporting to the Senate of the United States, said, somewhat floridly:

The miners' rules and regulations are not only well understood, but have been construed and adjudicated for now nearly a quarter of a century . . . By this great system established by the people in their primary capacities, and evidencing by the highest possible testimony the peculiar genius of the American people for founding empire and order, popular sovereignty is displayed in one of its grandest aspects, and simply invites us, not to destroy, but to put upon it the stamp of national power and unquestioned authority . . . The rules and regulations of the miners . . . form the basis of the present admirable system arising out of necessity; they became the means adopted by the people themselves for establishing just protection to all . . . The local courts, beginning with California, recognize these rules, the central idea of which was priority of possession.[8]

---

[7] *Ibid.*
[8] *Ibid.*

For eighteen years—from 1848 to 1866—the regulations and customs of California miners as enforced and molded by the courts and sanctioned by the legislation of the state constituted the law governing mines on public lands. All recognized discovery, followed by appropriation, as the foundation of the possessor's title. Retention of title was conditional upon his development of the claim by work done upon it.

Then came the Congressional Act of July 26, 1866, which recognized local mining customs and rules of miners when not in conflict with the laws of the United States and acknowledged and confirmed the miners' rights to their properties. It was not unopposed, for many members of Congress felt that miners should buy or lease their mineral land to help pay for Civil War debts. The Act of 1866 not only confirmed local usages and prescribed rules to protect the rights of miners, but it also established, and this was its primary object, a method by which patents from the United States granting mineral lands might be obtained. It provided that a claimant who had previously occupied and improved a vein or lode of quartz or rock-bearing gold, silver, or other valuable deposits, and had spent a specified minimum sum in actual labor and improvements, could file a diagram of his mine in the local land office and receive a patent giving him absolute ownership and the right to follow the vein or lode to any depth.

Subsequent acts of Congress, principally the Congressional Mining Act of May 10, 1872, define the entire subject of mining law, and court decisions followed the lines laid down by these acts. The Act of 1872, amending that of 1866 and actually codifying the common law of the miners, has retained its essential features to the present time. Under it "all valuable mineral deposits in lands belonging to the United States, both surveyed and unsurveyed, are ... free and open to exploration and purchase, and the lands in which they are found to occupation and purchase, by citizens of the United States and those who have declared their intention to become such, under regulations prescribed by law, and according to the local customs or rules of miners in the several mining districts, so far as the same are applicable and not inconsistent with the laws of the United States."[9]

Mining location and operation were carried on in California under these federal statutes of 1872 until 1909. On July 1, 1909, the state itself adopted legislation embracing the requirements of the Congressional Act of 1872, together with such additional matters as the posting and recording of notices of mining locations.[10] It is true that the state had years earlier given official recognition to miners' customs in its Code of Civil Procedure enacted March 3, 1872. Section 748 of this code referred to actions involving mining claims and was a reënactment of an old provision that existed long before the state's laws were codified.

To get a full picture of mining and mining titles we must take into consideration the Congressional Acts, the rules and regulations of the General Land Office, the California statutes of 1909, and federal and state court decisions bearing upon them. The professional examiner of mining titles, asked to render an opinion on the validity of the title to a particular unpatented mining claim,

---

[9] The general provisions of United States mining laws are set forth in *United States Revised Statutes*, sections 2319–2346. See *Public Land Statutes of the United States*, compiled by Daniel M. Greene (United States Department of the Interior, 1931).

[10] *The Civil Code of the State of California*, sec. 1426 *et seq.*

will need to be familiar with these acts, rules, statutes, and decisions. He will need also proper abstracts of title from the county recorder's and local land offices, the assistance of a surveyor, the testimony of witnesses concerning the consummation of certain acts—such as posting the location notice—and the existence of certain conditions that public records alone do not disclose. But first of all he will have determined from the records of the federal land office whether the mine is on public land open to mining. It could not be lawfully on state-owned land, nor within the boundaries of a Mexican or Spanish land grant, nor within a federal "railroad grant," nor within an Indian reservation, though it might be within a public forest reserve if the rules and regulations thereof had been complied with. The problems of mining titles have become intricate and complicated.[11]

As stated, the mining laws of the United States did not, and do not, apply to lands within the boundaries of Spanish or Mexican ranchos. The owners of these ranchos, whose titles had been confirmed by the United States and who had received their confirmatory patents, were the owners of the minerals as well as of the land. Hence discovery and development of a gold mine on a rancho by an enthusiastic 'forty-niner gave him no title nor a basis for title.

Rancho Las Mariposas, at the southernmost end of the Mother Lode, is the outstanding example of a Mexican rancho containing rich gold deposits and in which gold mines were located by invading prospectors. It was in the spring of 1849 that Colonel John C. Frémont set out from Los Angeles, with a party of Sonorans, to find out whether

---

[11] O. A. Rouleau, "Mining Law in California" (MS property of the Title Insurance and Guarantee Company, San Francisco).

there was gold on the remote ten-square-league rancho that Thomas O. Larkin had bought for him for $3,000 from Juan B. Alvarado who, in turn, had obtained it as a grant from the Mexican governor, Micheltorena. There was gold in plenty! Creek beds were so rich that Frémont's Mexicans scooped up flakes in cups and pans, and with their knives dug gold out of the crevices in the bedrock. The news of the strike spread and soon throngs of miners were all over the rancho. For several years prospectors mined at will and Frémont was without power to evict these trespassers, for his title had not yet been confirmed. Several valuable mines were developed on Las Mariposas by men who thought they had the same right there they had elsewhere in the Mother Lode country. In 1856 the Supreme Court of the United States finally upheld the validity of Frémont's title, based on the Mexican grant to Alvarado, thereby establishing full ownership of the "ten-million-dollar" rancho, and all its minerals, in John C. Frémont.

Litigation over Las Mariposas, and that over the Fernandez grant in Butte County, brought out interesting and important facts about the ownership of minerals in California, whether within or outside of ranchos.[12] Upon the separation of Mexico from Spain, the California Supreme Court found, the mines of gold and silver, which until that time had been vested in the Spanish crown, passed to and became vested in the Mexican nation. Under Mexican law, no interest in the minerals of gold and silver passed by a land grant from the government unless expressly so designated. Under Mexican mining ordinances, however, such government-owned minerals could pass to an individual through his registry

---

[12] 17 Cal. 200, Moore *v.* Smaw and Fremont *v.* Flower.

of discovery, or by proceedings upon "denouncement" when a mine once discovered and registered had been abandoned and forfeited. The mining laws of Mexico, during the time California was Mexican, were in part like those adopted by the United States and no doubt influenced their adoption. They were seldom used in Mexican California for there was little interest in mining. Gold and silver (as well as quicksilver)—the "precious metals"—owned by the Mexican nation, passed by cession, under the Treaty of Guadalupe Hidalgo, to the United States. The United States became the owner, but not in trust for the future state of California. Accordingly, a patent from the United States, issued in confirmation of a former Mexican land grant, invests the patentee with the ownership of the precious metals which the land may contain. This is true even though it gives the patentee *more* than he or his predecessor received under the Mexican grant. Today it is established law that such a United States patent issued without exceptions or reservations conveys the full title to the land including minerals and mineral rights.[13]

A quicksilver mine near San Jose that had been operated during the Mexican period—and that for long years thereafter continued to furnish mercury required in California gold mining—was the subject of a celebrated and long-drawn-out case heard before the United States Land Commission and the District and Supreme Courts. This mine was the New Almaden, named after the famous quicksilver mine in Spain. Andrés Castillero, owner of Santa Cruz Island, had acquired it under Mexican laws in 1845, through discovery and denouncement. Castillero claimed before the Land Commission not only the mine,

---

[13] 40 *Corpus Juris*, 759.

but a grant of land around its mouth. There were two other claimants to grants that also included the mine. Castillero and his lessee, the New Almaden Company—a British concern—finally lost out, though receiving partial payment in compensation, to the Philadelphia Quicksilver Company holding under another grant. This result is usually pointed to, and perhaps justly, as a glaring example of injustice and sharp practice on the part of the United States government which simply wished to wrest this important mine from British hands.[14]

Today when a man locates, claims, and develops a mine on public land he follows the rules and regulations that bearded miners of the Sierra Nevada adopted one hundred years ago. Those pioneers of 1849 and the 'fifties long ago left to prospect for "outcroppings of gold in the stars," as Joaquin Miller phrased it, but they left a heritage of common sense and good titles for today's miners.

[14] Gregory Yale, *Legal Titles to Mining Claims* (San Francisco, 1867), pp. 333–337; also John Walton Caughey, *California* (New York, 1940), p. 373.

CHAPTER XI

Land Grants to Railroads

"THE LAST RAIL is laid, the last spike is driven. The Pacific Railroad is finished."

So read the telegram sent President Grant on May 10, 1869, after a gold spike had been driven by Leland Stanford into a railroad tie, made of California laurel, at Promontory in northern Utah. This ceremony was in celebration of the meeting there, actually several days before, of the Central Pacific, which had been building east from Sacramento in California, with the Union Pacific which had been building west from Omaha in Nebraska. One thousand people were present on this occasion which heralded the completion of America's first transcontinental railroad. A new era opened for California and the West.

The building of this long-hoped-for, long-planned railroad and of the railroads that followed was made possible by federal aid in the form of subsidy to railroad companies in lands and bonds.

Promotion of railroad construction through federal grant of land from the public domain, or through the proceeds of the sale of such land, was a well-established government policy. It had antecedents in the grants of land for wagon roads and canals in the eastern part of the United States before the days of railroads. It originated in the enabling Act of April 30, 1802, which provided that one-twentieth part of the net proceeds from the sale by Congress of public lands in Ohio should be given to Ohio for the laying out of roads from navigable waters emptying into the Atlantic to the Ohio River. As early as 1823 Ohio was granted a right of way for a wagon road 120-feet wide, along with the equivalent of two strips of land a mile in width, one on each side of the projected road to be constructed from Lake Erie to the western boundary of the Connecticut Western Reserve. Lands were to be sold by Ohio for not less than $1.25 an acre. In 1827 Indiana was authorized to locate a canal to connect the Wabash River and Lake Erie with a grant of land equal to one-half of five sections in width, each alternate section being reserved to the United States. The area of a section is, of course, 640 acres. Beginning in 1835 Congress made many grants to railroad companies of rights of way through public lands, together with land for depot sites and terminals. In 1850 the grant to the Illinois Central provided for the transfer to the states affected of alternate sections of land for six miles on each side of a line of railroad extending from Illinois to Alabama. These sections were to be sold by the states and the money used by private corporations for the building of a railroad.[1]

[1] Benjamin Horace Hibbard, *A History of the Public Land Policies* (New York, 1924); Thomas Donaldson, *The Public Domain* (Washington, D.C., 1884); Daniel M. Greene, *Public Land Statutes of the United States* (Washington, D.C., 1931).

The first person to propose a transcontinental railroad seems to have been Hartwell Carver of Rochester, New York, who published articles in the New York *Courier and Independent* in 1832 and memorialized Congress from 1835 to 1839. The western terminus of his proposed railway was to be on the Columbia River—for California was still a Mexican province. Carver, who spent forty years and $23,000 on his dream, received in 1869, as his final reward, a free pass over the railroad that other men built.[2]

Many other individuals besides Carver, noteworthy among them being Asa Whitney, worked for a transcontinental railroad. The discovery of gold in California awakened fresh interest in the subject. It was talked about in Congress, and at the session of 1852–1853 the Secretary of War was authorized to employ engineers to find the most economical and practical route for a railroad to the Pacific from the Mississippi. In the spring of 1853 surveys of five possible railroad routes began, and in February, 1855, the Secretary of War laid his report before Congress. For several years the railroad question was discussed by Congressmen, and, while they talked, people in increasing numbers were going west the hard way; California, Oregon, Minnesota, and Kansas were acquiring statehood; and the southern states were seceding. In the popular mind the proposed Pacific railroad was a military necessity and one required to hold the nation together. The Pacific Coast was defenseless. The overland route to California was beset by dangers and Indians. The commercial aspects were given slight consideration.

Finally, in 1862, Congress passed a bill, effective July 1, "to aid in the construction of a railroad and telegraph

---

[2] Bancroft, *History of California*, VII.

line from the Missouri River to the Pacific Ocean, and to secure to the Government the use of the same for postal, military and other purposes." It was under the Congressional Act of July 1, 1862, as amended July 2, 1864, that the first transcontinental railroad was actually built—the ceremony of the driving of the golden spike on May 10, 1869, at Promontory, Utah, being the announcement to the country of successful accomplishment.

Hitherto, in the railroad grants, the states had been used as trustees and agents. The Act of 1862, called the Pacific Railroad Bill, provided a departure from established methods, for it empowered the Union Pacific Railroad Company and the Central Pacific Railroad Company of California to lay out, locate, construct, and maintain a railroad and telegraph line and to be the recipients of land grants. The Union Pacific was authorized to build the road from Nebraska to the western boundary of Nevada, and the Central Pacific was to build from the Pacific Coast, at or near San Francisco, or the navigable waters of the Sacramento River, to the eastern boundary of California. Each company, however, was authorized to continue construction until it met the other, whether at or beyond the California boundary line.

Each company, under the Act of 1862, as amended in 1864, was granted a right of way 200 feet in width on each side of the railroad—400 feet in all. In addition each received necessary grounds for stations, buildings, shops, depots, switches, sidetracks and turntables, together with the right to take from adjacent public lands earth, stone, timber, and other materials for construction purposes. The United States agreed to extinguish Indian titles where they conflicted with railroad titles. Furthermore, as an aid in the construction of the railroad and telegraph line and to secure the transportation of mail, troops, and munitions, each company was granted every alternate section of public land, designated by odd numbers, to the amount of ten alternate sections per mile on each side of the railroad and within the limits of twenty miles on each side. The railroad act specified that it did not apply to lands sold, reserved, or otherwise disposed of by the United States, or to which a preëmption or homestead claim may have attached at the time the line of the road was definitely fixed. Excepted from the grant, too, were "all mineral lands," though this was not to be construed as referring to coal and iron land. Granted lands unsold or undisposed of by the company within three years after completion of the railroad were to be open to settlement and preëmption, like other lands, at $1.25 per acre to be paid the company. With the completion of each forty consecutive miles of railroad and telegraph line, the United States was to issue to the company patents—that is, official conveyances—of the lands on each side of the completed road. A map of the general route was to be filed by the company with the Department of the Interior within two years, whereupon lands within twenty-five miles of the route were to be withdrawn by the Secretary of the Interior from preëmption, private entry, and sale.

To sum up: each of the two railroad companies secured a right of way 400 feet wide, the necessary depot sites, shops, and so on, and each received odd-numbered alternate sections of land to the amount of twenty sections per mile. Since each regular government section contained 640 acres, the acreage granted per mile was, in theory, 12,800 acres. Under the original act, the land grant, so far as California was concerned, was of little value, for only

200,000 acres of arable land could be obtained between Sacramento and the Nevada line. Hence the amendments of 1864, which gave the Central Pacific twenty sections per mile instead of the original ten and clarified the mineral land exception.[3] The land included within the right of way itself, it should be added, was not granted the railroad in absolute ownership, the railroad company's title being a limited fee, with a reversionary right remaining in the United States. (Later, after the Act of March 3, 1875, the right of way grants conveyed an easement only, with forfeiture for non-use.)

Of course, the federal subsidies of land were only part of the help given. The national government practically guaranteed a part of the bonded debt of the companies. Each company was allowed to issue first mortgage bonds on its railroad and telegraph line to the amount of the bonds issued by the United States to the company, the government subordinating its lien. These first mortgage bonds could be sold readily at the highest market rates. With the completion of every twenty miles, the government issued thirty-year bonds—each in the amount of $1,000, bearing interest at 6 per cent—and these totaled $16,000 a mile across the plains and increased to $48,000 per mile through the mountainous country which began less than seven miles from Sacramento. The California Legislature aided the Central Pacific and later railroad companies in many ways, for example, in providing land for terminal facilities, including submerged lands and tidelands. The California counties and municipalities also lent their assistance.

The story of the Central Pacific Railroad Company and of the successful completion of the first transconti-

---

[3] 12 *Stat.* 489; 13 *Stat.* 356.

nental railroad is, of course, much more than a story of land grants and financial aid. It is, first of all, a story of California men. One of these men was Theodore D. Judah, a construction engineer whose technical knowledge and enthusiasm for a Pacific railroad brought about the organization of the Central Pacific and, ultimately, a survey of a route through the Sierra Nevada. His skill as a lobbyist at Washington helped to shape and put through the Pacific Railroad bill. Judah was backed by the capable and extraordinary "Big Four": Collis P. Huntington, Leland Stanford, Charles Crocker, and Mark Hopkins who participated in the organization of the Central Pacific, and took over its control, along with that of the later organized Southern Pacific. These four men built the first transcontinental railroad—a titanic achievement—Huntington acted as financial agent and lobbyist in the eastern states, Stanford did the same work in California, Crocker was superintendent of construction, and Hopkins superintendent of supplies. The "Big Four" not only built a railroad but, expanding north and south, created in California an empire. In this empire the owners of the Southern Pacific dominated the state's economic and political life well into the twentieth century, though their railroad monopoly was successfully challenged in the late 'eighties by the entry of the Atchison, Topeka, & Santa Fe. The account of these dynamic figures who lived before the days of antitrust legislation, income tax returns, social "awareness" and planned "public relations," and of how the Southern Pacific demanded subsidies of cities, manipulated freight rates, and controlled governments and legislatures, is part of the railroad story of California and one that has received the attention of reformers and writers.

Congressional land subsidies for railroads began, as we have seen, in 1862 with the grants to the Central Pacific to help it build its share of the transcontinental railroad. There were several later land grants, however, involving a far greater area of the public land of California, but all these later grants followed somewhat the pattern established by the first.

The construction of a railroad and telegraph line through the Sacramento and Shasta valleys to Portland, Oregon, was provided for by the Act of July 25, 1866. Under it the California and Oregon Railroad Company, incorporated in California (later consolidated with the Central Pacific and operated by the Southern Pacific) was to build from a point on the Central Pacific Railroad in the Sacramento Valley to the north boundary of the State of California. Another company, organized in Oregon, was to work south from Portland. Each was authorized to continue construction until it met the other. The right of way granted was 100 feet on each side of the railroad—making a 200-foot strip—together with necessary depot sites, and so on. In addition, the companies were granted "every alternate section of public land, not mineral, designated by odd numbers, to the amount of twenty alternate sections per mile (ten on each side)." When any of these sections had already been granted, sold, reserved, occupied by homestead settlers, preëmpted, or otherwise disposed of, the companies were given the right to select other lands in lieu thereof, but these lands had to be alternate, odd-numbered sections nearest to and not more than ten miles beyond the zone of the grant. Patents would be issued to the companies whenever twenty or more consecutive miles of railroad had been completed.[4]

------

[4] 14 *Stat.* 239; 15 *Stat.* 80; 16 *Stat.* 47; 39 *Stat.* 218; 40 *Stat.* 593.

Not until December 17, 1887 could a "last spike" ceremony celebrate a junction completed between the California line and the Oregon line at Ashland, Oregon.

The Act of July 27, 1866, authorized the Atlantic and Pacific Railroad Company to construct a railroad and telegraph line from Missouri to the Pacific Coast, via Albuquerque and the Colorado River, and at the same time empowered the Southern Pacific Railroad to connect with the Atlantic and Pacific at such a point near the boundary line of the State of California as they would think suitable for a railroad line to San Francisco. The provisions for the right of way—100 feet wide on each side of the railroad—for the depot sites, and so on, for the grant of alternate sections, and for the "lieu" selections were similar to those in the act that gave the California and Oregon Railroad Company its authority.

The Southern Pacific immediately went ahead with its plans, filed a map of its proposed route with the Department of the Interior on January 3, 1867, and received Congressional authority on June 28, 1870, to proceed along that route. The articles of incorporation originally had called for a railroad to extend from San Francisco south along the coast to San Diego, thence east. Coast land, however, was mostly rancho land—and therefore not in the public domain. By switching to the central valley, not only would some of the richest agricultural districts in the state be opened up but the railroad could take advantage of the generous land-grant privileges in the Act. The switch was made and the California legislature approved the change of route.

The Atlantic and Pacific never entered California and, in 1886, Congress declared forfeited the lands granted it along the "uncompleted portions of the main line." Years later the charter of the Atlantic and Pacific Company was bought by the Atchison, Topeka, & Santa Fe which, though blocked by Southern Pacific interests, finally reached Los Angeles and San Diego in 1885.

By the Act of March 3, 1871, the Southern Pacific was authorized to construct a railroad from the Tehachapi Pass, by way of Los Angeles, to meet the Texas Pacific Railroad at or near the Colorado River. It was given all the rights, grants, and privileges of the Act of July 27, 1866. Under this act the city of San Francisco could connect with the Texas Pacific.[5]

By the Act of March 3, 1875, Congress granted a right of way through public lands to *any* railroad company duly organized under the laws of any state or territory or by Congress, to the extent of 100 feet on each side of the central line of the road. There were also granted certain rights to take material for construction purposes, along with ground adjacent to the road for station buildings, etc., not to exceed 20 acres for each station, to the extent of one station for each ten miles of road. To get the benefits of this act, a railroad company had to file a profile or map of its road with the district land office, under specified conditions, and to secure its approval by the Secretary of the Interior. Good use of this act was made by the Southern Pacific to relocate part of its line. Part of the original line was then abandoned.[6]

Congress took care of forfeited or abandoned railroad rights of way and railroad structures by the Act of February 25, 1909, and the Act of March 8, 1922. The last-mentioned act provided that when such rights of way or structures were no longer used or occupied for railroad

---

[5] 14 *Stat.* 292; 16 *Stat.* 382; 16 *Stat.* 573, 579; 24 *Stat.* 123.
[6] 18 *Stat.* 482; 31 *Stat.* 815.

purposes, whether by forfeiture or by abandonment by the railroad company, or by court decrees or by act of Congress, the public lands that had been granted for such purposes became vested—with certain exceptions— in the owners of the land crossed or occupied.[7]

Through federal land grants railroads received title to 11,585,534.28 acres of California land, or about 11.4 per cent of the state's area. In the United States as a whole 9.5 per cent of the public domain went to the railroads.[8] The tabulation of land grants to railroads published in the 1946 Annual Report of the Commissioner of the General Land Office gave these totals:

CALIFORNIA	ACRES
Central Pacific (Central Pacific)	978,091.22
Central Pacific (California and Oregon)	3,237,347.16
Central Pacific (Western Pacific)	462,130.18
Southern Pacific (Southern Pacific main line)	4,656,425.78
Southern Pacific (Southern Pacific branch line)	2,251,539.94
Total California	11,585,534.28

The lands granted to railroads were not outright gifts, for the railroads were required to haul mail and handle government traffic at less than regular charges—a deduction of immense importance to the federal government and the public. The Southern Pacific's own estimate is that by the end of World War II the land-grant rate reductions for all railroads in the United States reached a total in excess of one billion dollars, or more than eight times the $123,000,000 value of the lands at the time they were granted to the railroads.[9] The government bene-

---

[7] *35 Stat.* 647; *42 Stat.* 414.

[8] *Report of Commissioner of General Land Office,* June 30, 1943.

[9] Erle Heath, *Seventy-Five Years of Progress—Historical Sketch of the Southern Pacific* (San Francisco, 1945).

fited, too, in the increase in value of its retained alternate sections, owing to improved transportation. What the railroads received from the sale of lands granted them was only a fraction of the cost of building the railroads. Furthermore, financial subsidies from the government were not gifts but interest-bearing loans—loans that were paid off.[10] To get the over-all picture, it should be remembered that federal land grants were far from providing California with the railroad lines that now connect the cities of the state. Federal grants were applicable only to lands in the "public domain." Lands in Spanish and Mexican ranchos, for example, were unaffected. It was through direct purchase from private owners of land or through condemnation under statutory powers or through state permit when state-owned lands were involved—*plus* the federal grants—that California's vast railroad system was finally built up. In this connection the Southern Pacific and its predecessor corporations were the chief beneficiaries in California of federal land grants. The Santa Fe received land-grant aid in Arizona and New Mexico, but acquired its rights of way in California largely the hard way. The Needles-Mohave line, built by the Southern Pacific through land-grant help, was first leased, then the right of way was bought, by the Santa Fe.[11]

It is apparent that the story of the federal grants to railroads in California is much more than a legalistic recital of Congressional acts and their provisions. An important phase of the story is the clash of railroads with settlers in their path. It will be recalled that railroad companies were given no rights in lands subject to exist-

[10] Robert S. Henry, "The Railroad Land Grant Legend in American History Texts," *Mississippi Valley Historical Review*, September, 1945.

[11] James Marshall, *Santa Fe* (New York, 1945).

ing preëmption and homestead claims. Since several years might elapse between the grant and the building of the road, or between the establishing of the route and the building, it was inevitable that misunderstandings and differences of opinion should develop, especially in the undeveloped San Joaquin Valley. Add to this the hostility toward the Southern Pacific that had been growing during the construction era because the railroad did not always sell its lands at the price stipulated by the government—and we have the basis for drama as well as law suits. A climactic clash was the pitched battle on May 11, 1880, between settlers and officials seeking to evict the former on behalf of the Southern Pacific, at a place called Mussel Slough near the town of Hanford. California histories give considerable space to the incident—which seems to be the only important armed clash of its kind—and Frank Norris wrote a novel, *The Octopus,* around the tragic affair. As late as May 12, 1938, a central valley newspaper, *The Fresno Bee,* thought the story had sufficient appeal to recall it in a feature article that carried an interview with a ninety-year-old man who was at Brewer's Ranch, the scene of the shooting, a few minutes after five men had been shot dead, two others fatally wounded, and still another man slightly wounded. The newspaper illustrated its story with a photograph of the oak tree standing on the M. N. Doggett Ranch on the Laton–Grangeville Highway, beneath whose shade the dead and wounded were laid.

The tragedy had been in the making for at least ten years, during which time settlers had been laying irrigating ditches, developing ranches, and building homes on land that finally turned out to be federally granted railroad property. When the railroad appraisers included the improvements in the selling price of the land—ten dollars to forty dollars an acre—the settlers organized. They said they would pay the government-fixed price of $2.50 an acre but denied the right of the Southern Pacific to homes made valuable by years of toil. Suits in ejectment followed, with decisions favorable to the railroad. The settlers, it seems, had on occasion been highhanded, too, and had dispossessed some purchasers of railroad land. The aftermath of the battle was that a few men went to jail for a few months for resisting a United States Marshal and were then welcomed back with acclaim by 3,000 people assembled in Hanford Park. The Southern Pacific, on its part, made concessions to the settlers, reducing their price by 12½ per cent. From that time on, according to a Tulare County historian, "peace and prosperity prevailed."[12]

Most of the clashes between the Southern Pacific and settlers were settled in the courts rather than by physical combat. Some lands were patented to the railroad that were not within the scope of the grant. On the other hand, lands belonging properly to the railroad were patented to claimants under preëmption, homestead, or mining laws. In some instances the railroad sold lands it did not own. Many a settler, too, found it hard to believe that vast vacant territory could be anything but "open" land. Such cases came into the courts and often long years of litigation followed.

If the title story of any parcel of land within a railroad land grant is followed, much of what has been told here will be recapitulated and special features will be added. An example is the 160-acre quarter section legally de-

[12] "Brief Sketch of the Early History of Tulare County," *Official Historical Atlas Map of Tulare County* (Tulare, Thos. H. Thompson, 1892).

scribed as "the northeast quarter of Section 15, Township
1 South, Range 12 West, S.B.M.," now a heavily built up
Los Angeles County area.[13] This land, a part of the public
domain, was selected on January 12, 1876, by B. B. Redding, Southern Pacific agent, under the Congressional
Act of March 3, 1871, on List No. 1. The United States
issued its patent to the railroad company in March, 1876.
Six years later the company sold and conveyed it to the
Lake Vineyard Land and Water Association, with a reservation of a 200-foot right of way for the railroad. But,
alas for the Southern Pacific, the United States Supreme
Court later held the patent itself to be void. This was
because the land was within the limits of the grant to the
Atlantic and Pacific Railroad Company (by the Act of
July 27, 1866), this area not having been restored to the
public domain until the passage of the forfeiture Act of
1886. Accordingly, the Southern Pacific had no title to
convey. The Lake Vineyard Land and Water Association,
however, being a bona fide purchaser from the Southern
Pacific, suffered no loss. Its title was confirmed in 1902
through a court action brought by the United States
(under Act of Congress approved March 2, 1896, uphold-
ing "good faith" buyers of railroad land even though
patents had been issued erroneously to the railroad companies). The United States, in this particular case, recov-
ered from the Southern Pacific the purchase price of the
160-acre parcel with interest at 6 per cent and costs.

Without federal grants of land to railroads there would
have been no celebration at Promontory, Utah, in 1869,
a celebration that announced the completion of the first

---

[13] Reference is to the "Office Information Relating To Rights Of Way
Of Southern Pacific Railroad Company," unpublished MS compiled in
1930 for Title Insurance and Trust Company, Los Angeles, by W. W. Reyburn and J. Sam Hall.

transcontinental railroad and the achievement of national unity. With them, there were unloosed the energies of the country and of ambitious individuals. The West was quickly transformed from a wilderness to a place of civilization. For California—in spite of abuses that were by products—the federal land-grant policy to railroads made possible the beginnings of its present development and helped to speed that development.

CHAPTER XII

Land for Settlers

WHEN CALIFORNIA became a part of the United States the fine trickle of American settlers that had already set in toward the Pacific Coast became a stream and, finally, a flood. Full settlement by the pioneers of California's valleys and fertile slopes, of its timbered and desert lands, together with the development of the state's varied resources, awaited the segregation of all privately claimed lands—the ownership of which dated from the Mexican period—from those that were part of the public domain.

Segregation was a leisurely process. It began in the early 1850's, following the passage of the Act of March 3, 1851. It was accomplished through the activities and decisions of the Board of Land Commissioners and of the federal courts to which board decisions were appealed.

Meanwhile, even before the land commissioners got under way with their job, settlers were pouring into California where gold, newly discovered, was the principal lure. Most of the existing pueblos soon were bulging with newcomers, young towns were springing up at logical or convenient spots, especially in the gold-mining areas, and ranch and farm land was coming into demand. Settlers could not all wait on boards and courts. With land titles unsettled, there began a long period of uncertainty and conflict, while squatters had a field day wherever there was land that looked good to them.

Within two decades after 1848, however, what was and what was not public land had largely been determined. Thenceforth, if not before, federal laws applicable to the settlement of the public domain governed mining claims, railroad grants, federal townsites, preëmption rights, homesteads, desert, timber culture, and timber and stone entries, military bounty warrants, the use of scrip certificates, as well as forest reserves. Settlers' needs could be met, too, out of those lands granted from the public domain directly to the state to help California raise money for education and reclamation, as well as through purchase of privately owned lands.

Some of the settlers who came with the Gold Rush helped to expand the population of the pueblos of Sonoma, San Francisco, San José, Monterey, Santa Barbara, Los Angeles, and San Diego, though the last two were dormant until stimulated by the overflow from the northern immigration and the coming of railroads. The title story of California's seven pueblos, so far as it has to do with the land comprised in their original boundaries, is told elsewhere in this book. Land later annexed to these cities had its origin in Spanish or Mexican ranchos or in the public domain and its chain of title is no different from that of similar land outside town limits.

Others of the settlers of the Gold-Rush period helped to start mining camps, inland ports, and centers for farming, lumbering, or manufacturing. These places leaped into life as vigorous towns. Later the railroads and railroad enterprises fathered other California cities.

Many of these hearty pioneer towns, like Sacramento, Stockton, Mariposa, and Anaheim arose on what had been rancho land. The subdividing and selling of such privately owned property, either for the subdividers themselves or for other owners, was not greatly unlike a present-day undertaking in town making, though pioneer subdividers had no restrictions imposed by law on their activities and only such worries as were provided by squatters and unsettled land titles.

Many other early-day towns were spawned on public land as "federal townsites," and this calls for special comment. As early as 1812 Congress had been lending help to the formal establishment of townsites and the confirmation of title to the inhabitants. In California, Crescent City, Eureka, and Red Bluff, all born in the early 1850's, were the principal towns to avail themselves of the Townsites Act of May 23, 1844, which permitted the entry—that is, the placing on record in the proper form and place—of a claim to 320 acres, with provision for the sale of lots under rules and regulations established by the legislature of the state. This act, in effect, granted to towns preëmption rights similar to those that had been given individuals in 1841. It had provided that whenever any portion of surveyed public land was settled upon and occupied as a townsite, its authorities (or the judges of the county court, if unincorporated) could enter the land, at the proper land office and at the minimum price, in trust for the townsmen.[1]

---

[1] O. A. Rouleau, "Public Lands of United States Other Than Those Granted to the States," MS.

The act was superseded by that of July 1, 1864, providing for the establishment of townsites not exceeding 640 acres on either surveyed or unsurveyed public land. It set forth the kind of plat that was to be filed with the county recorder, the requirement that a transcript be transmitted to the General Land Office, it covered the public sale of town lots, with actual settlers given prior purchase privileges, and it provided for patents to be issued. Petaluma availed itself of the more elaborate method outlined in this act.

Federal townsite requirements were liberalized in 1865, 1867, and 1868, and the state itself designed a procedure for entry, procurement of title and transfer to conform to these liberalized provisions. A large number of California towns took advantage of the newer townsite laws. Among them were sturdy Nevada City, Grass Valley, San Rafael, Placerville, San Luis Obispo, Weaverville, and Lakeport. In Mendocino County there were two such townsites, one being the Town of Mendocino— under a United States patent issued to J. B. Lamar, county judge of Mendocino County, on November 10, 1868— the other the Town of Point Arena. A few federal townsites in the San Joaquin Valley are of recent origin.

The rise of towns and cities is only one part of the story of the settlement of California. Not all settlers were townsmen. Many were farmers or ranchers who bought lands in ranchos or within railroad grants or—and this is of present concern—who bought at auction sales for cash, or who filed preëmption or homestead claims, or who in other ways "took up" or purchased government land.

Since 1820 the United States had been selling its public domain at auction sales where the minimum price was $1.25 per acre. Later came preëmption and still later homesteading, and these methods of acquisition practically supplanted the sales system.

Preëmption was really a preferential right of purchase given actual settlers. Settling on government land without permission—squatting—had begun as soon as the Revolutionary War ended and emigrants started west. Out of this practice, and after tremendous pressure had been put on Congress, settlers finally won the legal right of preëmption, the right of settling on and improving unappropriated public lands and, later, of buying them at the minimum price without competition. The Act of September 4, 1841, the outgrowth of earlier legislation, recognized preëmption rights. It provided that preëmption could be initiated by taking possession of land and filing a declaration of intention within thirty days thereafter at the local land office. Such government land, in parcels of not more than 160 acres at $1.25 an acre, could be bought free from competitive bids by the head of a family or widow or single person over twenty-one years of age who had filed such a declaration and who undertook to settle, improve, build a dwelling, and pay the purchase price, within a given period, usually twelve months. A certificate of preëmption was issued, and later a United States patent.

Preëmption went west on March 3, 1853, when the Act of 1841 was applied by Congress to lands in California and other western states. There were various and later modifications, with the period of settlement extended to two years. Owing to abuses and fraudulent entries, and to the repeated recommendations of the Commissioner of the General Land Office, all preëmption laws were repealed March 3, 1891. Between 1853 and 1891, however, many titles in California were acquired and patents issued under the preëmption laws. Preëmption, accordingly, did play a part in the settlement of California, in the turning of unused areas into cultivated regions of farms and homes.

A greater part was played, however, by the settlement and cultivation of public lands in California under the homestead laws.

The demand for homesteads, that is, *free* land for actual settlers, was a natural outgrowth of preëmption concessions and of earlier leniency toward squatters and gifts to defenders of the frontier. Free land was a hot political issue in the United States from 1825, when Senator Benton of Missouri introduced a bill providing for the donation of certain lands to settlers, until May 20, 1862, when Abraham Lincoln signed the first homestead act. The Free Soil Party in 1848 had put forward a strong homestead plank in its platform and four years later the Free Soil Democrats were declaring that "all men have a natural right to a portion of the soil" and "that the public lands . . . should be granted in limited quantities, free of cost, to landless settlers." The Republican party in 1860 had declared in favor of homesteads. The opposition, stronger in the South than in the North, had seen in homesteading loss of revenue from the public domain, reduction in value of land already in private hands, the encouragement of immigration and emigration, and the crowding out of slavery in new territories.

Under the Homestead Act of 1862 settlers could acquire farms of 160 acres from unappropriated public lands free of all charges except a nominal filing fee to be paid when application was made at the proper land office. Five years of residence and cultivation were required of the settler before he would be entitled to a certificate or patent from the United States. The privilege of commuting also was permitted—that is, of converting the homestead with a preëmption right and of paying the regular price per acre. The Three Year Homestead Law of June 6, 1912, reduced the five-year period to three years and permitted a five-month leave of absence a year. Failure to establish residence within six months after the date of entry, or abandonment of the land by the settler for more than six months at any time, would result in the reversion of the property to the government.

Enlarged homesteads—320 acres or less, of nonmineral, nonirrigable, unreserved, and unappropriated surveyed public lands not containing merchantable timber—were provided for in a 1909 act which was made applicable to California in 1912. Stock-raising homesteads of 640 acres were provided for in 1916. Ten years earlier, June 11, 1906, provision had been made for the entry under the homestead laws of forest-reserve lands that were chiefly valuable for agriculture and which could be occupied for that purpose without injury to the forest.

Homesteading, of course, means something other than this recital of acts, amendments, definitions, and dates. It means men and women going into new, perhaps forbidding, country, overcoming the obstacles of terrain and weather, doing hard physical labor, using intellect, ingenuity, and patience, being self-sufficing, transforming valleys, plains, and hillsides into productive farms, ranches, homesites. It means man against nature, man triumphing over nature.

California settlers made extensive use of the homestead laws. To get land "free" was just what the people wanted. Free land helped to "spread the wealth" quickly and to make possible a landowning, home-owning population.

From the long-range viewpoint, however, homestead laws were part of an unscientific land policy that resulted in squandering the public domain.

Settlers made use, too, of the timber-culture laws, the theme of which was "plant trees and get land." They were adopted because the demand for timber was rapidly increasing whereas the supply was diminishing. The first timber-culture bill became a law March 13, 1873. It provided that a person could obtain title to a quarter section—160 acres—if he would plant forty acres of it to trees not more than twelve feet apart and would protect and keep them in a healthy growing condition for ten years. Amendments to the first act—culminating in the Act of June 14, 1878—reduced the time for cultivating the timber to eight years, the acreage from forty to ten, and prescribed easier specifications for the planting of trees. Timber-culture laws were admittedly a failure. They were easily taken advantage of by speculators, and were used by cattle owners to hold great tracts for range purposes. They were repealed March 3, 1891.

The desert-land laws came into being because homestead laws were ill-adapted to dry lands. A quarter section on a western mountain or on a western desert could hardly be of great use to a settler. Lassen County, California, was used as a guinea pig in a special act for desert-land disposal passed March 3, 1875. This act permitted the entry of a section, 640 acres, by persons who would undertake to conduct water on it for reclamation within two years, in which event they would receive title on payment of the minimum government price. Under the Act of March 3, 1877—the first that was generally applicable to California and the western states—a person could buy a section of desert land by paying twenty-five cents an acre and filing a declaration with the proper official that he intended to reclaim the tract by irrigating it within three years. The acreage he could get was later (March 3, 1891) reduced to 320 acres and the time for reclamation extended to four years. Desert lands, the law said, were those lands, exclusive of timberlands and mineral lands, which will not produce some agricultural crop without irrigation. Proof to the register and receiver of actual reclamation within the time set, together with payment of the additional sum of one dollar per acre, entitled the person to a patent. The amendments of 1891 specified that three dollars per acre had to be expended for reclamation and that one-eighth of the land had to be under cultivation before a patent could be issued. Other amendments covered necessary extensions of time for making final proof and protective clauses for men in military or naval service. There were, of course, abuses in desert entries. Land grabbing was aided. Stockmen, for example, sometimes got hold of desert land, by paying twenty-five cents an acre, only to hold it for several years as range land with no effort at reclamation. Between March 3, 1877, and June 30, 1947, desert-land entries had been made in California on 1,079,152 acres.

The government found still other ways of disposing of the public domain to settlers in California. Under the Act of June 3, 1878—the Timber and Stone Act—unoccupied, unimproved, surveyed, nonmineral public lands that were valuable chiefly for timber or for stone, but unfit for cultivation and, therefore, unfit for disposal under pre-emption or homestead laws, could be sold in quantities not exceeding 160 acres at the minimum price of $2.50 an acre. The purpose of the act, to stop timber depredations and to aid settlers and miners, was not accomplished.

Great tracts of forest lands in California were obtained fraudulently by lumber companies under this Timber and Stone Act. Far-sighted but unscrupulous lumber operators "employed cruisers, who went over and determined the value of the various legal subdivisions containing heavy stands of timber. They allowed the public to know that they would purchase timber land from any who might enter it under the Timber and Stone Act. In some cases they imported shiploads and carloads of their employees and other persons, furnishing them with the necessary funds to buy. These persons entered valuable contiguous quarter sections, and transferred them wholesale to their principals. A specific instance is that in Modoc County, California, where more than 85 per cent of about 25,000 acres of timberland entered in one calendar year was transferred before May 1, as was shown by a search in the recorder's office of the county. More than 14,000 acres of this went to one man, and the bulk of the rest to three others."[2]

Final timber and stone entries in California totaled 2,899,214 acres on June 30, 1945.

An "isolated" or "disconnected tract" of the public domain, not exceeding 320 acres, could be ordered into market by the Secretary of the Interior and sold at public auction in the land office of the district under an act approved March 9, 1928. The price could be not less than $1.25 an acre. So, too, "rough or mountainous lands," not exceeding 160 acres, were to be sold upon application of any person owning adjoining lands.

The use in California of government-issued military bounty land warrants and land scrip of various kinds

---

[2] From the *Report of the National Conservation Commission*, made in 1909 and referred to by Benjamin Horace Hibbard in *A History of the Public Land Policies* (New York, 1924).

helped settle the state and is an interesting part of the title story—one reserved for another chapter. So, too, that part of the story that has to do with land granted directly to the state and by it to individuals.

Not all of the public domain in California, however, was given away or offered for sale to settlers. Part of it eventually became forest reserves, or, as they are now called, national forests. Their creation in California came as a result of a state and national agitation for conservation and the preservation and supervision of forests. The first report of the California State Board of Forestry tells of the destructive effect on mountains and valleys of uncontrolled fires and floods, unrestrained timbering, and unlimited pasturing by sheep and cattle. It contained Chairman Abbott Kinney's recommendation that "the necessity of the hour is an intelligent supervision of the forest land and brush lands of California, with a view to their preservation in such proportion to the other lands of the state as scientific forestry may demonstrate to be necessary to the welfare of the commonwealth."[3] The national movement was activated by John Muir's magazine articles and by the American Forestry Association in 1889 calling for a Congressional investigation of the country's forest resources. Congress responded on March 3, 1891, by providing: "That the President of the United States may, from time to time, set apart and reserve, in any State or Territory having public land bearing forests, in any part of the public lands wholly or in part covered with timber or undergrowth, whether of commercial value or not, as public reservations; and the President shall, by public proclamation, declare the establishment of such

[3] W. W. Robinson, *The Forest and The People: The Story of the Angeles National Forest* (Los Angeles, 1946).

reservation and the limits thereof." Accordingly, the Department of the Interior appointed B. F. Allen special agent to investigate timbered lands and watersheds on the Pacific Coast, with a view to their reservation.

Today California has eighteen national forests and within their boundaries is one-fifth of the state's area. They are administered by the Forest Service of the United States Department of Agriculture.

As we have already seen, prospecting, under established regulations, and later, restricted homesteading, were permitted in these forest areas. Other legislation provided for "forest lieu selections." That is to say, if a tract covered by an unperfected bona fide claim or by a patent were included within the limits of a public forest reservation, the settler or owner could, if he wished, relinquish his tract to the government and "select in lieu thereof" a tract of vacant land open to settlement and not greater in area.

Part of the public domain or of later federally acquired areas is also in national parks—like Yosemite—and national monuments created to preserve scenery, natural and historic objects, and wild life.

The settlement of California, since it became a part of the United States, was begun by pioneers even before the Land Commission could begin the job of segregating privately held land from land that was public domain. It was speeded by the final settlement of land titles and by grants out of the public domain to railroads, to the state itself, and directly to the men and women who laid out the towns and developed the land. It was featured by heroic pioneering effort, as well as by exploitation on the part of railroad, timbering, and cattle interests and by the widespread waste of public resources. The "free land" days ended in 1935, with a conservation program now governing what is left of the public domain and providing that public lands may be disposed of only after appropriate classification. Instead of a General Land Office we now have, fittingly, the Bureau of Land Management. This program developed out of the passage by Congress of the Taylor Grazing Act of June 28, 1934, and the subsequent issuance of executive orders by President Franklin D. Roosevelt, on November 26, 1934, and February 5, 1935, withdrawing from private entry the entire 165,695,000 acres remaining in the nation's public domain.[4] The act had provided for the segregation of 80,000,000 acres—this figure was later increased to 142,000,000 acres—of the public grasslands to be organized into districts under the control of the Secretary of the Interior, with broad powers being given for the issuance of grazing permits, for soil-erosion control, and for the distribution of unneeded land. Though an era has ended, with only 16,062,192 acres of vacant public land remaining in California on June 30, 1945, the settlement of the state, town and country, still goes on, with the onrush of people to the Pacific Coast unabated. Today most of the early-day ranchos or other large land holdings have become fifty-foot lots, one-acre "estates," or small ranches—or they are in the process of becoming so. Some parts of the state, it is true, are remote from population centers and have been less affected by the pressure of population. In still other parts development of large-scale, "industrialized" farming has caused small holdings to become large. In recent years, then, California has had the smallest and some of the largest individually owned land areas in its history, but the over-all tendency seems in the direction of constant reduction and subdivision.

[4] Roy M. Robbins, *Our Landed Heritage* (Princeton, 1942).

CHAPTER XIII

Land Scrip

WHEN THOMAS B. VALENTINE, founder of a pioneer San Francisco printing establishment, arrived in the Golden State from New York in 1851, he did not head for the mines. Instead, he turned his hand to the real estate business, did very well, and among other purchases acquired title to the unconfirmed Rancho Arroyo de San Antonio in Sonoma County.

This purchase led ultimately to the issuance to him, by the General Land Office, of certain certificates of location—or "scrip"—which became known as Valentine scrip. Each certificate was assignable and entitled its owner, without homesteading obligations, to select forty acres in the public lands of the United States, provided the selection was made in an unoccupied, unappropriated, non-mineral area.

Since various kinds of land scrip have been issued by the United States—scrip being a piece of paper entitling the person to whom it is issued to a select amount of land in the public domain—and since several have played a part in the settlement of California, the Valentine incident is told here.

The three-square-league rancho bought by Thomas B. Valentine was situated on or near the site of present-day Petaluma. Originally it had been granted October 8, 1844, by Mexican governor Manuel Micheltorena to Juan Miranda, who took possession and made it his home.

When the United States Land Commission, set up in the 'fifties, passed upon the validity of private land claims originating in the Mexican and Spanish periods, the claim to Rancho Arroyo de San Antonio was among the claims rejected. Juan Miranda had a son-in-law named Ortega. Ortega's successors in interest had put in a claim before the commission that was adverse to Valentine's. Valentine withdrew, intending later to intervene in the district court, but a Supreme Court decision precluded him from asserting title by intervention. When the Ortega claim was rejected, the rancho automatically became a part of the public lands, to be disposed of as such, with the proceeds going into the Treasury.

Years went by, but energetic Valentine did not admit he was beaten. Able to prove his point, he took the matter to Congress which, on April 5, 1872, passed the Act for the Relief of Thomas B. Valentine.

The Ninth Circuit Court was authorized and required to hear the story and pass upon its merits. On January 6, 1873, this court upheld the Valentine contentions and a year later its decree was affirmed by the Supreme Court of the United States.

Under the provisions of the act of Congress, Valentine deeded to the United States all his rights to the particular rancho (his deed being recorded January 22, 1874, in

Sonoma County) and in return received from the General Land Office certificates of location, or scrip, entitling him to select other acreage from surveyed or unsurveyed public land equal in area to that of the rejected rancho—13,316 acres.

These certificates—Valentine scrip—made Thomas B. Valentine famous. What he did not use himself, he sold. Speculators got some, hiking the price, to peddle along with other types of scrip. In time Valentine scrip became too high-priced to be used on admittedly public lands, and scrip owners had to look for forgotten islands—"sleepers"—areas overlooked by government surveyors and with questionably held titles. During Florida's land boom scrip brought as much as $1,000 an acre and was used to acquire islands and keys along the coast.

An interesting and successful use of Valentine scrip in southern California in recent years took place when Frew Morton in 1929 acquired White Rock Island, off Catalina. This island is 50,000 square feet of rocky, marine plateau that early-day government surveyors overlooked when they surveyed the island of Catalina, itself a Mexican rancho. Morton, the holder of a piece of Valentine scrip represented by Certificate of Location E No. 173, surrendered it to a reluctant registrar at the Land Office in Los Angeles. In time he received a patent from the United States for 1.30 acres of land described as "Lot 1 of Section 30, Township 8 South, Range 15 West," which being freely interpreted means the guano-covered island that seagulls laid undisputed claim to long before any man, red or white, appeared on the near-by Isthmus of Catalina. Morton, or those he represented, is said to have paid $138, plus expenses, for White Rock Island.

Other types of land scrip—some assignable like the

Valentine, some not assignable—have been used or attempts have been made to use them in California.

Gerard scrip, for example, was issued under act of Congress, approved February 10, 1855, to the three children of Joseph Gerard, "a messenger of the United States to the Indians," who was killed in 1792. This scrip was in payment for his patriotic services and "in accordance with the spirit of the inducements authorized by President Washington to be held out to such persons as would consent to carry a message from Fort Washington, now Cincinnati, in seventeen hundred and ninety two to the hostile Indians of the then North West Territory."

The scrip entitled each of the three recipients—Reese A. P. Gerard, William Gerard, and Rachel Blue (formerly Rachel Gerard)—to enter one section of the public lands without payment. This privilege extended also to their heirs. William Gerard's original certificate was canceled and, in lieu thereof, the General Land Office issued him sixteen certificates on October 18, 1880, each good for one-sixteenth of a section or forty acres. Gerard scrip has made its appearance in California as late as 1947, with attempted use of it in connection with areas below tidewater, following the Supreme Court's ruling of June 23, 1947, and the possible implication that they were part of the public domain.

Sioux half-breed scrip is not unknown in California, its issuance having been authorized by Congress July 17, 1854. The relinquishment to the United States by the "halfbreeds or mixed bloods" of the Sioux Indians of their interest in a certain tract in Minnesota that had been set apart for their use in 1830 entitled these individuals to scrip for the same amount of land—not more than 640 acres, and not less than 40 acres each—to which they, individually, would be entitled in the event of a division of the reservation prorata among claimants. The certificates could not be assigned but could be used on unoccupied lands within the reservation *or* "upon any other unoccupied lands subject to preëmption or private sale, or upon any other unsurveyed lands, not reserved by the Government, upon which they have respectively made improvements."

Porterfield scrip, authorized April 11, 1860, has had California use or attempted use. Acting under a Congressional "relief" act, the Secretary of the Interior issued to William Kinney and Thomas J. Michie, executors of the last will and testament of Robert Porterfield, deceased, a number of warrants, equal to 6,133 acres of land, in quantities not less than forty acres. These could be located by them on unappropriated public lands where the minimum price did not exceed $1.25 per acre, and in accordance with directions in the will of the deceased.

The various types of scrip named so far have been more spectacular than important. They are typical of the scrip Congress had been issuing since 1806 to indemnify individuals whose land claims had been unsatisfied by reason of conflict with other claims, nonlocation, or reduction by deficient surveys. More important in the settlement of California lands that were part of the public domain were military bounty warrants—which were really in the nature of scrip—and agricultural college land scrip.

The giving of land bounties as compensation for military services dates from the colonial period, when Virginia gave one hundred acres in 1646 to the commander at Middle Plantation. Soon afterward came a plan to promote frontier settlements by land gifts to soldiers. During the Revolutionary War the gift of unoccupied land was first an inducement to desertion from the British army and later of enlistment in the Continental army. It was a way of building an army and of paying soldiers. Land bounties were offered in the War of 1812, in the Black Hawk Indian War—Abraham Lincoln was one soldier who was issued a bounty land warrant for his services—and again in the Mexican War. Liberalization, beginning in 1850, made bounty lands available to men of every rank and branch and for service in wars from 1790 to and including the Mexican War. They were given as a reward for services long past.

On March 22, 1852, all warrants for military bounty lands were made assignable—in recognition of the fact that most soldiers had no desire to be frontiersmen—and their principal use in California began from that date. These warrants empowered the holder to "locate" 160 acres upon any lands of the United States open to private entry and provided the means of purchase, for they were receivable by the government in lieu of cash at $1.25 an acre. If the minimum was greater than $1.25 per acre, the locator could pay the United States the difference.

The assignable warrant brought the speculator to the fore. In 1852 Mexican War land warrants, according to Benjamin Horace Hibbard, were selling at $110 to $115, whereas, on the basis of $1.25 an acre, they would have been worth $200. In 1857 New York City brokers were quoting them as low as 60 cents per acre. The broker's handling fee was 10 cents per acre. The Commissioner of the General Land Office reported that not one in five hundred land warrants was located by a soldier. They were used, instead, by nonsoldiers for speculation in the public lands of California and elsewhere. Scrip practically passed as currency in California and is said to have been widely bought by Henry Miller of Miller and Lux fame to extend his land empire in the San Joaquin Valley. Military bounty warrants helped put public land in private hands, helped settle California, helped put a little money in discharged soldiers' pockets and more money in those of claim agents, brokers, and speculators. After 1862, however, when the Homestead Act became law, these warrants had to compete with free land and were no longer issued.

To enable states and territories to establish colleges for the benefit of agriculture and the mechanic arts, Congress on July 2, 1862, enlarged its earlier land grants and at the same time provided that states without public land should receive an equivalent amount of land scrip to be sold and the money used for the purposes of the act. Scrip so sold could be used by its assignees for unappropriated public lands in other states.

Under this procedure California, of course, received no agricultural college land scrip, but its holders acquired title (by 1903) to 1,397,760 acres of California public lands.

Both military bounty warrants and agricultural college land scrip could be used, and were used, like cash in the payment of preëmption claims.

CHAPTER XIV

The State as Owner

CALIFORNIANS went to the polls on November 13, 1849, to ratify the constitution that had just been drafted by the convention at Monterey. Though they had to plod through the rain, nearly everyone went out to vote. They gave the constitution almost unanimous approval.

The delegates to this first convention had been thinking of the schools and universities that the new state would be needing and of how these needs could be met. Article IX, of the ratified constitution, which dealt with education, showed they were not overlooking the public-land gifts that might come from the United States for the support of schools, and that they were well aware of the 500,000 acres to which each new state automatically was entitled. The proceeds of such lands, the article provided—and still provides—were to be used for the support of common schools throughout the state. And, should there be a reservation or grant of other land by the United States for a university, then the funds from the rental or sale of such land—the 1849 constitution said—should remain a fund for the support of a university and its branches.

The delegates had wisdom and foresight. The United States did make several large grants of land out of the public domain to the State of California in the cause of *education*.

In addition, the state became the owner, by federal grant, of the "swamp and overflowed" lands in California, the proceeds of which were to be used for *reclamation*.

Besides these specifically granted lands, there is at least the qualified ownership which California has or had in lands under navigable streams or lakes or harbors or those between ordinary high tide and ordinary low tide, as well as the lands the state acquired and continues to acquire through purchase, condemnation, gift or other method of acquisition.

Much of the public land obtained by grant from the United States went quickly into private ownership—and probably too quickly—through sales conducted by the state. While the causes of education and reclamation were being furthered, thousands of owners of state-sold real estate were helping to settle and develop California.

In an act of Congress approved September 4, 1841, grants of 500,000 acres were made, in the interests of internal improvements, to Ohio, Indiana, Illinois, Alabama, Missouri, Mississippi, Louisiana, Arkansas, and Michigan. This act also provided that each new state, upon admission, would be accorded the same privileges as the states specifically named in the act. State legislatures were given the right of selection of these public lands so granted by the United States, but not until the land had been surveyed. They were to be located in parcels conforming to sectional divisions and subdivisions of not less than 320 acres in any one location, on any public land not reserved from sale. Thus when California was admitted to the Union it participated at once in the half million acres of public lands of which the constitution framers had been so well aware.

A few years later, on March 3, 1853, California received other and more important grants of public land from the United States to further the state's educational program. These included the grant of two sections—the sixteenth and the thirty-sixth—in each township "for the purposes of public schools"; another grant of 72 sections for the use of "a seminary of learning"; together with ten sections for "public buildings." Each section was, of course, 640 acres.

Nine years later, on July 2, 1862, another grant provided "colleges for the benefit of agriculture and the mechanic arts." Not only California but all the states were recipients of this federal generosity. Since the amount of land to be apportioned each state was 30,000 acres for each Senator and Representative in Congress to which the state was entitled under the census of 1860, California was allowed 150,000 acres of nonmineral land.

The most important of these grants was that of the two "school sections" in each township, which was to total five and a half million acres. In this connection, California in 1866 was permitted to select other lands in the public domain of equal acreage whenever the sixteenth and thirty-sixth sections "were settled upon prior to survey, reserved for public uses, covered by grants made under Spanish or Mexican authority, or by other private claims, or where such sections would be so covered if the lines of the public surveys were extended over such lands." Lands selected by the state under this provision are called "lieu lands."

These land grants by the United States had antecedents in America's colonial period and became the basis of California's educational development. The legislature of the state provided the machinery. It adopted uniform methods of selecting the specific lands from the public domain—where selection was required—and uniform methods of sale. It provided for the use of the funds resulting from sales, though limited by restrictions of the grants. On March 31, 1866, the legislature established an agricultural, mining, and mechanics arts college. On March 23, 1868, the University of California was created and organized, and the board of directors of the college was directed to transfer its property to The Regents of the University of California. The college was to retain for its benefit the funds from the sale of the "seventy-two sections" and the "ten sections" and was given power to select and dispose of the "150,000 acres" in the interests of the college. The land agent of the University, as the agent of the state, was given the duty of actual selection, under board instructions.

The donation to the University of the earlier College of California, which had been founded in Oakland, and the selection of a site of two hundred acres at Berkeley— which it took possession of on July 6, 1873—gave it a good start. Appropriations from the state and gifts from individuals have added and continue to add to what was made possible by land grants from the United States. Today the University of California has eight campuses: Berkeley, Davis, La Jolla, Los Angeles, Mt. Hamilton, Riverside, San Francisco, Santa Barbara—and forty thousand students.

As provided in the present constitution of California, which follows the lines laid down by the revised constitution of 1879, the University of California is declared to constitute "a public trust, to be administered by the existing corporation known as 'The Regents of the University of California,' with full powers of organization and government, subject only to such legislative control as may be necessary to insure compliance with the terms of the endowments of the university and the security of its funds." In this corporation is vested the legal title and the management and disposition of the property of the University. Article IX goes on to provide that "all moneys derived from the sale of public lands donated to this State by act of Congress approved July 2, 1862 (and the several acts amendatory thereof), shall be invested as provided by said acts of Congress and the income from said moneys shall be inviolably appropriated to the endowment, support and maintenance of at least one college of agriculture, where the leading objects shall be (without excluding other scientific and classical studies, and including military tactics) to teach such branches of learning as are related to scientific and practical agriculture and mechanic arts, in accordance with the requirements and conditions of said acts of Congress."

Before California could make specific selections out of the "500,000 acre grant," the "150,000 acre grant," the "72 sections grant" and the "10 sections grant," the public lands had to be surveyed, so that particular lands could be described. Lists of selected lands were then filed with the local land office. After being checked they were sent to the Commissioner of the General Land Office for his approval and the certification to the state by the Secretary of the Interior. Approved lists would then be sent back to the state authorities. The certified listing acted as a transfer of title to the state—and without patents being issued—effective when the selections were made and reported to the local land office. The state was then in a position to issue its own patents to purchasers of listed lands. It was the practice of the state to make a selection *after* it had received an application to purchase.

California thus reduced its "500,000 acre grant" to private ownership at so fast a rate that by June 30, 1880, the acreage selected amounted to 487,709 acres. The other grants were reduced in swift fashion, too.

As for the grant to California for public school purposes of the sixteenth and thirty-sixth section in each township—the largest grant—the title to the lands already surveyed passed to the state on the date of the Congressional Act—March 3, 1853. As for the unsurveyed lands, the title passed when the survey was approved by the United States Surveyor General. No patents were issued by the United States nor any certified listings.

In the grant of these "school sections" there was no specific exception of mineral lands, but the United States Supreme Court ruled that the intention was to convey agricultural lands and that lands then known to be mineral did not pass to the state.[1] Hence the title that the state got in a particular section was the complete title or no title at all. If the lands were not then known to contain minerals in sufficient quantity to justify the expenditure of funds for their extraction, the state got full title. Any later discovery of minerals did not affect the state's title. On January 25, 1927, however, Congress granted to the states the mineral school sections not then in controversy, with the restriction, among other restrictions, that the

---

[1] Ivanhoe Mining Co. *v.* Keystone Mining Co., 102 U.S. 167, 26 L. Ed. 126.

states should reserve the coal and other minerals when disposing of any of them.

As for the "lieu lands"—those selected by the state because a particular section sixteen or a particular section thirty-six was not available for one reason or another—their selection was made in the same way as the lands in the "500,000 acre grant." The state's list of selected lieu lands would be submitted to the land office, approval secured from the commissioner and certification to the state obtained from the Secretary of the Interior. These lists passed title to the state, without any patent from the United States and without regard to whether the lands were or were not mineral.

The sale of school lands made possible the school system of California and their use by purchasers, who received patents issued by the state, helped in the settlement and development of California.

California, it will be recalled, also received a grant of lands, the proceeds of which were to be used for reclamation. This was the grant of "swamp and overflowed" lands, and they were to amount to more than two million acres. The state received this grant less than three weeks after its admission into the Union.

The unruly Mississippi River was really responsible for the Act of September 28, 1850, by which California ultimately became the owner of those public lands subject to overflow which, unless assisted by drainage or embankment, could not be put to the profitable raising of crops. In 1849 Congress had passed an act to aid Louisiana in draining its swamp land. It met with such favor that in 1850 land classed as "swamp and overflowed" was ceded under the so-called Arkansas Act to other states, California among them.

Identification of such lands in California and their segregation from other lands through federally approved state surveys or federally made surveys, together with their certification to the state by the Commissioner of the General Land Office, was provided for in a later act of Congress approved July 23, 1866.

Patents to the state were issued upon request of the governor and after approval of survey by the General Land Office, and these conveyed full title to California. Purchasers from the state, in turn, received state patents.

Swamp and overflowed lands conveyed to California totaled 2,192,456.70 acres, according to the report of the Commissioner of the General Land Office to the Secretary of the Interior for the year 1945. Their reclamation in California has been less difficult than with similar lands along the Mississippi River. Most of the California swamp and overflowed lands were free from jungle growth and have been easily drained: for example, lands of this type abutting on the Bay of San Francisco and on the banks of the Sacramento and San Joaquin rivers emptying into it, as well as areas in more northerly and southerly parts of the state. There has sometimes arisen, however, the problem of distinguishing swamp land from tideland or of segregating swamp from upland.

Edward F. Treadwell, biographer of Henry Miller, "the cattle king," tells us that Miller, after forming a partnership in 1858 with Charles Lux, began a thirty-year program of land and cattle buying. The purchase of school sections, homestead and preëmption rights, bounty warrants, and swamp and overflowed lands all helped to build up a vast land empire in the central valley of California. He availed himself generously of the swampy areas, bordering the rivers, that had been granted to the state, these being purchasable at $1.25 an acre. Under state law, we are informed by Treadwell, Miller would make proof of his expenditure of the same amount for reclamation of these areas and thus obtain a repayment of the purchase price. Ultimately Henry Miller owned a hundred-mile, continuous strip of reclaimed swamp and overflowed land along the San Joaquin River and another fifty-mile strip along the Kern River.

So much, then, for the lands of the public domain which California received by direct grant from the United States in the interests of education and reclamation and which California—with little thought of conservation, of development, or of future income—largely disposed of within twenty years after becoming a state.

Until the precedent-shattering decision of the United States Supreme Court of June 23, 1947, California had considered itself the owner, by reason of its sovereignty, of lands beneath navigable waters within its boundaries. The 1849 constitution described California's area not only as including islands, harbors, and bays, but also as having a western boundary line that was offshore "three English miles." California's civil code, section 670, since 1872 has declared the state to be the owner of "all land below tidewater, and below ordinary high-water mark, bordering upon tidewater within the state" and "all land below the water of a navigable lake or stream." The basis for this claim to lands under navigable waters was that California had been admitted into the Union on *an equal footing* with the original thirteen states, these latter acquiring lands of such character from the Crown of England and holding them in trust for the public as an incident to their sovereignty.

The Supreme Court in 1947 declined to follow this

theory of ownership. It did not deny "that California has a qualified ownership of lands under inland navigable waters such as rivers, harbors, and even tidelands down to the low-water mark." It stated, however, that "California is not the owner of the three-mile marginal belt along its coast, and that the Federal Government rather than the state has paramount rights in and power over that belt, an incident to which is full dominion over the resources of the soil under that water area, including oil."

These oil-rich lands under navigable waters were, admittedly, the motivating force in the suit against the State of California that was brought—after the lapse of nearly a hundred years—by the United States.

As a result of California's assumption since 1850 that it was the owner of lands under navigable waters within its boundaries, whether inland or along the coast, an assumption that apparently had been backed by court decisions and acquiesced in by the United States, it had proceeded to use or dispose of some of these lands—subject, of course, to the public rights of navigation, commerce, and fishery.

Although forbidden under its constitution of 1879 from granting tidelands within two miles of any incorporated city or town and fronting on the waters of any harbor, estuary, bay or inlet, used for navigation, California did make, through its legislature, numerous grants to coastal municipalities or counties of tide and submerged lands lying in the Pacific Ocean or in entrances to bays, harbors, and rivers along the California coast, many of them extending three miles from shore. Examples are grants to Eureka, Santa Cruz, San Mateo County, Orange County, Monterey, San Diego, Long Beach, Los Angeles, Santa Barbara, and the Carmel Sanitary District. City authorities, under such legislative grants, developed harbors and made vast expenditures for improvements. Long Beach, for example, built a breakwater, its semicircular Rainbow Pier, and a municipal auditorium extending 1,400 feet into the Pacific Ocean and Bay of San Pedro. Begun in October, 1928, the project was completed in November, 1930, at a cost to the city of $1,067,000. In addition, working with the state and the county (of Los Angeles), Long Beach dredged the mouth of Alamitos Bay and put in improvements at a cost of $116,000.

Aside from the making of these grants of land, the State of California, under authority of a legislative act approved May 25, 1921, for a number of years granted permits to private individuals or corporations to prospect for oil and gas in tide and submerged lands and also entered into oil and gas leases covering such areas. Pursuant to the act and to later amendments, the state entered into leases of submerged land oil areas in the Summerland and Rincon fields in Ventura County and in the Elwood, El Capitan, Carpinteria, and Goleta fields in Santa Barbara County. Further new activity of this sort by the state was stopped May 28, 1929, but under the State Lands Act of 1938 California was given a restricted authority to lease tide and submerged lands containing oil or gas deposits that may be or are being drained by wells on adjacent lands not owned by the state. Drilling under such leases could take place only from upland or shore sites, with slant-drilling into tide and submerged lands.

The Federal Leasing Act of 1920 permits any person to file an application for an oil lease on public lands. Until 1936, the Department of the Interior had rejected such applications so far as California tidelands were concerned.

When one application of this sort, involving land off Huntington Beach, was then allowed to stand, the lid was off and "claimjumpers"—so called—filed nearly 200 applications in a short time. Some overlapped the areas already leased by the state to operating oil companies. "Let the courts decide" was the federal government's new view. And presently, in October of 1945, after several preliminary skirmishes, a suit was filed in the United States Supreme Court, with the State of California named as the sole defendant.

The United States Supreme Court's startling decision of 1947, involving the ownership and use of immensely valuable lands long claimed by California, also cast a cloud on claims of the nation's coastal and inland states to lands beneath navigable waters within their boundaries. A specific grant or quitclaim of such lands by Congress to the states—now under consideration—would settle one of the greatest state-versus-federal questions that has ever been raised.

In any event the disposition and use that has already been made of these lands, which California considered state-owned by reason of its sovereignty, has played a very large part in the building up of its port cities, the development of its resources, the expansion of its commerce, and the creation of its prosperity.

Aside from the lands to which California has claimed ownership through specific grants from the United States or by reason of its sovereignty, there are those to which the state acquires title through purchase, condemnation, dedication, gift or other acquisition. To give a few illustrations: state parks; lands deeded to the state by tax collectors because of owners' failure to pay taxes or assessments that have become delinquent; lands that have escheated or reverted to the state because of their having been deeded to aliens ineligible to citizenship; and lands described in the civil code as being "property of which there is no other owner." The problems arising out of present-day state ownership are complex and are outside the scope of this book. In passing, it should be mentioned that the California legislature on June 11, 1938, enacted the State Lands Act of 1938, a comprehensive piece of law-making relating to lands owned by the State of California. By it there was created a state lands commission to which was transferred the administration, sale and leasing of state lands. Under the act, deposits of oil and minerals in state-owned land (except land acquired upon sale for delinquent taxes) were reserved to the state. Therefore, conveyances or patents of such land issued by the state do not transfer oil and minerals—even if they contain no specific reservations. The state, under the act, was allowed to lease its lands for oil and gas development but, as already pointed out, no oil derricks could be erected on tide or submerged lands. In 1941 this important act was incorporated within the public resources code.

CHAPTER XV

Buying and Selling California

EVER SINCE there have been men and women in California it seems probable that claims to the occupancy or use of particular land areas have not only been fought over but have been bought and sold.

The more individualistic of California Indians are reported to have indulged occasionally in the real estate business even before the white invaders came. That is to say, the rights to use river land that was good for hunting deer or elk, or to use special acorn-gathering areas, fishing places along streams, redwood-plank houses on the Klamath River, or farm lands on the Colorado, were sometimes exchanged for strings of dentalium shells, beads, white deerskins, wives, or slaves.

There was apparently little buying or selling of land, whether in or outside of pueblos, during the Spanish period, 1769–1822, or in the early years of the succeeding Mexican period. Ranchos were obtained on petition to the governor of California and, if desirable property, usually remained in the family of the first grantee. If not desirable, they were abandoned, with reversion of title, and could be obtained by other petitioners. So, too, pueblo lots, when granted by the *ayuntamiento* or council to individual townsmen on petition. Such lots, if abandoned, could be picked up by other persons through "denouncement" and the issuance to them of official approval of new petitions. The pueblo archives of Los Angeles, for example, are full of such petitions and denouncements. The earliest is that of José Antonio Carrillo who, on June 22, 1821, asked the *comisionado* for a house lot in Los Angeles on the site of the present-day hotel known as The Pico House. It was near the plaza church then being built. Carrillo received his grant next day.

Enough has been said in other chapters about early California procedure in obtaining ranchos through petition to the governor. The method of getting title to lots in pueblos is well illustrated by the petition and the grant through which William Richardson became the first owner, in 1836, of a lot in Yerba Buena, predecessor of present-day San Francisco. The grant appears, in translation, in the addenda to John W. Dwinelle's *The Colonial History of San Francisco:*

Most Illustrious Ayuntamiento:

William Richardson, a citizen and resident of this Port, in due form represents that he is resolved to establish himself in Yerba Buena, and for that effect requires to build a house, for which he applies to your Superiority, by using your faculties to deign to grant him a lot of one hundred varas square, in Yerba Buena, in front of the Plaza and anchorage of the ships.

For which effect I request that you will deign to grant this my petition, which is on common paper, there being no stamp as corresponds.

SAN FRANCISCO, June 1, 1836.

(Signed) WM. RICHARDSON.

This Corporation being satisfied of the good services that the party requesting has rendered to this jurisdiction since his arrival in this country, with his different trades as bricklayer, surgeon and carpenter, and having married one of the first in the country, and that the said party has resolved to follow his good conduct, this Corporation has concluded to grant to Mr. William Richardson the lot of one hundred varas square, which he requests in Yerba Buena, so that he may establish himself there with his family.

Date as above.

JOSÉ JOAQUIN CARRILLO
Alcalde Constitutional.

The buying and selling of ranchos and of pueblo property was under way by the early 1830's. Property had become valuable in certain areas,—for example, land fronting on plazas. To put through a real estate deal, the buyer and the seller, with witnesses, went before an alcalde or a justice of the peace—these officers having the powers of notary. It was somewhat like "going into escrow" today. The deed was drawn up by the alcalde or justice of the peace. It was that officer's certified statement of all the facts about the conveyance, including the names of parties, the words of conveyance, a description of the property being conveyed, the consideration passing, and the warranties involved. He signed it, so did the witnesses and also the grantor—if the grantor knew how to write. If the consideration—say a certain number of barrels of brandy—could not be turned over immediately, another individual might be named responsible for full compliance of the terms. This individual, along with the certifying officer, had duties that remind us of a present-day "escrow agent." The original deed would remain—as under the Torrens system of land registration—in the alcalde's files, a certified copy being available to the purchaser. The completion of the deal included the reading aloud of the document to the persons present.[1]

The almost complete absence of professional surveyors in Spanish and Mexican California resulted in the use of vague or haphazard descriptions when conveying land. For ranchos, natural boundaries—a stream, the ocean, a sycamore tree, a road, a willow grove—were the best that could be expected. More often a rancho would be described vaguely like this: "the place known by the name of Las Salinas, with the Potrero Viejo, bounded by the Mission of San Francisco, the sea, and the lands of La Visitacion"; or "the tract within this vicinity called Corral Viejo del Rincon"; or "the place being vacant which is known by the name of San José, distant some six leagues, more or less, from the Ex-Mission of San Gabriel, a map of which place we will lay before your Excellency as soon as possible." For pueblo lots a reference to the neighbors on each side of the particular parcel was considered sufficient for identification. As an example, note how Ramon Orduno described a piece of property in Los Angeles which he deeded to Abel Stearns on December 22, 1834: "A lot 40 varas square and a house situate thereon which has 3 rooms half in ruins and a kitchen and is situated between the house of the widow Rita Villa on the west and the gulch on the east and the roads on the north and south."

---

[1] For full copy of a Mexican deed executed in 1841 and involving the sale of a Los Angeles city lot, see Historical Society of Southern California, *The Quarterly* (December, 1945).

There were at least two professional surveyors who did their bit toward helping California enter into the real estate business during the Mexican period. One was Jean Jacques Vioget, Swiss sailor and surveyor, who came to California in 1837. He made the first survey and map of Yerba Buena, in 1839, and from that date on his survey was used in the buying and selling of town lots. His survey in 1841 of New Helvetia for John Sutter, the first made of the Sacramento region, was so good that historian Bancroft thought it worthy of reproduction. The other surveyor was Jasper O'Farrell, for whom a street in San Francisco was named. He was an Irishman who came to California in 1843, made San Rafael his home, and occupied himself with making surveys of ranchos. He also mapped San Francisco in 1847, going far beyond the limits of the Vioget survey, and showing street names, an important step forward in making town lots merchantable. In southern California, under the name of "Don Gaspar Farrel," he handled the important partition, in 1846, of San José Rancho (Pomona Valley), between the three owners, Ricardo Vejar, Henry Dalton, and Ygnacio Palomares.

Ordinarily, however, surveying in early California was on a strictly amateur basis. Town lots did not absolutely require surveying and, for ranchos, the overseeing of the job fell frequently to the alcalde of the pueblo having jurisdiction. He would set forth, with or without a surveyor but accompanied by two chain bearers, all on horseback. A cord one hundred varas long was used—a vara was about thirty-three inches—and to each end was attached a wooden stake. Taking, say a black willow tree, as a starting point, the party would place between the limbs dry sticks in the form of a cross. From the willow tree they would proceed around the whole of the rancho, measuring hundred-vara lengths, and placing landmarks as they went.

The alcalde, as has been mentioned, was not only a notary, but a receiver and keeper of documents. Not only deeds, but mortgages, bills of sale, leases, powers of attorney, wills, petitions, and other instruments were in his safekeeping.

The raising of the United States flag at Monterey on July 7, 1846, did not end the Spanish Californian way of buying and selling land, for local government was little disturbed for several years. The forms, rules, and practices of the Mexican government carried on, though subject to the supervision of the American military governor. In fact, Commodore John D. Sloat's proclamation to Californians in 1846 included these words:

> I invite the Judges, Alcaldes, and other civil officers, to execute their functions as heretofore, that the public tranquility may not be disturbed, at least until the Government of the Territory can be more definitely arranged.

Between 1846 and 1850, people in California bought or sold land as they had been doing and the alcalde continued to play his part. Certified copies of many of the deeds executed in this period were later recorded with county recorders under the American recording system.

As a matter of fact, the subdividing of California lands for the purpose of sale did not wait on the importation of American systems of government or practice. There were many Yankees in California already and most of them were real-estate minded. This we have already seen in Yerba Buena. In a nontechnical sense, of course, subdivision is as old as landownership. The division of a selected area into house lots and their assignment to the first settlers of San José and Los Angeles was subdivision of a sort. So, too, the allotment to soldiers of parcels in a presidio, or, in later years, to Indian heads of families in an Indian pueblo. The early-day division or partitioning of a rancho or the splitting of a town lot is, informally, a "subdivision." But when real estate began to rise in value in San Francisco in the late 1840's, Thomas O. Larkin and Robert Semple, real-estate-minded gentlemen, bought a tract of rancho land on the Straits of Carquinez from Mariano Vallejo. They planned a town that would rival the growing peninsula city and in 1847 put it on the market as Benicia. Presently, promoter Semple was on the townsite supervising activities while promoter Larkin—who had been buying and selling land, on speculation, in Monterey, Yerba Buena and elsewhere—was persuading friends, relatives, officers of the American fleet, army men, and prospects in general to invest in "Benicia, the Queen City of the Bay." Then came the discovery of gold—and scrambling for lots at Benicia fell off. To Benicia, however, goes the honor of being California's first hundred-per-cent-promoter-inspired town.

As early as January 8, 1849, the first auction sale of lots at Sacramento was held. The town had been laid out in salable-sized lots by William H. Warner of the United States topographical engineers. The same year saw the survey of Stockton, founded earlier as Tuleburg.

Los Angeles, needing revenue, was eager to engage in the real estate business and to sell some of the land within its four square leagues. But it was unable to get under way until late in 1849, a decade or more after Yerba Buena's entry into the real estate field. The pueblo wanted to be subdivided but had no surveyor who could map the place. The military governor had ordered that sales of unappropriated pueblo lands should be by reference to a city map. The distressed ayuntamiento petitioned the Superior Territorial Government and was assigned Lieutenant E. O. C. Ord of the United States Army. Ord agreed to do the job for $3,000. Ord's Survey, Los Angeles' first, was formally turned over to the city on September 19, 1849. In November, following, the first auction of city lots was held, with $2,490 in cash realized. Many auctions were held later, and Los Angeles showed itself as careless of its patrimony in land as the United States was with its public domain.

There was a flurry of lot selling at La Playa and Old Town (San Diego) in 1849, but the next year the speculators obtained a grant of land south of the pueblo and laid out New San Diego. This new town was destined to stand still, however, until the coming of dynamic Alonzo Erastus Horton in 1867 when the modern city really got its start.

When California's first legislature met at San José on December 15, 1849, shortly after the first constitution had been ratified, it proceeded to organize the state government, it divided California into counties, provided for the incorporation of cities, and—to safeguard the ownership of land and facilitate land transfers—adopted the recording system. All these events took place early in 1850, after which California could begin to function exactly as though it were already a part of the Union.

This "recording system" was the same as that in use throughout the United States. It had had its origin in colonial America and was therefore strictly a home product. It was the American attempt to meet a problem which in many other nations or in other times was taken care of through a "registration system" or through some other workable system by which landownership could be proved. In ancient Greece, for example, there was a period when the record of a mortgage was kept on a stone pillar placed on the property of the borrower, to give notice to prospective buyers.

The public recording of a deed or other document— under the theory of the American recording system—gives "constructive" notice of its contents. All persons are conclusively presumed by law to have notice of instruments properly recorded, whether or not these persons have examined the public records. The county is the recording unit. Thus, a man buying land in Alameda County and receiving a deed, takes title subject at least to matters shown in the documents in the recorded chain of title on display in the office of the recorder of Alameda County. A document is "recorded" when, after being acknowledged or certified or verified, as may be required, it is deposited with the recorder to be transcribed by him in the proper book of records. After transcription, whether this is done by pen, typewriter, or camera, the *copy* becomes, so far as the public is concerned, the document itself. It is the recorder's duty also to index each document. The recording system, accordingly, establishes legal priority of rights in land and, with its adoption in California in 1850, it became a vital factor in the buying and selling of land and in the preservation of essential data about landownership. Since 1850 county recorders' offices in California have been the chief source of information not only about transfers of land but also about mortgages, deeds of trust, contracts of sale, leases, subdivision maps, and a multitude of other documents or instruments which under the law may be recorded: declarations of homestead, notices of action, notices of completion, powers of attorney, assignments of various kinds, and agreements of one kind or another. The American recorder's *copy* has supplanted the Mexican alcalde's *original*.

Shortly after the organization of the state government in California, Congress provided for the survey of the public lands in California. This was an important step in making it possible to identify lands and to describe selected areas exactly, so they could be readily transferred by the United States, by the State of California or by individuals. The Act of March 3, 1853, provided for a surveyor general for California, authorized to survey private land claims, after they had been confirmed, and public lands.

The extension to California of the rectangular system of survey brought to this state the benefits of a system that had its origin in an ordinance sponsored by the Continental Congress and passed in 1785. This had provided for the location of townships six miles square, each township to contain thirty-six sections of one mile square. Townships, under this first ordinance, were laid out in ranges extending northward from the Ohio River. Eleven years later Congress made provision for the appointment of a surveyor general and the numbering of sections beginning with number one in the northeast section and proceeding west and east alternately through each township. It was afterward directed that public lands be subdivided into quarter sections. As a part of the system of rectangular surveys, principal meridians and base lines were established. These bear local names. The meridian lines extend north and south and the base lines east and west.

The Humboldt meridian governs in northern California, the Mount Diablo meridian in central California, and the San Bernardino meridian in southern California. Tiers of townships are arranged north and south of the established base lines. Theoretically each township contains thirty-six sections, but in many cases Spanish or Mexican land grants cut into the townships and, where this is the case, the sections or parts of the sections which fall in the ranchos are omitted from the government maps of the townships.

From 1850 to the present time the subdivision and resubdivision of California has proceeded at an ever-faster pace—under the urge of an ever-increasing population. It is beyond the scope of this book to give the history of subdivision in California. To do so would require an account of the laying out of every city or town or community in the state—and many of them were started in the years 1846 to 1850—as well as of the innumerable later subdivisions and resubdivisions within these inhabited areas. It would require the retelling of city building which spread from the region of San Francisco Bay, and its tributary rivers, throughout the state—in the north directed at first by the rise of mining districts and the expansion of lumber and farming, in the south, initially, by the awakening of pueblos and the stimulation of railroad enterprise. The real estate subdivision, as we know it today, had its origin in the early years of the American period which began on July 7, 1846. It has had a flowering in each of the succeeding peak years, or boom years, of the major cycles in real estate sales activity. These high points have been, approximately, 1855, 1875, 1887, 1906, 1923, and 1946, or about twenty years apart—the real estate cycle itself averaging, as in the United States as a whole, about eighteen years. The maps recorded in the recorders' offices of the state tell the whole story. So, too, a trip throughout the state discloses that much of southern California and part of the San Francisco Bay region are becoming solidly built up "population areas," with town and country tending to merge through subdivision and common use. Subdivision has been engaged in by towns as well as individuals. This story of the buying and selling of California, until it is brought down to the twentieth century, is one of unregulated, uncontrolled cutting up and selling of land. In the greatest real estate boom in California history, that of the 1880's it was possible for a promoter to sit in his office, there prepare a map, without setting foot on ground, of some inaccessible mountaintop or of some worthless river-wash land which he owned, make his lots any size he wanted, record the map, and then sell. There was no official to say nay to any and all gullible comers.

Today the subdivider, the real estate broker, and the salesman toe the mark. Comprehensive laws control both the subdividing and the selling of land in the interests of the community and of all persons directly concerned. The activities of subdivider, broker, and salesman are defined and governed by the detailed provisions of the business and professions code of the state. Subdivisions are defined. Subdividers must meet the exacting requirements of the state, the county, and the municipality. They must follow regulations of city engineers, county surveyors, planning commissions, and governing bodies. They often find it advisable to have federal agency,—such as the Federal Housing Administration—approval if lot purchasers can be expected to seek federally insured construction loans. No sales may be made until the real estate commissioner has been given full information about the new subdivision that is about to be placed on the market.

This commissioner makes a public report of his findings and has the power to prohibit the sale or lease of lots or parcels if it is apparent that misrepresentation, deceit, or fraud of purchasers is involved.

The business of selling land in California is on a vast scale today. The number of real estate licenses issued during the peak year 1946–1947 totaled 70,662, as compared with the highest earlier total of 60,000 in the 1920's. New subdivisions launched during 1946–1947 and filed with the real estate commissioner numbered 1,777. These figures are those of the state real estate division.

Some of the glamour may have been taken from the buying and selling of land in California by "subdivision map acts," "California real estate acts" and the establishment of a "state real estate division" and a "real estate commissioner," but a greater degree of safety for purchasers has been added. To be sure, the apparently inevitable real estate cycle remains, and with it the same old opportunity to speculate, to make or lose fortunes in the land of California. Buying and selling California, a very old custom, will continue.

CHAPTER XVI

Insurance of Title

ONE OF the most important acts of California's first legislature, meeting at San José, was the adoption early in 1850 of the recording system. This system was to give California, which, under the Mexican regime, had been familiar only with rather crude registration, the benefits of a time-tried American device that had proved helpful throughout the United States in safeguarding the ownership of land and in making land transfers easy.

The significant points about recording, how it establishes legal priority of rights in land, and how vital a factor it was to become in the buying and selling of real estate in California, have been discussed in the preceding chapter.

Admittedly the public records system is an excellent device for keeping track of a multitude of interests in land. But, with increase in population and public offices, it becomes inevitably cumbersome. It does not provide machinery for the complete classification, according to land affected, or the interpretation, of the deeds and other documents that are daily recorded and transcribed in the recorder's office or of the day-by-day proceedings in the clerk's, the tax collector's, and numerous other governmental offices. It is apparent, too, that land titles are affected by many factors outside the province of the public records system of a county, such as actual occupancy of land by an individual who holds an unrecorded deed, lease, or contract of purchase.

Since the public records system could not meet all the needs of the public for specific title information, there arose in California, as elsewhere, auxiliary private agencies which took over the job of searching, classification, and interpretation. These agencies can be listed in order of development: the conveyancer; the abstracter; firms of attorneys and corporations equipped to furnish certificates of title; and, finally, title insurance companies.

Today there are large and ever-increasing populations, a multitude of public offices, and a myriad of laws and regulations—city, county, state or federal—that affect the holding of land. Hence the business of furnishing information about landownership and of insuring land titles has become big business. Corporations engaged in this business operate under the insurance laws of the state and are known as title insurance companies. Their services are more widely used in California than in any other state. Their activities are accepted as helping to make land a safe commodity to buy or sell. Accordingly, when a Californian buys a home, an apartment house, an office building, a factory, an oil well, or even a vacant lot, he first satisfies himself, through the medium of such a company, that the seller's ownership or title is clear of the claims of other persons. When a bank, a savings-and-loan association, or an individual loans money, with land as security, this lender requires evidence that the landowner has good title and relies upon the findings of the title insurance company as final proof. Even the government—whether city, county, state or federal—must know all about the ownership of the land it buys, condemns, or takes over and, in California, is in the habit of largely relying on the title company to segregate and interpret the public records and to insure the correctness of its findings.

The story of the rise of these private agencies auxiliary to the public recording system, culminating in California's modern title insurance companies, is a part of the title story of the state.

The directory of San Francisco issued for the years 1852–1853 carries this advertisement of Theodore Payne & Co.: "Real Estate Business in all its branches, for the conducting of which they esteem themselves peculiarly qualified by having given it their especial attention for over two years past, and made themselves familiar with all questions affecting titles, etc., etc." The directory of the same city for the year 1856 lists four "searchers of records and conveyancers." They were Joseph Clement, C. V. Gillespie, Gunnison & Parker, and G. W. Waugh. Gunnison & Parker who were "attorneys and counsellors at law," advertised: "We have prepared books containing a chain of title to every lot of land in the City and County of San Francisco, with maps of each subdivision and owners. We will give Abstracts of Title at the Shortest Notice." Waugh claimed to be a "Searcher of Records and Examiner of Titles," asserting that he had "compiled more information, and is better equipped than any man in the City in reference to the Validity of Titles in the

City and County of San Francisco." Gillespie announced himself as the "first notary public approved in California—commissioned July, 1848." He became associated with Giles H. Gray and, in the 1860–1861 directory of San Francisco, from their offices on Washington Street, "adjoining the Hall of Records," they advertised themselves as: "Examiners of Deeds, Searchers of Records for all incumbrances including Judgments and Taxes" and as "familiar with Titles to Real Estate in this City and County since February 1848."

From these early advertisements it is apparent that real estate men, notaries, and attorneys were taking care of the title needs of San Franciscans in the early years after California had organized itself as a state and had adopted the recording system. The transition from "conveyancing" to "abstracting" was already under way. The early-day conveyancer in California was either an attorney or a layman and, like his predecessors in other states, handled real estate transactions by checking a few records, drawing papers, and giving oral or written opinions that the title was clear. With the expansion of public records and of the business of conveyancing, the conveyancer or title lawyer often delegated the job of assembling title information to subordinates. These latter became skilled as abstracters, finally establishing offices of their own and submitting the results of their searching to attorneys for written opinions before advising customers.

Thus there came into use the "abstract of title" which was simply a written history of the recorded transactions affecting a piece of land. It consisted of summaries of each deed or other instrument in the chain of title, certified to by the abstracter as being complete up to a certain date, and sufficiently detailed so that an attorney could check it through and from it alone express his opinion in writing as to who owned the land and whether or not there were defects in the title or incumbrances. The abstract of title did not originate in California, for it had been used in the first quarter of the nineteenth century in other states. Throughout California it came to be used almost exclusively in real estate transactions, with the abstract business getting an early start in the larger and older county seats such as San Francisco, Sacramento, San José, Monterey, Los Angeles, San Bernardino, and San Diego. Early-day land transfers were often conducted by two attorneys: one representing the seller and preparing the abstract, the other representing the buyer and passing on the abstract. Abstracters, individually, or, later, organized into corporations, operated in each county seat where there was enough real estate business to justify their existence. The offices of abstract companies were usually as close to the courthouse as they could get and close also to the attorneys who wrote the opinions. In many cases the attorneys were in the offices, as staff members.

While the use of the abstract of title was expanding in California, with actual abstracting being done by both laymen and attorneys, there was another phase of the "title business" that remained exclusively in the hands of attorneys. The owners of ranchos whose ownership originated in the Mexican or Spanish period, as well as pueblo authorities, had to prove their claims before the United States Land Commission that had been provided for by Congress in 1851 and usually, also, before the courts to which board decisions were appealed. As a result, there grew up in California, and especially in San Francisco, where most of the board meetings were held, firms of attorneys that specialized in Spanish and Mexican titles. It was part of their job to submit transcripts of all the evidence in Mexican and Spanish archives that would prove ownership, as well as to secure witnesses, old-timers, and experts who could give convincing testimony bearing upon ownership. The transcripts usually included copies of *expedientes*, or land-grant files, obtained from the archives that had been assembled and deposited in the Surveyor General's Office in San Francisco, and were actually in the nature of abstracts of title. The handling of rancho titles made experts out of a large number of attorneys. Their title activities extended later to other fields, such as the public lands of the United States, where, in competition with land brokers and land agents, they helped purchasers, preëmptioners, homesteaders, squatters, miners, and others to get or prove ownership. "Special attention to business in the United States Land Office" was a typical advertisement of these attorneys.

Although the abstract of title is almost never used in California today it is still in wide use in other parts of the United States, especially in the Middle West. In California it gradually gave way to the "certificate of title," a short cut for those buying and selling land. The abstract was often ponderous—one covering the whole of Rancho San José (Pomona Valley) in Los Angeles County occupied thirty-seven large volumes—and the only part that was of importance was the attorney's opinion attached. It was only logical, therefore, that the opinion should be separated from the abstract, written as a complete statement, and then handed to the seller or buyer. The abstract itself, that is, the summaries of the recorded documents in the chain of title, remained in the abstracter's office, as a record of the searcher's work.

Certificates of title, giving, in one or two sheets, the net results of an examination of title, did not have their origin in California, but, since they were a natural outgrowth of the abstract, their use in California began as early as the 1870's. One issued at Los Angeles on January 23, 1875, from the "Office of Judson and Gillette, Examiners of Titles," was written informally on a letterhead bearing the names of "A. H. Judson, Att'y at Law" and "J. W. Gillette, County Recorder." It stated briefly:

The title of N.E.¼ S.E.¼ Sec. 16 Tp. 2S. R.13W. is vested in N. I. Orme, discharged of any & all liens or incumbrances. The only defect we discover is in the signature of Mrs. Schluter to the deed to Orme, the name 'Manilla' having been substituted for 'Manuella' (See Book 28, p.9). As names are entirely different we would suggest a rectification of the error by a new deed from Mr. & Mrs. Schluter.

Incidentally, the firm of Judson and Gillette, later to become Judson, Gillette, and Gibson, were pioneers in the Los Angeles title field, ultimately forming there a corporation—the Abstract and Title Insurance Company, incorporated in November of 1886—to carry on their work.

Brief statements of the kind quoted gave way to formal certificates of title prefaced by a statement such as this:

From examination of the records of Los Angeles County, California, in the offices of the County Recorder, County Clerk, County Auditor and County Tax Collector thereof, concerning the title to that certain real property in the County of Los Angeles, State of California, hereinafter described, The Abstract and Title Insurance Company of Los Angeles hereby certifies that the title thereto is now vested as follows.

By the 1880's the firms of attorneys that had been examining titles were incorporating, their certificates of title and abstracts of title being issued by corporations instead of by individuals. In these corporations were combined the functions of searcher, abstracter, and attorney. The real estate boom of 1887 gave great vogue to certificates of title and to the incorporated "title business." On the other hand the certificates themselves, one- or two-page documents telling everything a purchaser need know about his property, helped to make the fast "turn-over" in real estate possible.

It was in the 1880's that the present-day, large-scale business of furnishing information about land titles and of insuring such titles began to take shape. At that time the certificate of title—with coverage limited to public records—began to give way to "title insurance" which offered a buyer an *insured* statement of the condition of the title to the property he was buying.

In February of 1886 the California Title Insurance and Trust Company, with offices in San Francisco, was incorporated with capital stock of $250,000.00, and issued its first policy of title insurance on March 17, 1887. At the same time it distributed a pamphlet on the objects, plan, and advantages of title insurance as compared with abstracts of title. Title insurance was offered as a means of facilitating the transfer of real estate and at scheduled rates, based on the amount of insurance. The pamphlet was adorned with pungent paragraphs such as: "A bad title may appear perfect. The record does not show if a deed is forged or the act of an insane person." Again: "It is not safe to assume a title good because you are familiar with it. Good sense is not always good law." Or: "All men are fallible. The best of searchers and attorneys may err. A responsible guaranty is better than an opinion." Finally, quoting from *Macbeth:* "I'll make assurance doubly sure, And take a bond." This company, a pioneer in the "policy" field in this state, now carries on business as the California Pacific Title Insurance Company, with branch and affiliated offices in various cities of California.

In that same year of 1887 California corporations in the business of insuring titles to real estate were given specific recognition in the civil code of the state, and a new section required them to set apart annually a certain percentage of their premiums as a surplus fund for the security of policyholders. The office of Insurance Commissioner had been created earlier, in 1867, and corporations doing any kind of insurance business were obliged to obtain a certificate of authority. In 1907 the legislature defined the various kinds of insurance, including title insurance, and in 1935 all the insurance provisions of the civil and political codes were incorporated in one new code, the insurance code. Today a title insurance company organized in California must have a minimum capitalization of $100,000 and must make an initial deposit with the proper state official of $100,000 in cash or approved securities. It must also set apart annually, as a "title insurance surplus fund," a sum equal to 10 per cent of its premiums collected during the year, until this fund equals 25 per cent of the subscribed capital stock of the company. This fund—very substantial in the case of the larger and older companies—is maintained as a further security to the holders and beneficiaries of policies of title insurance.

Title insurance did not have its origin in California. The first use of title insurance was in Philadelphia in 1876. A Pennsylvania court, a few years earlier in the case of Watson *v.* Muirhead, had found a certain conveyancer and abstracter not liable for his failure to include certain money judgments in an abstract, though these were actually a lien on the particular parcel of land. This incident so disturbed Philadelphians that, when a real estate boom began, as a result of the approach of the Centennial Exposition, a group of conveyancers took decisive action. The outcome was the passage by the Pennsylvania legislature of a measure permitting a corporation to engage in the business of insuring titles. Then in 1876, the Real Estate Title Insurance Company was organized to insure "purchasers of real estate and mortgages against loss from defective titles, liens and incumbrances." Later this corporation was merged into the Land Title Bank and Trust Company, which is the oldest title insurance company in the world.

In the same year that San Francisco began to develop title insurance, Los Angeles saw the organization of the Abstract and Title Insurance Company. Out of this company's later merger with the Los Angeles Abstract Company came the birth in December of 1893, of Title Insurance and Trust Company, destined to become the largest insurer of titles in California and in the nation. For many years, however, it continued largely to issue certificates, though policies were available. This company is credited with developing the use of the "escrow," today an important business device in the buying and selling of land throughout California.

Although "escrow agents" have probably been functioning ever since man began exchanging or selling property—and we have seen traces of them in Mexican California—the flowering of "escrow service" in California as distinct from title service, seems to date from the 1890's. The late L. J. Beynon, a former official of Title Insurance and Trust Company, tells of the beginnings of escrow service there in these words: "One day in 1895 a man came into the office of the company and left an order for a certificate of title. He said he was obliged to leave town for a few days and asked if the order clerk would take his executed deed, deliver it to the buyer, together with the certificate of title, and collect from him the sum of $1000.00. This simple transaction was our first escrow." Soon afterward an escrow department was installed. Presently the employment of a title company to hold funds and documents and to see that proper payments and deliveries were made when the condition of the title met requirements, became common practice.

Going into escrow simply meant depositing purchase money and transfer papers in the hands of a responsible and impartial representative of buyer and seller to be held safe until all the instructions of both parties—and of a lender, if there was one—could be fully complied with. Not only title companies, but banks, began to offer escrow service. With the development of branch banking in Los Angeles County, a large part of this county's escrow business was taken over by the branch banks. Real estate brokers got in the habit of taking the parties to a real estate transaction to the bank nearest the property. Since loans, especially construction loans, were a common feature of such "deals," not only banks, but savings and loan associations, mortgage companies, and lenders in general in southern California, established escrow departments—using the mails or messenger service to get their title reports and their final policies from title insurance companies. A still later development was the entry into the escrow field of independent companies organized solely to handle escrows. Of course law firms and real estate companies also act as escrow agents. In central and northern California the escrow business is largely in title company hands.

Competition to the recording system and to the title services offered by private agencies, was offered in 1914 when optional *title registration* was provided for in the Land Title (Torrens) Act adopted in California in that year. Its purpose was to simplify real estate transactions. There had been an earlier law, adopted in 1897, following the report on the Torrens Land Transfer Act of Australia made by a commission appointed by the governor in 1893, but it had been too indefinite for general use. Registration of land titles, in various forms, existed in Europe for several centuries. It had been used in parts of the British Empire, and in Australia it had been made compulsory in 1858, owing to its promotion by Sir Robert Torrens, who gave his name to the system. As we have seen, too, Mexican California had a limited registration system in line with Spanish-American practice. Illinois in 1896 was the first state in the United States to adopt a registration law. Ultimately nineteen states were to pass land registration laws; Utah was the last, in 1917.

Under California's Land Title Act, a title may be registered when the ownership of the property is established by a judicial proceeding similar to a quiet title action. All persons known to have an interest in the property, together with adjoining owners, are made parties to this proceeding. Registration follows the obtaining of a decree, with a registrar's certificate of title issued. This certificate names the owner and any incumbrances shown by the decree. If this owner wishes to transfer his title he files or registers his deed with the registrar, along with the certificate. A new certificate is then issued to the new owner. Mortgages, deeds of trust, and other types of incumbrances must be registered, these being entered as "memorials" on the certificate. The law contemplated that registered property could not be taken from an owner because of a title defect, but that any person deprived of a valid interest because of registration would be reimbursed out of the public fund created under its provisions from filing fees.

The use of the registration system in California has been confined almost entirely to southern counties and of these Los Angeles County has been the largest user. The report of the State Land Commission on January 2, 1945, shows that in eighteen counties the registrar—who is also the county recorder—had issued certificates of title since the Torrens law had been in effect. Certificates in San Francisco totaled twelve, in Los Angeles County 133,993. Orange County was the nearest competitor to Los Angeles, with 10,111. The complete lack of interest in registration in San Francisco was due in part to the existence and use there of the McEnerney Act, adopted to meet the emergency created in April, 1906, by the burning of the public records following the earthquake. This act provided, like the Torrens, for a judicial procedure to establish ownership in a particular parcel, but, unlike the Torrens Act, thereafter the recording system was to be used. For a few years after 1914 there was an active campaign in Los Angeles County to bring property under the Torrens Act. Owners were recruited and urged to combine forces to reduce initial costs. Begining in 1923, however, new registrations began to decline, and since 1935 the act has been a dead letter so far as the initial registering of land is concerned. Land once registered may not be withdrawn. Accordingly, an extensive land registration department is maintained in the office of the recorder of

Los Angeles County to take care of land already registered.

The Land Title Act was adopted to simplify the buying and selling of land. Presently it was discovered that a Torrens-registered title was at least as complicated as an unregistered title and that auxiliary private agencies—brokers, attorneys, escrow agents, title companies—were being called upon, as with the recording system, to care for the needs of buyers and sellers. At that point interest in registration began to decline. Many other factors played their part, among them the complete liquidation of the assurance fund to satisfy one judgment for $48,000, obtained in Imperial County against the fund; the limited coverage and protection of Torrens certificates of title as compared with policies of title insurance; the rigidity of the Torrens system; the fact that the operating costs of the system are borne largely by the general public instead of by persons using it; and certain apparently fundamental conflicts with the American recording system, with the separation (in the United States) of the legislative and the judicial functions, and with the constitutional provision that no person can be deprived of property without due process of law. Today it is general practice in California for buyers, sellers, and lenders to rely on private agencies for title information and title insurance whether the land in question happens to be registered or unregistered.

The 1948 directory of the California Land Title Association, the trade organization of the title companies of the state, lists seventy-six separate companies having one hundred offices throughout California. It makes the statement that California "is, practically speaking, on a solid title insurance basis." The tendency of recent years has been for small companies to become merged with the larger or to secure from the latter the underwriting or the issuance of their policies of title insurance. Thus insurance of title is available to real estate buyers, sellers, and lenders in almost any part of the state. Mass demand for, and mass production of, policies of title insurance have kept costs down as compared with title costs in other states. The broadening of coverage, brought about largely through insistence of out-of-state life insurance companies engaged in making nation-wide loans on real estate, has been another important development.

Most of the title insurance companies in California today are the outgrowth of earlier companies, firms, and individuals who began selling title service almost as soon as California was admitted into the Union. The letterhead of one San Francisco Company—Title Insurance and Guarantee Company—says: "Established 1848." This corporation, though not incorporated until 1902, succeeded to the pioneer "plants" of C. V. Gillespie, and of F. A. Rouleau (father of the late O. A. Rouleau). Early-day title "plants" of these companies have been vastly enlarged, so that today some title insurance companies can boast of having "complete title plants"—these being, in effect, classified histories of the land transfers that have taken place in a county since 1850. Such are made possible through the day-by-day segregation and posting of essential information concerning property or people to be found in the recorded or filed papers, or in the proceedings, of all the many offices of the public records system of the county. The use by experienced searchers or examiners of this storehouse of local history enables the corporation employing them to offer insurance of title to anyone buying or selling real property in California.

CHAPTER XVII

Title Story of Two Cities

THE STORY of the rise of California's two metropolitan giants—San Francisco and Los Angeles—is one of dramatic contrasts. From their beginnings as pueblos, in the days when California was not a part of the United States, the physical aspects of the two cities have presented striking differences. Since these first days, too, their development has presented patterns that are equally varied.

Something of the story of the beginnings of presidios and pueblos has been told already, and of how presidios became pueblos and of the four square leagues of land to which, under Spanish law, they were each entitled. As a part of it, there was the founding in 1776 of a military outpost near a high and perpendicular cliff that overlooked San Francisco Bay. Also included was the starting in 1781 of a farming community in the fertile valley of the Porciuncula River to help supply the garrisons of California. So began San Francisco and Los Angeles. As the story continues, we find the population of the presidio

shifting, in 1835, to a sheltered cove near by and becoming
Yerba Buena, which in 1847 was to retake the name of
San Francisco and to stride forward as a seaport. Los Angeles meanwhile kept to its location and its name and was
already the center of the cattle country, with great ranchos
round about. As the two cities developed, San Francisco,
under the impetus of the Gold Rush leaped to maturity.
Los Angeles remained a pastoral pueblo until the railroad
came to it. Ultimately the northern metropolis was to find
almost full development within its original four square
leagues for which it had to fight bitterly. The southern
metropolis, winning its pueblo title to land with ease,
spread over all the surrounding ranchos and mountains
and valleys until its original four-square-league area was
merely the hub.

The setting up by Congress in 1851 of the Board of
Land Commissioners authorized to segregate private land
claims from public domain was the signal for the pueblos
of the north and the south to bestir themselves. Pueblo
authorities were in the same position as were the owners
of ranchos. All had to prove claims to land that originated
in the Spanish or Mexican periods.

Early in 1852 the Land Commission began hearings in
San Francisco. There was a rush to file claims. San Francisco, as successor to the pueblo of Yerba Buena, put in
its claim on July 2. The Los Angeles claim was filed October 26 when the board was in session in the southern city.

San Francisco, asserting ownership of four square
leagues of land, received a rebuff on December 21, 1854.
Confirmation came from the government but only for
the region north of the "Vallejo line," which ran approximately from Rincon Point on the bay to Point Lobos on
the ocean. The balance of the claim was rejected, the

decision being influenced by the government's acceptance of the "Zamorano document"—afterward proved spurious—in which General Vallejo in 1834 had purportedly suggested that line to Governor Figueroa as a boundary for the planned establishment of the pueblo of Yerba Buena.

Both the city and the United States appealed to the District Court. On September 5, 1864, the case was transferred to the United State Circuit Court where it was argued before Stephen J. Field, Justice of the United States Supreme Court, who some years before had participated in another celebrated case (Hart *v.* Burnett, 15 Cal. 530) where the city's title was also involved. His decision, presenting the views he had expressed in the earlier case, found the claims to four square leagues to be valid. "The confirmation is in trust," Judge Field found, in the decree entered May 18, 1865, "for the benefit of the lot-holders under grants from the pueblo, town or city of San Francisco, or other competent authority, and as to any residue, in trust for the use and benefit of the inhabitants of the city." While appeals from this decree to the United States Supreme Court were pending, Congress, on March 8, 1866, relinquished and granted to the city and its successors the land confirmed, and upon the trusts that had been set forth. The appeals were then dismissed.

The title of San Francisco to four square leagues of land rests, therefore, upon this decree of the Circuit Court, entered in 1865, and upon the confirmatory act of Congress in 1866. Confirmation was for an area bounded on three sides by the ordinary high-water mark as it was in 1846, excepting military reservations and a few private claims. A survey was made in 1867–1868. Disputes arose about the location of the easterly line of the pueblo at the mouth of Mission Creek and other estuaries. It was not until June 20, 1884 that the United States issued its patent for 17,754.36 acres, in accordance with court decree and Congressional act, with an additional patent, on March 6, 1887, covering 238.95 acres.

This bare recital of board rulings, appeals, court decrees, Congressional acts, surveys and patents entirely skips what was actually happening to the population of San Francisco, not only during the years between 1852 and 1866, when the principal contests over titles were taking place, and between 1866 and 1887, when minor issues were under dispute, but also during the earlier years beginning in 1849 when the city was feeling the full impact of the Gold Rush.

It is to the court contests, however, that we are indebted for our knowledge of the early title story of San Francisco. These court disputes had drawn the attention of the best students of Spanish and Mexican law, for the existence of the municipality itself, the approval of its past acts, and the well-being of its future were at stake. The story, as revealed in courtrooms, tells of the patrimony of four square leagues of land to which each Spanish American pueblo was entitled under the Laws of the Indies, it tells of the establishment of the presidial pueblo of San Francisco in 1776, and the organization there for the San Francisco area of an ayuntamiento in 1834. It continues with the settlement in the following year of Yerba Buena (within the limits of the pueblo of San Francisco) and the gradual shifting of population to that more sheltered area. It goes on with the suspension of the ayuntamiento in 1838, because the population requirements had been raised, but shows that alcaldes and justices of the peace continued to grant lands down into 1846. It points out that on July 7, 1846, the date of the conquest of California by the Americans, the pueblo was in existence, that it was recognized as such, and that its ayuntamiento was restored in 1847 and continued to function until April 15, 1850, when San Francisco was organized as a municipal corporation by act of the legislature of the new State of California, whereupon old officials gave way to mayor and aldermen.

It was John W. Dwinelle, city attorney of San Francisco, who presented the case for his city against the United States in the district and circuit courts, and it was he who made available much of the exhaustive material that was drawn upon in proving the pueblo's claim. His brief, which he published in four editions from 1863 to 1867 as *The Colonial History of San Francisco,* is a history of San Francisco's Spanish and Mexican periods, supported with documents of the greatest importance in the history of California land titles.

In this action against the United States, material used in the earlier case of Hart *v.* Burnett was drawn upon. Here the establishment of title under a sheriff's deed to several pueblo lots was involved originally, but this was submerged in the larger issue when the matter was appealed to the California Supreme Court. It was the big opportunity for the city and for property owners to come in and defend their titles and prove San Francisco's claim to four square leagues. So vast was the research, so great the compilation of laws and documents, so skillful the presentation, and so much was at stake, that the action of Hart *v.* Burnett has been called the *cause célèbre* in the annals of California land titles. The California court's decision was that San Francisco was a fully organized pueblo and as such entitled to four square leagues of land.

The reasoning that led to this decision led also to the later one in the case against the United States.

Mention has been made of the sale of land in Yerba Buena. This took place both before and after the first official survey made in 1839 by John (Jean Jacques) Vioget. This survey covered the portion of present-day San Francisco between Pacific and Sacramento streets and between the bay and Grant Avenue, to which was added certain "one hundred vara" lots adjacent to this area. Deeds came from alcaldes, prefects, and justices of the peace. It was Alcalde Washington A. Bartlett who employed Jasper O'Farrell to revise and extend the Vioget Survey; the new map was finished in 1847 and termed the Bartlett Map. Bartlett was also responsible for the change in the name on January 30, 1847, of Yerba Buena to San Francisco.

When the city lots were about gone, and San Francisco needed money, it did what every other city with land on its hands does. It called in another surveyor. This time it was William M. Eddy, who was appointed city surveyor in 1849. He assembled earlier surveys, dipped further into the surrounding lands, and prepared what is known as the second official map of San Francisco. It is referred to as the Eddy Map of 1851, for it was adopted by the legislature in 1851, and sometimes as the Red Line Map. The same legislature made certain grants of tideland rights within the red lines of the Eddy map to San Francisco. Later, in 1868, the state legislature was to provide for a board of tideland commissioners to have charge and disposition of salt marsh and tidelands of the state in San Francisco, pursuant to which blocks covering a considerable area of tidelands, conforming to the city blocks, were laid out and the lands sold to individual purchasers.

The Gold Rush had brought not only population but squatters to San Francisco and by 1852, when the city first asserted its claim before the Land Commission, they were an active horde whose tools often were the blanket and the gun. Beyond the lands surveyed by William M. Eddy lay a great unsurveyed area. It lay west of Larkin Street and southwest of Ninth Street but was within the charter boundaries of the city as defined in 1851. Professional landseekers concentrated on this region, on the wise assumption that it must belong either to San Francisco or to the United States. Prior possession, they thought, would be a forerunner of later confirmation by one or the other. Some bolstered their claims with guns and entrenchments. Some supported their claims to parcels of 40, 80, or 160 acres, by making entries under federal preemption laws or state laws governing "school land" selections. "Between 1850 and 1854 this section of the city," comments O. A. Rouleau, "was covered with several hundred of these notices and copies of surveys." Procedure for getting title simply did not exist, since the city's ownership had not been finally upheld.

The result was a compromise between "squatters" and city officials. It was effected by what is called the Van Ness Ordinance, passed during the administration of Mayor Van Ness. There were really three ordinances, adopted in 1855 and 1856, but they are considered as one. By it the title of persons who could prove possession of land in this "Western Addition" between January 1, and June 20, 1855, was upheld and confirmed, so far as the city was concerned. Early alcalde grants also were confirmed. Provision was made for the protection of city rights in the laying out and reservation of streets, parks, and grounds for various public purposes. State confirmation of the ordinance came in 1858, and the Congressional act of July 1, 1864 was an endorsement of its purposes. Later state legislation provided for the issuance of city deeds to those who could qualify.

Westerly and southerly of the lines established by the Van Ness Ordinance lay still other lands that were a part of the city's four square leagues. To this acreage, also a place favored by squatters, was given the term "Outside Lands," for it was originally outside the city's jurisdiction. Its western boundary was the ocean, and the four-square-league line was the southern boundary. Because squatters needed counsel and loans, many possessory rights in this area came into the hands of prominent lawyers and financiers. To "quiet title" here and do away with shotgun rule was the purpose of the Outside Lands Ordinance which was drafted shortly after the circuit court and Congress had upheld the city's pueblo title. Proof of possession on March 8, 1866, and of payment of taxes for five years preceding July 1, 1866, was required of the possessory claimants. The city was to have a park to contain not less than a thousand acres and land for other public purposes. Confirmation came from the legislature. The Committee on Outside Lands, under power given it, issued deeds to several hundred persons, among whom were names well known to this day.

In this manner San Francisco's patrimony in land passed into private hands. "Beneficent" and "wise" were the terms historian Theodore H. Hittell applied to the legislation making it possible. Critics have called it "unconditional surrender" to squatters and a "billion dollar steal." They point to Golden Gate Park as a silent reminder of all that is left of a wonderful heritage. It seems apparent, however, that San Francisco officials took a realistic view of a title situation that had become intolerable through no fault of their own. By their action they ended the era of squatter violence and made possible the orderly settlement and building up of the modern city.

Part of the title story of San Francisco also concerns the numerous adverse claims to its lands that were filed before the Board of Land Commissioners. These claims were either rejected or found to be fraudulent on appeal to the federal courts. They, too, helped to keep things unsettled and to interfere with the buying and selling of land. The fabulous claims of José Y. Limantour included most of the city, islands adjoining, and other property. When the Land Commission, finding the documents and testimony apparently in order, approved these claims in 1856, San Francisco was in an uproar. Some citizens rushed to get quitclaims from Limantour. Fears were quieted, however, when the district court found the purported grant from Governor Micheltorena covering the San Francisco area to be a forged document and that fraud and false testimony had been used extensively. So flagrant were the various Limantour claims that, in rejecting them, Judge Ogden Hoffman described the cases as being "without parallel in the judicial history of the country."

In the title story of California's southern metropolis, a city that has the largest population of any California city and one of the greatest areas of any city in the world, we turn from great court battles and squatter violence to activities that are more in keeping with the pastoral manner of living.

Los Angeles shares with San José the distinction of having been founded as one of the original Spanish pueblos in California and not as a presidio.

On August 1, 1852, Mayor John G. Nichols went before the Los Angeles Council to remind the members that the Land Commission would be meeting in the city in a few weeks. "We have but little time," he said "to procure from the archives in San Francisco the copies of such documents as may be needed. When we consider the value of the city claims amounting to not less than a million dollars it would seem only proper that some provision should be made for its protection to the utmost extent. I therefore recommend to the council early and efficient action." J. Lancaster Brent, attorney and Democratic leader, was engaged to represent the city, whose claim was filed with the board on October 26, 1852.

In submitting its case to the board, Los Angeles presented the history of its founding as a pueblo in 1781 under the specific directions of Governor Felipe de Neve, the giving of formal possession to the settlers four years later, the raising of the pueblo to the rank of city in 1835 by act of the Mexican Congress, and the incorporation on April 4, 1850, by an act of the state legislature which provided that the city should succeed to all the rights, claims, and powers of the pueblo with respect to property.

Los Angeles claimed not just four square leagues but, with a longing even then to be the biggest city, *sixteen* square leagues—or about 112 square miles. It interpreted the laws governing the establishment of a pueblo as meaning four leagues square rather than four square leagues, and based its interpretation on the language of the 1789 plan for the establishment of the town of Pitic in Sonora, which was cited, together with the governor's instructions in 1791 to the presidios to measure their "four common leagues" from the center of the presidio square.

The board was prepared to accept most of the assertions

in the petition, readily admitted that Los Angeles had been regularly incorporated and had been declared to be the capital of California on May 23, 1835, and that the city was in existence on the important date of July 7, 1846. The only disagreement was in the extent and limits of the city's claim.

Eminent citizens—Agustín Olvera, José Antonio Carrillo, Manuel Requena, Antonio F. Coronel—had made interesting and agreeable depositions, filled with references to rodeos, judges of the plains, Spanish place names, and rancho living. They unanimously understood that the boundaries of their town extended two leagues in each direction from the center of the plaza, but they could not recall that the common lands of the pueblo had ever been assigned or the designation of boundaries completed.

The opinion of the board, delivered by Commissioner Farwell, was that no foundation had been laid, by the evidence, for presuming an assignment to the city beyond the four square leagues to which it was entitled by law. On February 5, 1856, it confirmed Los Angeles' title to four square leagues only—one-fourth of what had been asked.

There were appeals to the District Court, and petitions for review filed by Brent, and, on behalf of the United States, by Pacificus Ord, brother of Surveyor Ord. On February 2, 1858, both sides signed and filed a stipulation accepting the board's decision as final.

Los Angeles had not waited for confirmation of title, not even for the legislative authority which came in 1850, before going ahead with the sale of its lands. In 1849 it had heeded an order issued by the military governor that no grants of unappropriated pueblo lands should be made without reference to the city map. It employed Lieutenant E. O. C. Ord of the United States Army to survey "the City of Los Angeles and to lay out streets and blocks, where there are no buildings, from the Church to the last house before the vineyard of Celis, and from the vineyards to the hills. . . . from the Church northerly to the ravine beyond the house of Antonio Ygnacio Abila." Ord, assisted by William R. Hutton, made his survey. The city's first auction of lots took place in November of 1849, the ayuntamiento having picked fifty-four to offer. Part of these lots were in the old "upper district"—that is, north of the plaza—in the blocks that were bounded by Bull, Eternity, Virgin, and Short streets. Part were in the new "lower district," south of the plaza and within the blocks bounded by Second, Fourth, Spring, and Hill streets. Buyers paid from fifty to two hundred dollars for lots having a width of 120 feet and a depth of 165 feet. The new district brought better prices than the old, for "business" had begun to move south. Purchasers included John Temple, Benjamin D. Wilson, and Francisco Figueroa.

So began the city's prodigal practice of raising its funds through selling its lands. Auction followed auction with purchasers paying cash and receiving city deeds executed by the president and secretary of the council.

The Ord map had included only the heart of the pueblo's four square leagues. It had been extensive in its covering of the vineyards, cornfields, and gardens that lay between Main Street and the Los Angeles River. It had laid out blocks as far south as unlabeled Pico Street, as far west as Grasshopper (Figueroa) Street, and almost as far north as the old cemetery. Many of the blocks shown had not been numbered or divided into lots. Accordingly, other surveyors were called upon to supplement Ord's work, notably Henry Hancock, George Hansen, A. F.

Waldemar, and Frank Lecouvreur, with the city council taking over the job of numbering Ord's unnumbered blocks and supplying street names.

As early as August 13, 1852, the city had passed an ordinance providing for the disposition of vacant city lands, with a limit of 35 acres to one person, the applicant obligated only to make two hundred dollars worth of improvements within a year. This ordinance was repealed in less than two years and another adopted which provided for putting up at public auction lands applied for, with a minimum bid of one dollar an acre for thirty-five-acre (Hancock's Survey) lots, and with a rising scale of minimum bids for smaller lots. Purchasers would receive a quitclaim from the mayor. On March 28, 1854, the city ceded "all the right she may have in favor of the persons who by themselves or their ancestors may have occupied them without interruption, peaceably and in good faith, for the term of twelve years, with house, fence or cultivation." Following this action there was confirmation of many old titles, for example, that of the tract in the city which Antonio Ygnacio Abila claimed to hold under grant from the governor made in 1817, later confirmed by the ayuntamiento in 1839. The city granted lands to various individuals and corporations for services rendered or conditional upon services being rendered—as to the Pioneer Oil Company for drilling for oil; to the Canal and Reservoir Company for constructing a ditch and a dam; to Phineas Banning for boring an artesian well, he to pay ten dollars an acre if successful. The largest of such grants was made in 1864 to O. W. Childs in payment for his construction of a new and important *zanja* or canal. He received practically all the blocks between Main, Figueroa, Sixth, and Twelfth streets, a stupendous conveyance of what is now called "down-town" property.

Los Angeles, like San Francisco, was successful in the rapid disposition of its patrimony. Today it has left Pershing Square, Elysian Park, and the old plaza.

Apparently there was little concern over the city's title at any time between 1849, when sales began, and 1856, when confirmation of pueblo ownership was obtained. Occasionally the mayor would ask Lancaster Brent about when action might be expected from the Land Commission, but aside from that the title situation in Los Angeles was serene. Everyone took it as a matter of course that the city's title was good. Squatter troubles were remote, too, though a few of the surrounding ranchos were to have difficulties of this sort before the United States or the surveyor general could get around to a settlement of their problems. The serenity of the land situation was due to the fact that gold seekers did not come to Los Angeles. Only the "backwash" from the Gold Rush came, and this consisted largely of gamblers who conducted their business from adobe buildings near the plaza. Here there was even more sin than sunshine, according to all contemporary accounts, with days and nights filled with the sounds of chinking fifty-dollar gold pieces, discordant music, and pistol shots, rather than the voices of men discussing the Los Angeles title situation.

After the title to Los Angeles' four square leagues had been confirmed, the boundaries had to be surveyed before a patent could be issued by the United States. Henry Hancock did the surveying in September, 1858. Conforming with it, a patent bearing the signature of President Andrew Johnson was issued by the United States on August 9, 1866. At first held invalid by the United States

Land Office, upon a technicality, with a new one being issued August 4, 1875, this 1866 patent was later upheld as the true and valid patent of the city's lands.

Long before Los Angeles concerned itself with its own title or with the United States at all, it was the center of California's cattle industry. It was surrounded with ranchos, several of them dating from the Spanish period. Practically the whole of what is now Los Angeles County, if we except part of the Santa Monica Mountains, part of the Mohave Desert, and the Angeles National Forest, was included in ranchos owned by Spanish Californians and by a few Anglo-Saxons who had become Mexican citizens. Beyond these county boundaries were the ranchos of other counties. The pueblo of Los Angeles was the hub of these ranchos, a trading center, and around its plaza, which was dominated by a church, were shops and the town houses of rancheros.

With confirmation of its pueblo title, Los Angeles continued to be the center of the "cow counties," and its geographical growth from that date was largely through the annexation of, or the consolidation with, areas that had rancho origins. This growth, however, did not mean that Los Angeles was acquiring the ownership of lands beyond its original pueblo boundaries. It merely acquired jurisdiction over annexed or consolidated territories, as these came within city limits.

There had been various changes in the boundaries of Los Angeles after the state legislature passed the act of incorporation on April 4, 1850, but on July 28, 1855, they had been fixed as including all lands belonging to the former pueblo. In 1859 the state authorized Los Angeles to extend itself 1,500 yards or less on any or all sides. Los Angeles availed itself of this opportunity and took in 400 yards on the south. This first annexation of August 29, 1859 is known as the "Southern Extension."

Los Angeles did not embark on its vast program of annexation and consolidation, however, until 1895, when the Highland Park area, adjoining the old pueblo boundaries on the northeast, became a part of the city and with it 904 more acres. Touching the high spots of the program, which was carried out, of course, at the request of the persons affected, expressed at the polls, the "Shoestring" annexation of 1906 should be mentioned. This annexation, together with the consolidation of Wilmington and San Pedro with Los Angeles in 1909, gave the city frontage on the ocean and a harbor. And then, as one writer said, Los Angeles dug a harbor "by its bootstraps" and filled it with world commerce. The Hollywood consolidation of 1910 is important, not only because it brought the motion-picture center within the city limits, but because it was the only action of this sort that brought in a lot of people. Hollywood came in because its population was becoming dense and it needed an outfall sewer and water from the Owens River basin, both of which Los Angeles could offer. Other areas and communities "joined up" for similar reasons. In 1913 water that had been brought 250 miles came plunging down the open aqueduct at San Fernando Reservoir, and two years later, on May 22, 1915, the greater part of the San Fernando Valley was annexed to Los Angeles. Since the aqueduct would not come to the city, the city had gone to the aqueduct. That single act brought nearly 170 square miles of new territory into the city, overwhelmingly the largest annexation. Sawtelle, Hyde Park, Eagle Rock, Venice, Watts, and Tujunga were among the towns that came in through the consolidation route. All had been communities that had sprung up on old ranchos. The bigger city offered what the small communities needed.

An important part of the saga of these annexations is the fact that Los Angeles upon its establishment as a pueblo had been entitled under Spanish law to certain water rights. These were prior or preferential rights in the waters of the Los Angeles River which passed through the pueblo boundaries—so far as these waters were necessary for the purposes of the town and the use of the townsmen. Los Angeles succeeded to all the pueblo rights and they expanded with the annexation of new territory. Rulings upon the water rights of the city were obtained from California's Supreme Court in the cases of Los Angeles *v.* Hunter and Los Angeles *v.* Pomeroy.

By 1945 ninety-five annexations or consolidations had given Los Angeles an area of more than 450 square miles. It had started out with 28! Among the ranchos contributing territory to the city's jurisdiction were the San Pedro, the Sausal Redondo, La Ballona, La Brea, Rincón de los Bueyes, Las Cienegas, Ex-Mission de San Fernando, El Encino, Providencia, and Los Felis—names that roll pleasantly off the tongue and carry us back to the pastoral age that flourished here before fifty-foot lots, stuccoed houses, filling stations, shops, food markets, and heavy automobile traffic filled the Los Angeles panorama.

The title story of San Francisco and Los Angeles from pueblo days as presented here is one of essential contrasts. If other phases of the rise and development of California's two greatest cities had been followed, however, there would be similarities: today both are on the march, both have the unlimited enthusiasm and energy of their citizens, and both have greater roles to play.

Appendixes

APPENDIX I

Boundary and Property Provisions of the Treaty of Guadalupe Hidalgo, 1848

The Treaty was signed at Guadalupe Hidalgo, February 2, 1848; ratifications were exchanged at Queretaro, May 30, 1848; and proclamation was made July 4, 1848.[1]

Article V.

Boundary line between the two republics established.

The boundary line between the two republics shall commence in the Gulf of Mexico, three leagues from land, opposite the mouth of the Rio Grande, otherwise called Rio Bravo del Norte, or opposite the mouth of its deepest branch, if it should have more than one branch emptying directly into the sea; from thence up the middle of that river, following the deepest channel, where it has more than one, to the point where it strikes the southern boundary of New Mexico; thence, westwardly, along the whole southern boundary of New Mexico (which runs north of the town called *Paso*) to its western termination; thence, northward, along the western line of New Mexico, until it intersects the first branch of the River Gila; (or if it should not intersect any branch of that river, then to the point on the said line nearest to such branch, and thence in a direct line to the same;) thence down the middle of the said branch and of the said river, until it empties into the Rio Colorado; thence across the Rio Colorado, following the division line between Upper and Lower California, to the Pacific Ocean.

Southern and western limits of New Mexico, as referred to in this article, defined.

The southern and western limits of New Mexico, mentioned in this article, are those laid down in the map entitled *"Map of the United Mexican States, as organized and defined by various acts of the Congress of said republic, and constructed according to the best authorities. Revised edition. Published at New York, in 1847, by J. Disturnell."* Of which map a copy is added to this treaty, bearing the signatures and seals of the undersigned plenipotentiaries. And, in order to preclude all difficulty in tracing upon the ground the limit separating Upper from Lower California, it is agreed that the said limit shall consist of a straight line drawn from the middle of the Rio Gila, where it unites with the Colorado, to a point on the coast of the Pacific Ocean distant one marine league due south of the southernmost point of the port

[1] The text is from the *U. S. Statutes at Large*, vol. 9, pp. 922 ff.

of San Diego, according to the plan of said port made in the year 1782 by Don Juan Pantoja, second sailing-master of the Spanish fleet, and published at Madrid in the year 1802, in the Atlas to the voyage of the schooners *Sutil* and *Mexicana*, of which plan a copy is hereunto added, signed and sealed by the respective plenipotentiaries.

A commissioner and surveyor to be appointed by each government to run and mark the boundary lines, who shall meet at San Diego within one year from exchange of ratifications.

In order to designate the boundary line with due precision, upon authoritative maps, and to establish upon the ground landmarks which shall show the limits of both republics, as described in the present article, the two governments shall each appoint a commissioner and a surveyor, who, before the expiration of one year from the date of the exchange of ratifications of this treaty, shall meet at the port of San Diego, and proceed to run and mark the said boundary in its whole course to the mouth of the Rio Bravo del Norte. They shall keep journals and make out plans of their operations; and the result agreed upon by them shall be deemed a part of this treaty, and shall have the same force as if it were inserted therein. The two governments will amicably agree regarding what may be necessary to these persons, and also as to their respective escorts, should such be necessary.

They shall keep journals, &c.

Boundary line to be religiously respected.

The boundary line established by this article shall be religiously respected by each of the two republics, and no change shall ever be made therein, except by the express and free consent of both nations, lawfully given by the general government of each, in conformity with its own constitution.

ARTICLE VIII.

Mexicans established in territories ceded to the United States to be free to continue where they are, or to remove at any time, retaining their property or disposing of the same at pleasure.

Mexicans now established in territories previously belonging to Mexico, and which remain for the future within the limits of the United States, as defined by the present treaty, shall be free to continue where they now reside, or to remove at any time to the Mexican republic, retaining the property which they possess in the said territories, or disposing thereof, and removing the proceeds wherever they please, without their being subjected, on this account, to any contribution, tax, or charge whatever.

Those who remain may either retain the title and rights of Mexican citizens or become citizens of the United States.

Election to be made within one year.

Those who shall prefer to remain in the said territories, may either retain the title and rights of Mexican citizens, or acquire those of citizens of the United States. But they shall be under the obligation to make their election within one year from the date of the exchange of ratifications of this treaty; and those who shall remain in the said territories after the expiration of that year, without having declared their intention to retain the character of Mexicans, shall be considered to have elected to become citizens of the United States.

Property to be inviolably respected.

In the said territories, property of every kind, now belonging to Mexicans not established there, shall be inviolably respected. The present owners, the heirs of these, and all Mexicans who may hereafter acquire said property by contract, shall enjoy with respect to it guaranties equally ample as if the same belonged to citizens of the United States.

ARTICLE IX.

How Mexicans remaining in the ceded territories may become citizens of the United States.

Mexicans who, in the territories aforesaid, shall not preserve the character of citizens of the Mexican republic, conformably with what is stipulated in the preceding article, shall be incorporated into the Union of the United States, and be admitted at the proper time (to be judged of by the Congress of the United States) to the enjoyment of all the rights of citizens of the United States, according to the principles of the constitution; and in the mean time shall be maintained and protected in the free enjoyment of their liberty and property, and secured in the free exercise of their religion without restriction.

APPENDIX II

ACT FOR THE ADMISSION OF CALIFORNIA INTO THE UNION
(Approved September 9, 1850)[1]

Preamble.

Whereas the people of California have presented a constitution and asked admission into the Union, which constitution was submitted to Congress by the President of the United States, by message dated February thirteenth, eighteen hundred and fifty, and which, on due examination, is found to be republican in its form of government:

California declared to be one of the United States.

Be it enacted by the Senate and House of Representatives of the United States of America in Congress assembled, That the State of California shall be one, and is hereby declared to be one, of the United States of America, and admitted into the Union on an equal footing with the original States in all respects whatever.

Entitled to two representatives until an enumeration is made.

SEC. 2. *And be it further enacted,* That, until the representatives in Congress shall be apportioned according to an actual enumeration of the inhabitants of the United States, the State of California shall be entitled to two representatives in Congress.

Admitted into the Union upon certain expressed conditions.

SEC. 3. *And be it further enacted,* That the said State of California is admitted into the Union upon the express condition that the people of said State, through their legislature or otherwise, shall never interfere with the primary disposal of the public lands within its limits, and shall pass no law and do no act whereby the title of the United States to, and right to dispose of, the same shall be impaired or questioned; and that they shall never lay any tax or assessment of any description whatsoever upon the public domain of the United States, and in no case shall non-resident proprietors, who are citizens of the United States, be taxed higher than residents; and that all the navigable waters within the said State shall be common highways, and forever free, as well to the inhabitants of said State as to the citizens of the United

Proviso.

States, without any tax, impost, or duty therefor: *Provided,* That nothing herein contained shall be construed as recognizing or rejecting the propositions tendered by the people of California as articles of compact in the ordinance adopted by the convention which formed the constitution of that State.

APPROVED, September 9, 1850.

---

[1] The text is from the *U. S. Statutes at Large,* vol. 9, p. 452. The following provision appears in an act approved September 28, 1850, *ibid.,* p. 521: "That all laws of the United States which are not locally inapplicable shall have the same force and effect within the said State of California as elsewhere within the United States."

APPENDIX III

ACT TO ASCERTAIN AND SETTLE THE PRIVATE LAND CLAIMS IN THE STATE OF CALIFORNIA

(Approved March 3, 1851)[1]

Commission constituted.

Be it enacted by the Senate and House of Representatives of the United States of America in Congress assembled, That for the purpose of ascertaining and settling private land claims in the State of California, a commission shall be, and is hereby, constituted, which shall consist of three commissioners, to be appointed by the President of the United States, by and with the advice and consent of the Senate, which commission shall continue for three years from the date of this act, unless sooner discontinued by the President of the United States.

Secretary.

Duties.

SEC. 2. *And be it further enacted,* That a secretary, skilled in the Spanish and English languages, shall be appointed by the said commissioners, whose duty it shall be to act as interpreter, and to keep a record of the proceedings of the board in a bound book, to be filed in the office of the Secretary of the Interior on the termination of the commission.

Clerks.

SEC. 3. *And be it further enacted,* That such clerks, not to exceed five in number, as may be necessary, shall be appointed by the said commissioners.

Agent for United States.

Duties.

Ante, p. 616.
Compensation.

Duties.

Notice of taking of depositions to be given to such agent.

SEC. 4. *And be it further enacted,* That it shall be lawful for the President of the United States to appoint an agent learned in the law, and skilled in the Spanish and English languages, whose special duty it shall be to superintend the interests of the United States in the premises, to continue him in such agency as long as the public interest may, in the judgment of the President, require his continuance, and to allow him such compensation as the President shall deem reasonable. It shall be the duty of the said agent to attend the meetings of the board, to collect testimony in behalf of the United States, and to attend on all occasions when the claimant, in any case before the board, shall take depositions; and no deposition taken by or in behalf of any such claimant shall be read in evidence in any case, whether before the commissioners, or before the District or Supreme Court of the United States, unless notice of the time and place of taking the same shall have been given in writing to said agent, or to the district attorney of the proper dis-

---

[1] The text is from the *U. S. Statutes at Large*, vol. 9, p. 631.

trict, so long before the time of taking the deposition as to enable him to be present at the time and place of taking the same, and like notice shall be given of the time and place of taking any deposition on the part of the United States.

SEC. 5. *And be it further enacted,* That the said commissioners shall hold their sessions at such times and places as the President of the United States shall direct, of which they shall give due and public notice; and the

marshal of the district in which the board is sitting shall appoint a deputy, whose duty it shall be to attend upon the said board, and who shall receive the same compensation as is allowed to the marshal for his attendance upon the District Court.

SEC. 6. *And be it further enacted,* That the said commissioners, when sitting as a board, and each commissioner at his chambers, shall be, and are, and is hereby, authorized to administer oaths, and to examine witnesses in any case pending before the commissioners, that all such testimony shall be taken in writing, and shall be recorded and preserved in bound books to be provided for that purpose.

SEC. 7. *And be it further enacted,* That the secretary of the board shall be, and he is hereby, authorized and required, on the application of the law agent or district attorney of the United States, or of any claimant or his counsel, to issue writs of subpœna commanding the attendance of a witness or witnesses before the said board or any commissioner.

SEC. 8. *And be it further enacted,* That each and every person claiming lands in California by virtue of any right or title derived from the Spanish or Mexican government, shall present the same to the said commissioners when sitting as a board, together with such documentary evidence and testimony of witnesses as the said claimant relies upon in support of such claims; and

it shall be the duty of the commissioners, when the case is ready for hearing, to proceed promptly to examine the same upon such evidence, and upon the evidence produced in behalf of the United States, and to decide upon the validity of the said claim, and, within thirty days after such decision is rendered, to certify the same, with the reasons on which it is founded, to the district attorney of the United States in and for the district in which such decision shall be rendered.

SEC. 9. *And be it further enacted,* That in all cases of the rejection or confirmation of any claim by the board of commissioners, it shall and may be lawful for the claimant or the district attorney, in behalf of the United States, to present a petition to the District Court of the district in which the land claimed is situated, praying the said court to review the decision of the said commissioners, and to decide on the validity of such claim; and such petition, if presented by the claimant, shall set forth fully the nature of the claim and the names of the original and present claimants, and shall contain a deraignment of the claimant's title, together with a transcript of the report of the board of commissioners, and

Form of petition.

of the documentary evidence and testimony of the witnesses on which it was founded; and such petition, if presented by the district attorney in behalf of the United States, shall be accompanied by a transcript of the report of the board of commissioners, and of the papers and evidence on which it was founded, and shall fully and distinctly set forth the grounds on which the said claim is alleged to be invalid, a copy of which petition, if the same shall be presented by a claimant, shall be served on the district attorney of the United States, and, if presented in behalf of the United States, shall be served on the claimant or his attorney; and the party upon whom such service shall be made shall be bound to answer the

Answers to petitions.

same within a time to be prescribed by the judge of the District Court; and the answer of the claimant to such petition shall set forth fully the nature of the claim, and the names of the original and present claimants, and shall contain a deraignment of the claimant's title; and the answer of the district attorney in behalf of the United States shall fully and distinctly set forth the grounds on which the said claim is alleged to be invalid, copies of which answers shall be served upon the adverse party thirty days before the meeting of the court, and thereupon, at the first term of the court thereafter, the said case shall stand for trial, unless, on cause shown, the same shall be continued by the court.

Proceedings thereon.

SEC. 10. *And be it further enacted,* That the District Court shall proceed to render judgment upon the pleadings and evidence in the case, and upon such further evidence as may be taken by order of the said court, and shall, on application of the party against whom judg-

Appeal to Supreme Court.

ment is rendered, grant an appeal to the Supreme Court of the United States, on such security for costs in the District and Supreme Court, in case the judgment of the District Court shall be affirmed, as the said court shall

Security for costs.

prescribe; and if the court shall be satisfied that the party desiring to appeal is unable to give such security, the appeal may be allowed without security.

On what principles
commissioners are
to act.

SEC. 11. *And be it further enacted,* That the comis-
sioners herein-provided for, and the District and Supreme Courts, in deciding on the validity of any claim
brought before them under the provisions of this act,
shall be governed by the treaty of Guadaloupe Hidalgo,
the law of nations, the laws, usages, and customs of the
government from which the claim is derived, the principles of equity, and the decisions of the Supreme Court
of the United States, so far as they are applicable.

Proceedings to
authorize petition
to District Court.

SEC. 12. *And be it further enacted,* That to entitle
either party to a review of the proceedings and decision
of the commissioners hereinbefore provided for, notice
of the intention of such party to file a petition to the
District Court shall be entered on the journal or record
of proceedings of the commissioners within sixty days
after their decision on the claim has been made and
notified to the parties, and such petition shall be filed
in the District Court within six months after such decision has been rendered.

All lands in Cali-
fornia to which
claims are not
established to be
taken as public
lands.

SEC. 13. *And be in further enacted,* That all lands, the
claims to which have been finally rejected by the commissioners in manner herein provided, or which shall
be finally decided to be invalid by the District or Supreme Court, and all lands the claims to which shall not
have been presented to the said commissioners within
two years after the date of this act, shall be deemed,
held, and considered as part of the public domain of
the United States; and for all claims finally confirmed

Patent to issue for
lands, claims to
which are con-
firmed.

by the said commissioners, or by the said District or
Supreme Court, a patent shall issue to the claimant
upon his presenting to the general land office an authentic certificate of such confirmation, and a plat or
survey of the said land, duly certified and approved by
the surveyor-general of California, whose duty it shall
be to cause all private claims which shall be finally con-

Location and
survey of claims.

firmed to be accurately surveyed, and to furnish plats
of the same; and in the location of the said claims, the
said surveyor-general shall have the same power and
authority as are conferred on the register of the land
office and receiver of the public moneys of Louisiana, by
the sixth section of the act "to create the office of surveyor of the public lands for the State of Louisiana,"
approved third March, one thousand eight hundred and

1831, ch. 116.
Provision where
a claim is contested
by some other
person.

thirty-one: *Provided, always,* That if the title of the
claimant to such lands shall be contested by any other
person, it shall and may be lawful for such person to
present a petition to the district judge of the United
States for the district in which the lands are situated,

plainly and distinctly setting forth his title thereto, and praying the said judge to hear and determine the same, a copy of which petition shall be served upon the adverse party thirty days before the time appointed for hearing the same. *And provided, further,* That it shall and may

be lawful for the district judge of the United States, upon the hearing of such petition, to grant an injunction to restrain the party at whose instance the claim to the said lands has been confirmed, from suing out a patent for the same, until the title thereto shall have been finally decided, a copy of which order shall be transmitted to the commissioner of the general land office, and thereupon no patent shall issue until such decision shall be made, or until sufficient time shall, in the opinion of the said judge, have been allowed for obtaining the same; and thereafter the said injunction shall be dissolved.

SEC. 14. *And be in further enacted,* That the provisions of this act shall not extend to any town lot, farm lot, or pasture lot, held under a grant from any corporation or town to which lands may have been granted for the establishment of a town by the Spanish or Mexican government, or the lawful authorities thereof, nor to any city, or town, or village lot, which city, town, or vil-

lage existed on the seventh day of July, eighteen hundred and forty-six; but the claim for the same shall be presented by the corporate authorities of the said town, or where the land on which the said city, town, or village was originally granted to an individual, the claim shall be presented by or in the name of such individual, and the fact of the existence of the said city, town, or village on the said seventh July, eighteen hundred and forty-six, being duly proved, shall be prima facie evidence of a grant to such corporation, or to the individual under whom the said lotholders claim; and where any city, town, or village shall be in existence at the time of passing this act, the claim for the land embraced within the limits of the same may be made by the corporate authority of the said city, town, or village.

SEC. 15. *And be in further enacted,* That the final decrees rendered by the said commissioners, or by the District or Supreme Court of the United States, or any patent to be issued under this act, shall be conclusive between the United States and the said claimants only, and shall not affect the interests of third persons.

SEC. 16. *And be in further enacted,* That it shall be the duty of the commissioners herein provided for to ascertain and report to the Secretary of the Interior the tenure by which the mission lands are held, and those held by civilized Indians, and those who are engaged in agriculture or labor of any kind, and also those which are occupied and cultivated by Pueblos or Rancheros Indians.

Compensation.
Commissioners.

Secretary.

Clerks.

SEC. 17. *And be it further enacted,* That each commissioner appointed under this act shall be allowed and paid at the rate of six thousand dollars per annum; that the secretary of the commissioners shall be allowed and paid at the rate of four thousand dollars per annum; and the clerks herein provided for shall be allowed and paid at the rate of one thousand five hundred dollars per annum; the aforesaid salaries to commence from the day of the notification by the commissioners of the first meeting of the board.

Secretary to receive
no fees except in
certain cases.

SEC. 18. *And be it further enacted,* That the secretary of the board shall receive no fee except for furnishing certified copies of any paper or record, and for issuing writs of subpœna. For furnishing certified copies of any paper or record, he shall receive twenty cents for every hundred words, and for issuing writs of subpœna, fifty cents for each witness; which fees shall be equally divided between the said secretary and the assistant clerk.

APPROVED, March 3, 1851.

Bibliography

LAND TENURE AND LAND CLAIMS OF INDIANS

THE GENERAL subject of land tenure among the American Indians is discussed in *Handbook of American Indians North of Mexico*, Bulletin 30, Smithsonian Institution, Bureau of American Ethnology, Washington, D.C. (1907–1910), edited by Frederick Webb Hodge. For a specific account of the ideas upon real property ownership that prevailed among the various tribes and groups of California Indians, consult *Handbook of the Indians of California* (1925), by A. L. Kroeber. S. F. Cook's *The Conflict Between The California Indian and White Civilization* (1943), an analysis of the tragic extermination of a race, also has a bearing on the subject of land titles.

Indian Land Cessions in the United States, by Charles C. Royce (in the 18th Annual Report of the American Institute of Ethnology) contains a year-by-year account of what lands the Indians of California gave up to the United States and what were set aside for them between 1851 and 1894. Daniel M. Greene's *Public Land Statutes of the United States* (1931) continues the listing of cessions to 1931. See also the subject of "Indians" in the *United States Code*.

William Carey Jones' report on land titles, in Senate Ex. Doc. No. 18, 31st Cong., 1st sess., 1850, and *The Colonial History of San Francisco* by John W. Dwinelle (1863), have information on the provisions in Spanish law relating to Indian rights in land and to Indian pueblos. So, too, *Land Commission Case No. 3,* involving Archibald Ritchie's claim to Rancho Suisun granted in 1842 to an Indian, Francisco Solano, which reviews Indian rights to own land in California.

Joseph J. Hills' *The History of Warner's Ranch And Its Environs* (1927) tells the story of the struggle of one Indian group to hold title to its land. *History and Proposed Settlement Claims of California Indians* by Robert W. Kenny, Attorney General of California (1944), is an important compilation. For a summary of the bewildering multiplicity of present-day laws governing Indians in the United States, see Felix S. Cohen's *Handbook of Federal Indian Law* (1945).

Annual reports of the Commissioner of Indian Affairs should be consulted. C. E. Kelsey's *Report of the Special Agent for California to the Commissioner of Indian Affairs, March 21, 1906,* is a first-hand account of land allotments, community ownership, and reservations. Warren K. Moorhead's *The American Indian in the United States* (1914) has pertinent data, along with John Collier's *The Indian of the Americas* (1947). Frances E. Watkins tells the story of the *Sequoya League* in *The Quarterly* of the Historical Society of Southern California for June-September, 1944.

The unhappy story of the California Indians, with indirect bearing on the subject of their title to land, has been told by many writers from Benjamin Davis Wilson, in his "Report as United States Indian Agent, Southern District, 1853," printed later in the Los Angeles *Star,* and J. Ross Browne, who was appointed Inspector of Indian Affairs on the Pacific Coast in 1855, down to the present time. Important material appears, of course, in Hubert Howe Bancroft's *History of California* and *The Native Races,* as well as in the works of Helen Hunt Jackson, Abbot Kinney, and Charles F. Lummis.

MISSION TITLES

Books about the missions of California are many, but they go little into titles or claims to land. For this latter, the report of William Carey Jones in Senate Ex. Doc. No. 18 (1850) should be read, along with the proceedings in *Land Commission Case No. 609* involving the claim of Archbishop Alemany on behalf of the Church (District Court Cases Nos. 425, N.D., and 388, S.D.), together with John W. Dwinelle's *The Colonial History of San Francisco* (1863), as well as Hubert Howe Bancroft's *History of California* and Theodore H. Hittell's *History of California.* All of these sources and histories consider the nature of mission titles under Spanish law. See, too, the comment and rulings of the California Supreme Court during its October term, 1856, in the case of Nobili *v.* Redman (6 Cal. 325). The story of secularization and of the later disposition of mission lands is to be found in Dwinelle, Bancroft, Hittell, and in H. W. Halleck's report in House Ex. Doc. No. 17 (1850). A good source, too, is Volume 12 of Henry E. Wills' *California Titles,* collected pamphlet material on deposit in the Huntington Library, San Marino. Another useful source is Charles Anthony (Zephyrin) Engelhardt's *The Missions and Missionaries of California* (1908–1915), together with his individual histories of the missions.

PRESIDIO AND PUEBLO TITLES

Information about presidio and pueblo titles, like mission titles, can be found both in histories and in the proceedings of law courts. A most satisfactory reference on the subject is the much thumbed *The Colonial History of San Francisco* (1863) by John W. Dwinelle. It carries, in Spanish and English, those Spanish laws—from the Laws of the Indies—which assigned four square leagues to each organized pueblo, together with a wealth of basic material about the titles of presidios and pueblos. Along with the case of Hart *v.* Burnett (15 Cal. 530), it presents San Francisco's claim to a pueblo's four square leagues. The nature of the title held by a pueblo is revealed in that law suit and also in Welch *v.* Sullivan (8 Cal. 165), San Francisco *v.* Canavan (42 Cal. 541), and City of Monterey *v.* Jacks (139 Cal. 542). *Land Titles in San Francisco* (1860), by "a member of the California Bar," concerned with the Hart *v.* Burnett and the Holliday *v.* Frisbie cases, has extracts from the Laws of the Indies and from Mexican law on pueblo titles. The standard histories of California, beginning with Bancroft, also tell something of the title story of presidios and pueblos, as well as much about their beginnings and their development. San Francisco's first days are revealed in several volumes edited or written by Herbert Eugene Bolton: *Historical Memoirs of New California* (1926); *Anza's California Expeditions* (1930), *Outpost of Empire* (1931), and *Font's Complete Diary* (1933). Los Angeles data can be found in Volume XV of the annual publications of the Historical Society of Southern California, commemorating the 150th anniversary (in 1931) of the founding of Los Angeles. See also *The History of San José* by Frederic Hall (1871). City Council minutes and ordinances are a helpful source. William M. Caswell's *Revised Charter and Compiled Ordinances and Resolutions of the City of Los Angeles* (1878) is especially useful in Los Angeles' title history. Also the Los Angeles City Engineer's map showing territory annexed and data about annexations, together with the explanatory manuscript *History of the Formation of the City of Los Angeles* by John R. Prince. O. A. Rouleau's "History of Land Titles in San Francisco," an unpublished manuscript, the property of the Title Insurance and Guarantee Company, San Francisco, is an important compilation.

Translations from the Laws of the Indies are included in Joseph M. White's *A New Collection of Laws, Charters and Local Ordinances of the Governments of Great Britain, France and Spain* (1839). Frederic Hall's *The Laws of Mexico* (1885) also is an important summary.

RANCHO TITLES AND THE LAND COMMISSION

A wealth of material, general and specific, about the acquisition of title to ranchos during the Spanish and Mexican periods, as well as an account of the activities of the United States Land Commission, is uncovered in a volume-by-volume perusal of Bancroft's seven volumes and Hittell's four volumes on the history of California. Bancroft is the most rewarding of all the historians on the subject of ranchos and land titles, though every California historian gives substantial space to this topic. John Walton Caughey has successfully summarized it in less than fifteen pages in his *California* (1940).

The most important economic and social study of the rancho period is *Cattle on a Thousand Hills* (1941) by Robert Glass Cleland. Although concerned largely with the southern California ranchos, and with concentration on the Stearns group, it presents an over-all picture, beginning with the land concessions of 1784 and gives considerable space to grants, titles, the Act of 1851, and the Land Commission, as well as offering a general picture of life on the ranchos.

The sources on the subject, drawn upon by all the historians, are the reports of Jones and of Halleck already referred to. These reports present the first adequate assemblage in English of the Spanish and Mexican laws bearing on the subject of land titles in California. To them may be added

John W. Dwinelle's invaluable material in *The Colonial History of San Francisco*. The third edition (1866) has the largest amount of supplemental documents and data. Alfred Wheeler's *Land Titles in San Francisco and The Laws Affecting The Same* (1852) should also be added. Wheeler's book is largely a listing of land grants within San Francisco's limits, but it presents summaries of the author's research in the Laws of the Indies and in other sources.

Land Commission and court proceedings involving individual ranchos, together with other court proceedings and decrees, state and federal, are primary source material, of course, but they cannot well be enumerated here. So, too, original Spanish and Mexican archives material in the National Archives, Washington, D.C., and copies available in the Capitol Building, Sacramento, in the Bancroft Library, Berkeley, and in the office of the United States District Court, San Francisco.

For a listing of claims before the Land Commission, consult the appendix in Ogden Hoffman's *Report of Land Cases Determined in the United States District Court for the Northern District of California* (1862). This table of claims gives information about each claim's origin, as well as the commission and court case numbers, thus enabling the investigator to get off to a good start when "running down" any particular rancho. A revision of this Hoffman index was made by J. N. Bowman in 1941, his "Private Land Cases" a manuscript available in the Bancroft Library, Berkeley, as well as in the office of the United States District Court, San Francisco. Dr. Bowman has also compiled an "Index of California Private Land Grants and Private Land Grant Papers" (1942), also in manuscript. Several early-day indexes to land grants and a one-volume *Index to Land Cases* were among the records transferred in 1937 to The National Archives, Washington, D.C. (See March, 1944, issue of *The Quarterly* of the Historical Society of Southern California.)

Various official lists of private land grants, mostly ranchos, have been published, none of them entirely perfect. At an early date the maps of California issued by the United States Department of the Interior showed the location of these grants together with a marginal listing of them. This practice has been continued, the latest being the 1944 map, which presents a numerical and an alphabetical list of 544 land grants. The numbers assist the investigator to find the rancho on the map. (This government list is reproduced in W. W. Robinson's *Ranchos Become Cities* (1939), along with a list of the private land grants within the present boundaries of Los Angeles County, and an account of the granting of the first ranchos in the state as disclosed by Land Commission proceedings.) The State of California has also issued its lists, in the reports of the surveyor general. These include the names of the ranchos or grants, the area, the location, and usually the confirmee of each. Since the latest list of the state was made on February 25, 1886, when many of the cases were still pending in the courts, the list is necessarily incomplete.

San Diego County ranchos are covered in *A History of the Ranchos* of San Diego County, California (1939), by R. W. Brackett, and a compilation by Roscoe D. Wyatt, *Names and Places of Interest in San Mateo County,* made in 1936, gives information about some of the ranchos in that county. Brief summaries of the stories of many ranchos throughout the state are to be found in Phil Townsend Hanna's *The Dictionary of California Land Names* (1946) and in Mildred Brooke Hoover's and H. E. and E. G. Rensch's *Historic Spots in California* (1948), the latter with emphasis on the northern counties. County histories and volumes in the American Guide Series should also be consulted.

Many publications have told the story of particular ranchos. Examples: *Heritage of the Valley, San Bernardino's First Century* (1939), by George William Beattie and Helen Pruitt Beattie; *The Place Called Sespe* (1939), by Robert Glass Cleland; *Ranchos Become Cities* (1939), for Los Angeles County ranchos, by W. W. Robinson; *Caminos Viejos* (1930), by Terry E. Stephenson, together with the publications of the Orange County Historical Society and the writings of William W. McPherson for Orange County ranchos; *The Story of El Tejon* (1942), by Helen S. Giffin and Arthur Woodward; *The Salinas* (1945) by Anne B. Fisher; *From Cowhides to Golden Fleece* (1946) by Reuben L. Underhill, and *One Hun-*

dred Years in the Pajaro Valley (1934), by F. M. Atkinson. A good portrayal of the ranchos of California and New Mexico is to be found in *Shepherd's Empire* (1945), by Charles Wayland Towne and Edward Norris Wentworth. Popular treatment of the rancho theme is to be found in *Romance and History of California Ranchos* (1935), by Myrtle Garrison, and *Romance of the Ranchos* (1939), by Palmer Conner.

An unmatched collection of early pamphlet material on land titles and the Land Commission is in the nineteen volumes of Henry E. Wills' *California Titles,* deposited in the Huntington Library, San Marino. This material originated, apparently, in the early-day law office of the San Francisco firm of Halleck, Peachy, and Billings.

A good summary of the land grant, Land Commission, story is William W. Morrow's pamphlet, *Spanish and Mexican Private Land Grants* (1923), as is also Senate Report No. 426, 72d Cong., 1st sess., issued in pamphlet form in 1932. The *Memoirs of Elisha Oscar Crosby* (1945) has pertinent comment about the Land Commission. Henry George expresses his views in *Our Land Policy, National and State* (1874). Good source material is to be found in *Speeches of Mr. Gwin, of California, in the Senate of the United States, on Private Land Titles in The State of California* (1851), and in William Carey Jones' *Letters in Review of Attorney General Black's Report to the President of the United States on the subject of Land Titles in California* (1860). Thomas Donaldson's *The Public Domain* (1884) gives a brief account of private land claims in California. Alfred Chandler in *Land Title Origins* (1945) gives one short chapter to California.

For the Mexican period, there is Eugene B. Drake's compilation, published in 1861 at San Francisco, covering, as stated on the title page: *Jimeno's and Hartnell's Indexes of Land Concessions, From 1830 to 1846; Also Toma de Razon, or Registry of Titles, For 1844–45; Approvals of Land Grants by the Territorial and Departmental Assembly of California, From 1835 to 1846, and A List of Unclaimed Grants Compiled from the Spanish Archives in the U. S. Surveyor-General's Office.* Jones' report in Senate Ex. Doc. No. 18, already referred to, lists private grants as recorded in the archives at

Monterey. A list and description of the grants made by Manuel Micheltorena while governor of California from 1843 to 1845 are in *Land Grants in Upper California* (San Francisco, 1858).

SQUATTERISM

The squatter riots and squatter troubles that came with the Gold Rush and continued for another twenty years receive due space from California historians. Hittell, for example, gives one chapter in the third volume of his *History of California* to the subject. Bancroft presents numerous squatter incidents. County and local histories are sprinkled with stories of violence arising out of squatterism and the unsettled land titles of the early days of the American occupation. So, too, personal accounts, like William Heath Davis' *Seventy-five Years in California* (1929). Local squatter problems have a place in Rockwell D. Hunt's *John Bidwell* (1942), in C. C. Baker's article on Henry Dalton in the 1917 publication of the Historical Society of Southern California, in Reuben L. Underhill's *From Cowhides To Golden Fleece* (1939 and 1946), in George William Beattie's and Helen Pruitt Beattie's *Heritage of the Valley* (1939), to name but a few publications.

Attention is focused on the causes of early-day squatterism in William H. Brewer's *Up and Down California in 1860–64* (1930), in Robert Glass Cleland's *The Cattle on a Thousand Hills* (1941), and in Henry George's *Our Land and Land Policy* (1871).

The chapters, "Some Call It Eden" and "Who Owns California," in Oliver Carlson's *A Mirror for Californians* (1941) throw light on early-day and more recent difficulties, along with Carey McWilliams' *Factories in the Field* (1939). John Steinbeck's novel *The Grapes of Wrath* (1939) has a bearing on present-day squatting.

Newspaper files are a source of information about squatters actually on the land. Consult the Los Angeles *Times* for October 21, 22, 28; November 1, 1897; January 11, 1901; April, 1929; and July 25, 1937, for accounts of modern squatting in California. In this connection, Senate Report No. 426 is important.

Spokesmen for those who, in recent years, have believed California land grants to be invalid and for those who, accordingly, settled upon various Los Angeles County and Orange County ranchos, include Clinton Johnson in his *Fraudulent California Land Grants* (1926); H. N. Wheeler in the pamphlet series issued during or about 1931 under the general title of *Mexican Grant or United States Public Domain?* and in the pamphlet *California Lands* (1933); the editor of *Facts,* a weekly paper published in 1932 in Los Angeles; Williamson S. Summers, in his *In the Matter of the Application to Homestead Certain Land in Los Angeles County, California* (1926), and in his testimony before the Committee on Public Lands and Surveys, United States Senate, disclosed in *Mexican Land Grants* issued in 1927 by the Government Printing Office, Washington, D.C.

MINING TITLES

Required reading on the subject of mining titles would include Gregory Yale's *Legal Titles to Mining Claims and Water Rights, in California, Under The Mining Law of Congress, of July 1866* (1867), Charles Howard Shinn's *Mining Camps, A Study in American Frontier Government* (1885 and 1947), and Bancroft's *History of California* and *California Inter Pocula.* Thomas Donaldson's *The Public Domain* (1884) gives a brief account of local mining laws and the development of mining legislation. Also to be consulted are the mining laws of the United States as set forth in *United States Revised Statutes,* Sections 2318 to 2346, together with government-issued regulations thereunder relative to the reservation, exploration, location, possession, purchase, and patenting of mineral lands in the public domain. See *Public Land Statutes of the United States,* as compiled in 1931 by Daniel M. Greene, also the subject of "Mineral Lands and Mining" in the *United States Code,* and also the provisions of California law regarding mining claims in Section 1426 *et seq.* in *The Civil Code of the State of California.* O. A. Rouleau's "Mining Law in California," (property of Title Insurance and Guarantee Company, San Francisco) is a valuable summary. Important California Supreme Court rulings to be found in 17 Cal. 200 (Moore *v.* Smaw and Fremont *v.* Flaver), set forth the ownership of minerals in California under Mexican and American law.

Idwal Jones' *Vermilion* (1947), three-generation novel with a setting of a California quicksilver mine (suggested by the New Almaden) is pertinent. On-the-spot descriptions of mining are given by J. H. Carson in his *Early Recollections of the Mines and a Description of the Great Tulare Valley* (1852) and by Daniel B. Woods in his *Sixteen Months at the Gold Diggings* (1851).

John A. Rockwell's *A Compilation of Spanish and Mexican Law, in Relation to Mines, and Titles to Real Estate, in force in California, Texas and New Mexico* (1851) covers mining titles before California became a part of the United States, and the appendix has important material on early California titles in general.

PUBLIC LANDS, STATE LANDS

For a general as well as a specific consideration of all the topics embraced in the broad subject of public lands or public domain, the two most useful books are Thomas Donaldson's *The Public Domain,* issued by the Government Printing Office at Washington in 1884, and Benjamin Horace Hibbard's *A History of Public Land Policies* (1924). A third interesting treatment of the whole subject and one that is more nearly up to date is *Our Landed Heritage—The Public Domain,* by Roy M. Robbins, issued in 1942 by Princeton University Press. For a convenient reference to the innumerable acts of Congress disposing of the public domain there is Daniel M. Greene's compilation made in 1931, *Public Land Statutes of the United States.* The annual reports of the Commissioner of the General Land Office and, now, of the Director of the Bureau of Land Management, are mines of statistical and other important data. Bulletins also issuing from these offices are useful; for example, *Bulletin No. 3* (reprint 1944) on "Homesteading in Continental United States," and another, dated January, 1945, on "Vacant Public Lands." *Land of the Free* issued from the General Land Office by Fred W. Johnson, Commissioner, is a short, illus-

trated summary of the story of the public domain. The public
land laws of general interest are now published in the *United
States Code*. Necessary information about surveying and
mapping the public domain (all about townships, ranges, sections and the history of the system of rectangular surveys) is
to be found in the government's *Manual of Instructions for
the Survey of the Public Lands of the United States* and in
the popular treatment given the subject in 1944 by David
Greenhood in his *Down to Earth: Mapping for Everybody*.

Railroad titles are discussed in the general books on the
public domain already listed, in the standard histories of
California, in Nelson Trottman's *History of the Union Pacific* (1923), and, specifically, in the various acts of Congress
creating them. The most important of the Congressional acts
granting titles to railroads are in the *Statutes at Large:* 12
Stat. 489, amended 13 *stat.* 356 (Union Pacific and Central
Pacific); 14 *Stat.* 239, 15 *Stat.* 80, 16 *Stat.* 47, 39 *Stat.* 218, 40
Stat. 593 (Oregon and Pacific Railroad); 14 *Stat.* 292, 16 *Stat.*
382, 16 *Stat.* 573, 579, 24 *Stat.* 123 (Atlantic and Pacific, Southern Pacific); 18 *Stat.* 482 (any railroad company); and 35
Stat. 647, 42 *Stat.* 414 (forfeiture and abandonment). An important United States Supreme Court decision, holding that
an exception or reservation in a patent without statutory
authority is void and that the excepted matter will nevertheless pass to the patentee, is to be found in 234 U. S. 669 (Burke
v. Southern Pacific Railroad Company). Books about railroad
companies are legion, but they have little to add to the subject of railroad titles. The "Battle of Mussel Slough," given
emphasis because it offered real drama, is described in Oscar
Lewis' *The Big Four* (1938), furnishes inspiration for two
novels: *The Octopus* (1901), by Frank Norris, and *The Feud
of Oakfield Creek* (1887), by Josiah Royce. It is also the subject of an article, "Notable Memorials to Mussel Slough," by
Irving McKee, in the February, 1948, issue of *The Pacific
Historical Review*. A slight reference to railroad titles occurs
in *Santa Fe* (1945) by James Marshall.

The settlement of the public lands of California was made
possible by various acts of Congress and of the state legislature. The title story of these lands is revealed, therefore, not

only by such authorities and commentators as Donaldson, Hibbard, and Robbins, already cited, but by the statutes themselves. In connection with federal townsites, the Act of May 23, 1844, is found in *United States Statutes at Large,* Volume V, p. 657. The desert land act applicable to Lassen County is in Volume XVIII, p. 497, of these statutes. Otherwise, Greene's convenient compilation of public land statutes, with an index to statutes and to subjects, will be found to cover adequately the federal statutes involving federal townsites, preëmptions, homesteads, timber culture laws, desert land laws, the Timber and Stone Act, military bounty land warrants, land scrip, railroad grants, national forests, forest lieu selections, national parks, national monuments, and lands granted to the State of California. See Robbins for the story of the Taylor Grazing Act of 1934. In connection with Valentine land scrip, see the article entitled "The Strange Case of Thomas Valentine," by W. W. Robinson, appearing in *Westways,* March, 1946. Summaries of federal and state laws and court decisions involving lands originating in the public domain and lands owned or claimed by the state make up O. A. Rouleau's "Public Lands of the United States Other Than Those Granted to the States," his "Public Lands of State—School Land Grants," his "Title to Tide Lands," and his "Title of the State to Swamp and Overflowed Lands," manuscript volumes in the possession of Title Insurance and Guarantee Company, San Francisco.

The Cattle King (1931), by Edward F. Treadwell, telling the story of Henry Miller, of Miller and Lux fame, and *Factories in the Field* (1939), by Carey McWilliams, already referred to, and concerned primarily with industrialized farming, have sidelights on titles to public and state lands in California.

Recent court battles over tidelands and submerged lands, culminating in the United States Supreme Court action of United States of America *v.* State of California, resulted in the assemblage by opposing counsel of a large body of historical material on the history and use of such lands in California and elsewhere. Outstanding are the *Answer of State of California* (1946), by Attorney General Robert W. Kenney, the

Brief for the State of California in Opposition to Motion for Judgment (1947), by Attorney General Fred N. Howser, Assistant Attorney General William W. Clary, Assistant Attorney General C. Roy Smith, *Counsel* (Homer Cummings, Max O'Rell Truitt, Louis W. Meyers, Jackson W. Chance, Sidney H. Wall, *of Counsel*), and the *Brief for the United States in Support of Motion for Judgment* (1947), by Attorney General Tom C. Clark and Special Assistant to the Attorney General Arnold Raum. An article in the *Los Angeles Bar Bulletin,* February, 1946, entitled "The Submerged Lands Controversy," by William W. Clary, gives the background and a condensed history of the dispute. Two booklets—Sheridan Downey's *Truth About The Tidelands* (1948) and Fred N. Howser's *This Can Happen To Any State* (1948)—are pointed summaries of the current situation.

The Civil Code, Code of Civil Procedure, and Public Resources Code, as well as the Constitution of the State of California, are sources of information about state ownership and state acquisition, use and disposition of land.

RECORDING, REGISTRATION, AND INSURANCE OF TITLES

Land Title Assuring Agencies in the United State (1937), by Daniel D. Gage, is an adequate handling of the historical and economic aspects of the American recording system, abstracts and certificates of title, and the rise of title insurance, including state title insurance. It is a pioneer in the field, with a value that is enhanced by an extensive bibliography. Briefer consideration of some of the same topics is to be found in the chapters entitled "Escrows," "Land Title History—Recording System," and "Title Insurance" in Melvin B. Ogden's *Escrow and Land Title Law in California* (1938), and in the chapter "Titles to Real Property," by James E. Sheridan, appearing in *Handbook of Real Estate* (Prentice-Hall, Inc., 1947). *Pinning Down Your Property* (1936), by Edmund D. Pitts and published by the California Land Title Association, is a popular treatment of the subject of title protection, and T. W. Haymond's "Title Insurance Risks of Which the Public Records Give No Notice," appearing in *Southern California Law Review,* July and December, 1928, and Lawrence L.

Otis' "What Protection *Is* Title Insurance," published in the *Los Angeles Bar Bulletin*, December, 1946, are technical analyses. "How California Went Title Insurance Over Night," by James R. Ford, in *Title News* for November, 1932, is a historical item. Cardinal Goodwin's *The Establishment of State Government in California—1846–1850* (1914) is widely useful.

In *Torrens Titles and Title Insurance,* reprinted from the *University of Pennsylvania Law Review* of April, 1937, Edward H. Cushman offers a short history and analysis of both. Other pamphlet material on the registration of titles includes the *Report of the Commission for the Purpose of Examining the Torrens Land Transfer Act of Australia* (Sacramento, 1895); *Registration of Titles to Real Estate in Massachusetts, Illinois and California, and Suggestions Applicable to New York* (1935), by Frederick C. Tanner; and *A Brief Review of the Torrens Experiment in the United States* (1938), by Edward D. Landels. "Registration of Land Titles" is discussed by C. H. Harbes, Superintendent of Land Registration in the office of the County Recorder of Los Angeles County, in the August, 1945, number of the *Los Angeles Bar Bulletin.* The April, 1913, issue of *Case and Comment* issue concerns land titles, including Torrens laws, abstracts of title, marketable titles, and so on.

Published material on the history of the title business in California is almost nonexistent. Early directories, newspapers, an occasional magazine article about a particular company, a few scanty manuscript copies of company histories, the records of individual companies—these are the source materials. Official activities or proceedings of the trade organization—California Land Title Association—are preserved in an annual publication issued after the annual convention.

Legal literature in the field of real property is abundant, published textbooks and manuals directed to men who examine titles or handle escrows, or directed to their customers, are few in number. The most widely used are Melvin B. Ogden's *Escrow and Land Title Law in California* (1938), already mentioned, and W. W. Robinson's *Title Insurance and Trust Company's Handbook for Title Men* (1948), the latter appearing in earlier editions as *California Land Titles.* Walter Home's *Escrow–Land Title Procedure* (1948) points up the use and handling of escrows. Earlier manuals are Norman Rulien's *Escrows and Title Transfer* (1929), E. L. Farmer's *Escrows* (1931), and W. D. Reyburn's *The Title Man's Reference Book of Practical Engineering Problems* (1934). Planned for 1949 publication is Melvin B. Ogden's basic and comprehensive textbook for title examiners and title attorneys: *Land Title Law in California.*

Index

Indians: population, 5, 13, 16 and n. 1; land tenure, 6; property beliefs, 6–9, 10; property transfers, 9; games, 9; culture, 10, 12; missionization, 11–12, 13, 25–26, and secularization, 13, 30; rights of California, to occupy lands, 11, 13, 95; pueblos, 13, 42, 61; Mexican grants of ranchos, 13, 71, and lots, 45–46; subject to U. S. jurisdiction, 13; tribal lands, 13–14; commissioners to effect settlement, 14; treaties, 14–15, 19, 20; restricted homestead rights, 17; allotments, 17–18; squatting, 18; schools, 18; appropriations for relief, 18; 1928 Jurisdictional Act, 19, and fund to compensate, 19–20; recognized in Laws of the Indies, 75; titles conflicting with railroad titles extinguished, 150. *See also* Indian reservations; Treaties

Jackson, Helen Hunt, 18
James, John M., 128
Jimeno Index, 82
Jones, William Carey: explains temporary nature of mission titles, 28; to classify Mexican and Spanish grants, 72, 92; arrival in Monterey, 91–92; report on land titles, 93–97; counsel for Frémont, 98; son, 98
Jordan, David Starr, 18
Juarez, Cayetano, owner of Rancho Yokaya, 71
Judah, Theodore D., 153
Judson, A. H., Judson, Gillette, and Gibson, 219
Jurisdictional Act, California Indians', of 1928, 19

Karoks: individualistic, 5; culture, 10
Kelsey, C. E., 18–19 and n. 3
Kinney, Abbott, recommendation for forest supervision, 173
Kinney, William, Porterfield scrip issued to, 181
Knight, William, 64
Kroeber, A. L.: Indian cultures, 6 ff.; missionization of Indians, 12

Lake Vineyard Land and Water Association, 161
Lamar, J. B., patent for Town of Mendocino, 166
Land Commission proceedings: San Pascual, 76–77, 82, 85; U. S. patents in confirmation of Spanish or Mexican titles incontestable, 90, 178; Bowman's report, 105–106; 800 claims, 106, 112; squatters and delay in titles, 116, 125
Land Commissioners, Board of: Indian failure to present claims, 15–16; missionary titles before, 28; Act of 1851 creates, 31, 100, 112, 130, 230; authorized to segregate privately owned land from public domain, 31, 230; Church claims, 31 and n. 1; partial rejection of San Francisco pueblo title, 36; 800 claims before, 55–56; liberal attitude, 69; patents, 69, 106; members, 85, 102; duties, 100–102; early claims before, 102; meetings, 102–103; search of titles, 103; proof of possession and use of land, 105; work summarized, 130; segregation, 163; claims filed to San Francisco lands, 237; Los Angeles claims, 238–239
Land Office, Federal, 143

282 *Index*

Mason, Governor Richard B., 97, 134; order to abolish Mexican laws on denouncement of mines, 136

Mexican province, California as a: Spanish rule yields to Mexican, 2, 13; Spanish grants respected, 2, 13, 94; period of ranchos, 2, 61; secularization of missions, 13, 29–30, 61; governors answerable to central government, 51; land grants to Mexican citizens, 61, 69, 94; 1824 and 1828 rules for colonization, 65–66, 69, 77, 78, 94; size of grants, 92, 112; method of application for grant, 94–95; no reservations of mineral rights, 95, 143, 144–145; validity of titles under, 107, 109, 125; Supreme Court upholds U. S. patent in confirmation of grant under, 125, 145; mining laws, 144–145. *See also* Guadalupe Hidalgo, Treaty of

Mexican War: close of, 13; Treaty of Guadalupe Hidalgo, 13

Micheltorena, Governor Manuel: attempt to restore twelve missions, 30; grant to Garfias, 84; "grant of gold mines" to Alvarado, 95, 114; grant to Miranda, 178; grant to Limantour forged, 237

Michie, Thomas J., 181

Miller, Henry, Miller and Lux, 183, 192

Miller, Joaquin, 146

Mining: ownership of mineral rights under Mexican laws, 95, 143, 144–145; gold discovery, 133, and Gold Rush, 134 ff.; phases, 135; camp meeting rules, 136–137; size of claims, 137; source of title, 137; regulations of Rock Ditch and Mining District, 138–139; notices, 139; race restrictions, 139; local jurisdiction, 140; 1848–1866 regulations and customs, 141; Act of 1866 confirms miners' rights, 141; Act of 1872 codifies common law of miners, 141–142; 1909 California statutes on titles, 142–143; mineral lands excepted from Railroad Act, 151, from school lands, 190–191

Miranda, Juan, Micheltorena's grant of Rancho Arroyo de San Antonio to, 178

Missions: twenty-one Franciscan, 11, 23–24; Serra's plan for chain of, 11–12, 23, 24; Indians at, 11, 12, 13, 25–26; secularization, 13, 24–25, 29–30, 58, 61, and ensuing land rush, 30; life, 24; temporary character, 24–25, 95; El Camino Real connecting, 25; land monopolizing by, 25, 28; system, 25; area, 25; self-sufficing units, 25–26; feudal activities, 25–26; oppose rancho movement, 26–28; Micheltorena's attempt to restore, 30; governmental decrees for sale and renting, 30, 67 and n. 4; Church claims of acreage, 31 and n. 3; list of, 31 n. 3; villages spring up out of decay of secularized, 61; 1845 and 1846 governmental decrees authorizing disposition of land, 67 and n. 4; transformed into parish churches, 76; Jones report, 95

Mofras, Duflot de, description of a presidio, 35

Mohaves: an organized tribe, 5; farm land, 8–9, and title disputes, 9

Monterey presidio: Spanish flag yields to Mexican, 2; building of presidio 34; title upheld by U. S., 60; Sloat takes possession, 69, 105, 204; 1849 description, 91; constitutional convention, 92, 185; deserted by gold seekers, 134

Moraga, José Joaquín de: founding of pueblo of San José, 37; commissioner, 40

Moraga, Vicente, 79
Moran, Michael, 115
More, Thomas, owner of Rancho Sespe, 127
Mormon settlers: owners of Rancho San Bernardino, 127; and squatters, 127–128; as miners, 134
Morrell, Benjamin, on population of San Francisco presidio, 36
Morrow, William W., on validity of land grants, 105–106, 109
Morton, Frew, acquires White Rock Island with scrip, 179
Muir, John, agitation for forest reserves, 173
Mussel Slough, 159–160

National Indian Association, 18; schools, 18
Navarro, Galindo, opinion on land grants, 51
Neve, Felipe de: site hunting for pueblos, 37; *Reglamento* for pueblo establishment, 38–39, 238
New Helvetia, Sutter's private "fortress," 60–61
New York *Courier and Independent,* Hartwell's articles for transcontinental railroad, 149
Nichols, John G., urges Los Angeles claims, 238
Nieto, Manuel Pérez: Mission San Gabriel objects to, 27; grant from Fages, 48–50; owner of Los Nietos (La Zanja), 56
Norris, Frank, story of Mussel Slough in *The Octopus,* 159

Oakland: Rancho San Antonio site of, 53, 116; squatters, 116
O'Farrell, Jasper: maps San Francisco, 203; partition of San José Rancho, 203
Olvera, Agustín, 31, 85, 239
Ord, E. O. C., survey of Los Angeles, 206, 240
Ord, Pacificus, 239
Orduno, Ramon, description of property deeded to Stearns, 202
Ortega, José Francisco de, El Refugio Rancho granted to, 53, 56; son José María, 53
Otay, most southerly rancho, 63
Outside lands, 46; Laws of the Indies on grants of, 51; Outside Lands Ordinance, 236

Padrés, José María, attempt to colonize Alta California, 29, 31
Pala Valley reservation: a "mission" reservation, 17; forced removal of Indians to, 20, 22
Palomares, Ygnacio, part owner of Rancho San José, 30, 203
Partridge, Clarence L., 21
Pasadena: original site, 87; beginning of, 88–89; name, 89
Peralta, Domingo, 102
Peralta, Luís María: quarrel with Mission Dolores, 27; Rancho San Antonio granted to, 53, 57; advice to sons on Gold Rush, 133
Peralta, Pablo, part owner of Rancho Santiago de Santa Ana, 55, 56
Peralta, Vicente, 102

Wilson, James, 102
Wilson John, 64, owner of Rancho Cañada de los Osos Pecho y Islay, 71
Woodland, J. M., 123
Wozencraft, O. M., negotiations with Indians, 14

Yankee rancheros, 64
Yerba Buena: within four square leagues of presidio, 36, 229–230, 232; town lots granted, 36; name change, 36, 230; Vioget survey, 203, 234; ayuntamiento, 232–233. *See also* San Francisco
Yorba, José Antonio: in Fages' Catalonian volunteers, 55; Rancho Santiago de Santa Ana, 55, 56
Yuroks: individualistic, 5, 7; real and personal property, 7, 10; northwestern culture, 10

Zamorano, Agustín V., 81; Zamorano document, 231